D1094461

# I BELIEVE

*The Personal Philosophies of Certain Eminent Men and Women of Our Time*

Edited, with an Introduction and Biographical Notes, by
CLIFTON FADIMAN



19 39

SIMON AND SCHUSTER · NEW YORK

*Published by Simon and Schuster, Inc.*

*386 Fourth Avenue, New York, N. Y.*



MANUFACTURED IN THE UNITED STATES OF AMERICA

BY THE HADDON CRAFTSMEN, INC.

# *Contents*

# *Illustrations*

# Introduction

*Almost exactly a decade ago the publishers of this book (acting jointly with the editors of* The Forum) *sent an invitation to a number of the world's most notable men and women. The heart of that invitation read as follows:*

> *Briefly, we should like to secure from you a statement of your personal credo; that is to say, a statement of your convictions and beliefs concerning the nature of the world and of man. In a sense, this would be a spiritual and intellectual last will and testament to our generation—a brief apologia, necessarily subjective, touching intimately on your own hopes and fears, the mainsprings of your faith or the promptings of your despair. Such an article, together with others of like nature from a selected group of the most penetrating minds of our era, would form an invaluable legacy to thoughtful readers everywhere, for they would indicate the valid principles, the personal philosophy, by which the great men and women of our day have guided their own lives and work.*

*A somewhat similar invitation was extended to a group of younger men.*

*The result was the publication, in 1931, of twenty-two essays, collected under the title of* Living Philosophies. *The contributors were Albert Einstein, Sir James Jeans, Theodore Dreiser, James Truslow Adams, Sir Arthur Keith, Beatrice Webb, Fridtjof Nansen, Robert Andrews Millikan, Hilaire Belloc, George Jean Nathan, Bertrand Russell, John Dewey, H G. Wells, H. L. Mencken, Julia Peterkin, Irving Babbitt, Joseph Wood Krutch, Lewis Mumford, Hu Shih, J. B. S. Haldane, Irwin Edman, and William*

*Ralph Inge. The book itself was remarkably successful; apparently the American public was eager to read and ponder just such a series of professions of faith or unfaith by some of the clearest and weightiest intellects of the day.*

*That day, in retrospect, seems paradisiacal. Despite the economic crisis in which, during the early thirties, the whole world was caught, there seemed no special reason to doubt that mankind was adequate to cope with its difficulties. But with the rise of the totalitarian powers, unquestionably the most important historical event of the century so far, a change has come over the minds of men. In a word, the entire cultural tradition upon which our twenty-two "living philosophers," despite their differences, implicitly rested, was challenged, and, in parts of the world, apparently defeated. The world of 1939 and that of 1929 are distinct. As Einstein, in his statement to be found in this book, puts it: "In these ten years confidence in the stability, yes, even the very basis for existence, of human society has largely vanished. One senses not only a threat to man's cultural heritage, but also that a lower value is placed upon all that one would like to see defended at all costs."*

*It occurred to the publishers of this book, therefore, that it might be interesting and even of some social and intellectual significance to get together another series of Living Philosophies, by a new group of eminent men and women. This new group would perhaps reflect, implicitly or explicitly, the experiences we have all gone through during this last decade. In any case, we felt, in the dark days amidst which we find ourselves, there might come from these distinguished men and women a profession of faith, a renewal of the covenant, a challenge to the anti-intellectual movement of our time. And so, with the co-operation of* The Nation *(in whose pages most of these essays, usually in shortened form, were first published), the book you hold in your hands came into being.*

*These twenty-one contributors are, quite candidly, all intellectuals. That does not mean they are not men and women of action. It simply means that they believe in the intellect. Put them in a room together and they would disagree violently on many important matters. But on one thing they would agree: that man, at his best, is a reasoning animal. None of them has much faith in thinking with the blood.*

*It occurred to us also, as we thought about this book, that perhaps the original contributors had revised or modified their views in the intervening decade. We thereupon invited short contributions from them, and publish them herewith. Of the original twenty-two, Irving Babbitt and Fridtjof Nansen had died in the interval; Dean Inge and Hilaire Belloc could not contribute; and Sir James Jeans wrote us quite simply that his fundamental philosophy had not changed. Seventeen "revised philosophies," therefore, are available for the reader's consideration, and he will find it interesting to compare them both with the 1931 statements and with the longer essays by the newer group.*

*Of this newer group, one or two things may be said. An attempt has been made at variety. There are young, middle-aged, and venerable contributors. From the point of view of nationality, there are seven American citizens, and of these Mr. Stefansson is of Icelandic background, Mr. van Loon of Dutch, Professor Boas of German; there are eight Englishmen and Englishwomen; there are two Germans; two Frenchmen; one Chinese; and there is Mr. Santayana, who is a kind of citizen of the world. These confessions or professions are by novelists, poets, anthropologists, economists, biologists, teachers, critics, historians, theologians, philosophers, explorers, and humorists. Yes, humorists; for no special apology is needed to explain the presence of James*

*Thurber in the company of such names as Mann and Santayana and Romains and Maritain. The point of view of the humorist is in its way as valuable and pertinent as that of the technical philosopher.*

*The reader will find no special agreement among these twenty-one minds. Each has written in entire ignorance of what the others were writing. No censorship or limitation was placed upon any contributor. There are men of Right, Left, and Center in this book; there are orthodox believers, agnostics, and atheists; there are optimists (but not many) and pessimists; there are men who, like Mr. Auden and Mr. Hogben, seem to have divested themselves of a* personal *philosophy or at any rate identify their own subjective feelings with a larger social affirmation; and there are those who, like Pearl Buck, offer a creed that is intensely, candidly, and movingly subjective. Some of these essays are almost mathematical in their rigor; some profoundly serious; some, like those of Mr. Thurber, Mr. van Loon, and Mr. Forster, couched in lighter vein, though nonetheless serious for all that.*

*There are twenty-one temperaments here. Yet, in a sense, they divide into two main classes. There are those who, like Ellen Glasgow and Pearl Buck and Lin Yutang and Emil Ludwig and Jacques Maritain, find themselves interested in what may be termed the permanent qualities of man. And there are those who, like Lancelot Hogben and Franz Boas and Stuart Chase, are more concerned with his present tragic dilemma. Some, like Thomas Mann, seem able to combine both angles of vision. But none of them, even the most detached, even the most individualistic, stands untouched by the events of the last ten years, untroubled by some fear for the future, untinctured by doubt. Even those who, like Maritain, possess the support of a strong and orthodox faith, feel the chill of the black shadow of our times—the shadow of unreason, the shadow of organized cruelty to mankind.*

*These views are not proposed to the reader that he may choose among them. They are not "helpful" in that sense. How can one put it better than in Havelock Ellis's words? "The reward of being simple and sincere with what seem the facts of one's universe is that one sheds abroad an influence that may be incalculable. It is worth while."*

*And so one reader may take fire from Thomas Mann's prophetic words, the words of a very great artist in whom lives a sense of the future of mankind. Another will rejoice with Pearl Buck as she utters her Everlasting Yea to life. The operational philosophy, with its conscientious engineer's note, of Stuart Chase, will appeal to still another. Catholics and non-Catholics alike will want to ponder the humane words, so genuinely Christian, of Jacques Maritain. For others, particularly younger readers, the creed of the scientific humanist like Lancelot Hogben or Julian Huxley will possess a clean, decisive, forward-looking quality; while more skeptical and less activist temperaments will savor the ironies of Hendrik van Loon, Lin Yutang, and George Santayana. Women readers should find a special interest in the original (and beautifully written) essay contributed by Rebecca West.*

*Socialists will agree with the ideas expressed by Harold Laski and John Strachey; non-Socialists may disagree, but will surely find their views worth considering. The perhaps overly rational spirit of the younger generation is condensed, surprisingly enough, in the almost consciously cold formulations of a poet: the young W. H. Auden. E. M. Forster writes a subtle, nonoratorical defense of democracy. Havelock Ellis offers his "vision of harmonious conflict," Ellen Glasgow her warm, nondogmatic idealism, Emil Ludwig his romantic and mystical symbolism, derived from his master Goethe. Jules Romains, one of the greatest novelists of our period, brings his unanimist and "group" theories up to date. Franz Boas illuminates the intellectual background out of which his important researches have grown. Finally, taking a viewpoint radically different from any of his colleagues, Vilhjalmur Stefansson suggests a new way of approaching the problem of the good life. There is something here for any man or woman of good will, and nothing for those in love with death or who have little but contempt for the aspiring spirit of man.*

—CLIFTON FADIMAN

April 14, 1939

# W. H. AUDEN

*Since the death of William Butler Yeats, W. H. Auden, despite his youth, is by many good judges accounted the greatest living figure in English poetry. His verse combines a fruitful reverence for the great tradition of English verse with a remarkable power of utilizing that tradition to express in a mingled tone of beauty, indignation, and irony the tragic world of today. Auden's regenerative influence on his contemporaries, both poets and prose writers, has been profound. Without desiring to do so, he has become the leader of a school and bids fair to occupy a position in his generation similar to that T. S. Eliot occupied in his.*

*Wystan Hugh Auden was born in England in 1907. He was educated at Gresham's School, Holt, and at Christ Church, Oxford. He lists himself as a schoolmaster but has engaged in other occupations, including journalism. In 1928 and 1929 he lived in Berlin, in 1937 visited war-torn Spain, and in 1938 traveled in China. Since 1935 he has been married to Erika, daughter of Thomas Mann.*

*He has written 'Poems' (1930); 'The Orators' (1932); 'The Dance of Death' (1933); 'The Dog Beneath the Skin,' with Christopher Isherwood (1935); 'On This Island' (1937); 'The Ascent of F 6' (1937); 'Letters from Iceland,' with Louis MacNeice (1937); 'On the Frontier,' a play (1939); 'Journey to a War,' with Christopher Isherwood (1939). He has edited 'The Poet's Tongue,' with John Garrett (1934); and 'The Oxford Book of Light Verse' (1938).*

*Robert Disraeli*

W. H. Auden

# *W. H. Auden*

*Everything that lives is Holy.*—BLAKE.

I

1) GOODNESS is easier to recognize than to define; only the greatest novelists can portray good people. For me, the least unsatisfactory description is to say that any thing or creature is good which is discharging its proper function, using its powers to the fullest extent permitted by its environment and its own nature—though we must remember that "nature" and "environment" are intellectual abstractions from a single, constantly changing reality. Thus, people are happy and good who have found their vocation: what vocations there are will depend upon the society within which they are practised.

There are two kinds of goodness, "natural" and "moral." An organism is naturally good when it has reached a state of equilibrium with its environment. All healthy animals and plants are naturally good in this sense. But any change toward a greater freedom of action is a morally good change. I think it permissible, for example, to speak of a favorable mutation as a morally good act. But moral good passes into natural good. A change is made and a new equilibrium stabilized. Below man, this happens at once; for each species the change toward freedom is not repeated. In man, the evolution can be continued, each stage of moral freedom being superseded by a new one. For example, we frequently admire the "goodness" of illiterate peasants as compared with the "badness" of many townees. But this is a romantic confusion. The goodness we admire in the former is a natural, not a moral, goodness. Once, the life of the peasant represented the highest use of the powers of man, the farthest limit of his freedom of action. This is no longer true. The townee has a wider range of choice and fuller opportunities of using his power. He frequently chooses wrongly, and so becomes morally bad. We are right to condemn him for this, but to suggest that we should all return to the life of the peasant is to deny the possibility of moral progress. Worship of youth is another romantic pessimism of this kind.

2) Similarly, there is natural and moral evil. Determined and unavoidable limits to freedom of choice and action, such as the necessity for destroying life in order to eat and live, climate, accidents, are natural evils. If, on the other hand, I, say, as the keeper of a boardinghouse, knowing that vitamins are necessary to health, continue, for reasons of gain or laziness, to feed my guests on an insufficient diet, I commit moral evil. Just as moral good tends to pass into natural good, so, conversely, what was natural evil tends, with every advance in knowledge, to become moral evil.

3) The history of life on this planet is the history of the ways in which life has gained control over and freedom within its environment. Organisms may either adapt themselves to a particular environment—e.g., the fleshy leaves of the cactus permit it to live in a desert—or develop the means to change their environment—e.g., organs of locomotion.

Below the human level, this progress has taken place through structural biological changes, depending on the lack of mutations or the chances of natural selection. Only man, with his conscious intelligence, has been able to continue his evolution after his biological development has finished. By studying the laws of physical nature, he has gained a large measure of control over them and insofar as he is able to understand the laws of his own nature and of the societies in which he lives, he approaches that state where what he wills may be done. "Freedom," as a famous definition has it, "is consciousness of necessity."

4) The distinguishing mark of man as an animal is his plastic, unspecialized "foetalized" nature. All other animals develop more quickly and petrify sooner. In other words, the dictatorship of heredity is weakest in man. He has the widest choice of environment, and, in return, changes in environment, either changes in nature or his social life, have the greatest effect on him.

5) In contrast to his greatest rivals for biological supremacy, the insects, man has a specialized and concentrated central nervous system, and unspecialized peripheral organs, i.e., the stimuli he receives are collected and pooled in one organ. Intelligence and choice can only arise when more than one stimulus is presented at the same time in the same place.

6) Man has always been a social animal living in communities. This falsifies any theories of Social Contract. The individual *in vacuo* is an intellectual abstraction. The individual is the product of social life; without it, he could be no more than a bundle of unconditioned reflexes. Men are born neither free nor good.

7) Societies and cultures vary enormously. On the whole, Marx seems to me correct in his view that physical conditions and the forms of economic production have dictated the forms of communities: e.g., the geographical peculiarities of the Aegean peninsula produced small democratic city-states, while the civilizations based on river irrigation like Egypt and Mesopotamia were centralized autocratic empires.

8) *But* we are each conscious of ourselves as a thinking, feeling, and willing whole, and this is the only whole of which we have direct knowledge. This experience conditions our thinking. I cannot see how other wholes, family, class,

nation, etc., can be wholes to us except in a purely descriptive sense. We do not see a state, we see a number of individuals. Anthropological studies of different communities, such as Dr. Benedict's work on primitive American cultures, or that of the Lynds on contemporary Middletown, have shown the enormous power of a given cultural form to determine the nature of the individuals who live under it. A given cultural pattern develops those traits of character and modes of behavior which it values, and suppresses those which it does not. But this does not warrant ascribing to a culture a superpersonality, conscious of its parts as I can be conscious of my hand or liver. A society consists of a certain number of individuals living in a particular way, in a particular place, at a particular time; nothing else.

9) The distinction drawn by Locke between society and government is very important. Again, Marx seems to me correct in saying that sovereignty or government is not the result of a contract made by society as a whole, but has always been assumed by those people in society who owned the instruments of production.

Theories of Rights arise as a means to attack or justify a given social form, and are a sign of social strain. Burke, and later thinkers, who developed the idealist theory of the state, were correct in criticizing the *a priori* assumptions of Social Contract and in pointing out that society is a growing organism. But, by identifying society and government, they ignored the power of the latter to interfere with the natural growth of the former, and so were led to denying the right of societies to revolt against their governments, and to the hypostatization of the *status quo*.

10) A favorite analogy for the state among idealist political thinkers is with the human body. This analogy is false. The constitution of the cells in the body is determined and fixed; nerve cells can only give rise to more nerve cells, muscle cells to muscle cells, etc. But, in the

transition from parent to child, the whole pack of inherited genetic characters is shuffled. The king's son may be a moron, the coal heaver's a mathematical genius. The entire pattern of talents and abilities is altered at every generation.

11) Another false analogy is with the animal kingdom. Observed from the outside (how it appears to them no one knows), the individual animal seems to be sacrificed to the continuance of the species. This observation is used to deny the individual any rights against the state. But there is a fundamental difference between man and all other animals in that an animal which has reached maturity does not continue to evolve, but a man does. As far as we can judge, the only standard in the animal world is physical fitness, but in man a great many other factors are involved. What has survival value can never be determined; man has survived as a species through the efforts of individuals who at the time must often have seemed to possess very little biological survival value.

12) Man's advance in control over his environment is making it more and more difficult for him, at least in the industrialized countries with a high standard of living, like America or England, to lead a naturally good life, and easier and easier to lead a morally bad one.

Let us suppose, for example, that it is sometimes good for mind and body to take a walk. Before there were means of mechanical transport, men walked because they could not do anything else; i.e., they committed naturally good acts. Today, a man has to choose whether to use his car or walk. It is possible for him, by using the car on an occasion when he ought to walk, to commit a morally wrong act, and it is quite probable that he will. It is despair at finding a solution to this problem which is responsible for much of the success of Fascist blood-and-soil ideology.

## II

1) A society, then, is good insofar as

*a*) it allows the widest possible range of choices to its members to follow those vocations to which they are suited;

*b*) it is constantly developing, and providing new vocations which make a fuller demand upon their increasing powers.

The Greeks assumed that the life of intellectual contemplation was the only really "good" vocation. It has become very much clearer now that this is only true for certain people, and that there are a great many other vocations of equal value: human nature is richer and more varied than the Greeks thought.

2) No society can be absolutely good. Utopias, whether like Aldous Huxley's Brave New World or Dante's Paradiso, because they are static, only portray states of natural evil or good. (Someone, I think it was Landor, said of the characters in the *Inferno*: "But they don't want to get out.") People committing acts in obedience to law or habit are not being moral. As voluntary action always turns, with repetition, into habit, morality is only possible in a world which is constantly changing and presenting a fresh series of choices. No society is absolutely good; but some are better than others.

3) If we look at a community at any given moment, we see that it consists of good men and bad men, clever men and stupid men, sensitive and insensitive, law-abiding and lawless, rich and poor. Our politics, our view of what form our society and our government should take here and now, will depend on

*a*) how far we think the bad is due to preventable causes;

*b*) what, if we think the causes preventable, we find them to be. If we take the extremely pessimistic view that evil is in no way preventable, our only course is the hermit's, to retire altogether from this wicked world. If we take a fairly pessimistic view, that badness is inherited (i.e., that goodness and badness are not determined by social relations), we shall try to establish an authoritarian regime of the good. If, on the other hand, we are fairly optimistic, believing that bad environment is the chief cause of badness in individuals, and that the environment can be changed, we shall tend toward a belief in some sort of democracy. Personally I am fairly optimistic, partly for reasons which I have tried to outline above, and partly because the practical results of those who have taken the more pessimistic view do not encourage me to believe that they are right.

4) *Fairly* optimistic. In the history of man, there have been a few civilized individuals but no civilized community, not one, ever. Those who talk glibly of Our Great Civilization, whether European, American, Chinese, or Russian, are doing their countries the greatest disservice. We are still barbarians. All advances in knowledge, from Galileo down to Freud or Marx, are, in the first impact, humiliating; they begin by showing us that we are not as free or as grand or as good as we thought; and it is only when we realize this that we can begin to study how to overcome our own weakness.

5) What then are the factors which limit and hinder men from developing their powers and pursuing suitable vocations?

*a*) Lack of material goods. Man is an animal and until his immediate material and economic needs are satisfied, he cannot develop further. In the past this has been a natural evil: methods of production and distribution were too primitive to guarantee a proper standard of life for everybody. It is doubtful whether this is any longer true; in which case, it is a moral and remediable evil. Under this head I include all questions of wages, food, housing, health, insurance, etc.

*b*) Lack of education. Unless an individual is free to obtain the fullest education with which his society can provide him, he is being injured by society. This does not mean that everybody should have the *same* kind of education, though it does mean, I think, education of some kind or other, up to university age. Education in a democracy must have two aims. It must give vocational guidance and training; assist each individual to find out where his talents lie, and then help him to develop these to the full—this for some people might be completed by sixteen—and it must also provide a general education; develop the reason and the consciousness of every individual, whatever his job, to a point where he can for himself distinguish good from bad, and truth from falsehood—this requires a much longer educational period.

At present education is in a very primitive stage; we probably teach the wrong things to the wrong people at the wrong time. It is dominated, at least in England, by an academic tradition which, except for the specially gifted, only fits its pupils to be schoolteachers. It is possible that the time for specialization (i.e., vocational training) should be in early adolescence, the twelve-to-sixteen group, and again in the latter half of the university period; but that the sixteen-to-twenty age group should have a general education.

*c*) Lack of occupations which really demand the full exercise of the individual's powers. This seems to me a very difficult problem indeed. The vast majority of jobs in a modern community do people harm. Children admire gangsters more than they admire factory operatives because they sense that being a gangster makes more demands on the personality than being a factory operative and is therefore, for the individual, morally better. It isn't that the morally better jobs are necessarily better rewarded economically: for instance, my acquaintance with carpenters leads me to think carpentry a very good profession, and my acquaintance with stockbrokers to think stockbroking a very bad one. The only jobs known to me which seem worthy of respect, both from the point of view of the individual and society, are being a creative artist, some kind of highly skilled craftsman, a research scientist, a doctor, a teacher, or a farmer. This difficulty runs far deeper than our present knowledge or any immediate political change we can imagine, and is therefore still, to a certain extent, a natural rather than a moral evil, though it is obviously much aggravated by gross inequalities in economic reward, which could be remedied. I don't myself much like priggish phrases such as "the right use of leisure." I agree with Eric Gill that work is what one does to please oneself, leisure the time one has to serve the community. The most one can say is that we must never forget that most people are being degraded by the work they do, and that the possibilities of sharing the duller jobs through the whole community will have to be explored much more fully. Incidentally, there is reason for thinking that the routine manual and machine-minding jobs are better tolerated by those whose talents are for book learning than by those whose talents run in the direction of manual skill.

*d*) Lack of suitable psychological conditions. People cannot grow unless they are happy and, even when their material needs have been satisfied, they still need many other things. They want to be liked and to like other people; to feel valuable, both in their own eyes and in the eyes of others; to feel free and to feel responsible; above all, not to feel lonely and isolated. The first great obstacle is the size of modern communities. By nature, man seems adapted to live in communities of a very moderate size; his economic life has compelled him to live in ever-enlarging ones. Many of the damaging effects of family life described by modern psychologists may be the result of our attempt to make the family group satisfy psychological needs which can only be satisfied by the community group. The family is based on inequality, the parent-child relationship; the community is, or should be, based on equality, the relationship of free citizens. We need both. Fortunately, recent technical advances, such as cheap electrical power, are making smaller social units more of a practical possibility than they seemed fifty years ago, and people with as divergent political views as the anarchists and Mr. Ford are now agreed about the benefits of industrial decentralization.

The second obstacle is social injustice and inequality. A man cannot be a happy member of a community if he feels that the community is treating him unjustly; the more complicated and impersonal economic life becomes, the truer this is. In a small factory where employer and employees know each other personally, i.e., where the conditions approximate to those of family life, the employees will accept without resentment a great deal more inequality than their fellows in a modern large-scale production plant.

## III

1) Society consists of a number of individual wills living in association. There is no such thing as a general will of society, except insofar as all these individual wills agree in desiring certain material things, e.g., food and clothes. It is also true, perhaps, that all desire happiness and goodness, but their conceptions of these may and do conflict with each other. Ideally, government is the means by which all the individual wills are assured complete freedom of moral choice and at the same time prevented from ever clashing. Such an ideal government, of course, does not and could not ever exist. It presupposes that every individual in society possesses equal power, and also that every individual takes part in the government.

2) In practice, the majority is always ruled by a minority, a certain number of individuals who decide what a law

shall be, and who command enough force to see that the majority obeys them. To do this, they must also command a varying degree of consent by the majority, though this consent need not be and never is complete. They must, for example, have the consent of the armed forces and the police, and they must either control the financial resources of society, or have the support of those who do.

3) Democracy assumes, I think correctly, the right of every individual to revolt against his government by voting against it. It has not been as successful as its advocates hoped, firstly, because it failed to realize the pressure that the more powerful and better educated classes could bring to bear upon the less powerful and less educated in their decisions—it ignored the fact that in an economically unequal society votes may be equal but voters are not—and secondly, because it assumed, I think quite wrongly, that voters living in the same geographical area would have the same interests, again ignoring economic differences and the change from an agricultural to an industrial economy. I believe that representation should be by trade or profession. No one person has exactly the same interests as another, but I, say, as a writer in Birmingham, have more interests in common with other writers in Leeds or London than I have with my next-door neighbor who manufactures cheap jewelry. This failure of the geographical unit to correspond to a genuine political unit is one of the factors responsible for the rise of the party machine. We rarely elect a local man whom we know personally; we have to choose one out of two or three persons offered from above. This seems to me thoroughly unsatisfactory. I think one of our mistakes is that we do not have enough stages in election; a hundred thousand voters are reduced by a single act to one man who goes to Parliament. This must inevitably mean a large degree of dictatorship from above. A sane democracy would,

I feel, choose its representatives by a series of electoral stages, each lower stage electing the one above it.

4) Legislation is a form of coercion, of limiting freedom. Coercion is necessary because societies are not free communities; we do not choose the society into which we are born; we can attempt to change it, but we cannot leave it. Ideally, people should be free to know evil and to choose the good, but the consequences of choosing evil are often to compel others to evil. The guiding principle of legislation in a democracy should be, not to make people good, but to prevent them making each other bad against their will. Thus we all agree that there should be laws against theft or murder, because no one chooses to be stolen from or murdered. But it is not always so simple. It is argued by laissez-faire economists that legislation concerning hours of work, wages, etc., violates the right of individual wills to bargain freely. But this presupposes that the bargaining powers of different wills are equal, and that each bargain is an individual act. Neither of these assumptions is true, and economic legislation is justified because they are not.

But there are other forms of legislation which are less justified. It is true that the individual will operating in a series of isolated acts is an abstraction—our present acts are the product of past acts and in their turn determine future ones—but I think the law has to behave as if this abstraction were a fact, otherwise there is no end to legislative interference. Take the case, for instance, of drink. If I become a drunkard, I may not only impair my own health, but also that of my children; and it can be argued, and often is, that the law should see that I do not become one by preventing me from purchasing alcohol. I think, however, that this is an unjustifiable extension of the law's function. Everything I do, the hour I go to bed, the literature I read, the temperature at which I take my bath, affects my character for good or bad and so, ultimately, the characters of those with whom I come in contact. If the legislator is once allowed to consider the distant effects of my acts, there is no reason why he should not decide everything for me. The law has to limit itself to considering the act in isolation: if the act directly violates the will of another, the law is justified in interfering; if only indirectly, it is not. Nearly all legislation on "moral" matters, such as drink, gambling, sexual behavior between adults, etc., seems to me bad.

5) In theory, every individual has a right to his own conception of what form society ought to take and what form of government there should be and to exercise his will to realize it; on the other hand, everyone else has a right to reject his conception. In practice, this boils down to the right of different political parties to exist, parties representing the main divisions of interest in society. As the different sectional interests cannot form societies on their own—e.g., the employees cannot set up one state by themselves and the employers another—there is always coercion of the weaker by the stronger by propaganda, legislation, and sometimes physical violence; and the more evenly balanced the opposing forces are, the more violent that coercion is likely to become.

I do not see how in politics one can decide *a priori* what conduct is moral, or what degree of tolerance there should be. One can only decide which party in one's private judgment has the best view of what society ought to be, and to support it; and remember that, since all coercion is a moral evil, we should view with extreme suspicion those who welcome it. Thus I cannot see how a Socialist country could tolerate the existence of a Fascist party any more than a Fascist country could tolerate the existence of a Socialist party. I judge them differently because I think that the Socialists are right and the Fascists are wrong in their view of society. (It is always wrong in an absolute sense to kill, but all killing is not equally bad; it does matter who is killed.)

Intolerance is an evil and has evil consequences we can never accurately foresee and for which we shall always have to suffer; but there are occasions on which we must be prepared to accept the responsibility of our convictions. We must be as tolerant as we dare—only the future can judge whether we were tyrants or foolishly weak—and if we cannot dare very far, it is a serious criticism of ourselves and our age.

6) But we do have to choose, every one of us. We have the misfortune or the good luck to be living in one of the great critical historical periods, when the whole structure of our society and its cultural and metaphysical values are undergoing a radical change. It has happened before, when the Roman Empire collapsed, and at the Reformation, and it may happen again in the future.

In periods of steady evolution, it is possible for the common man to pursue his private life without bothering his head very much over the principles and assumptions by which he lives, and to leave politics in the hands of professionals. But ours is not such an age. It is idle to lament that the world is becoming divided into hostile ideological camps; the division is a fact. No policy of isolation is possible. Democracy, liberty, justice, and reason are being seriously threatened and, in many parts of the world, destroyed. It is the duty of every one of us, not only to ourselves but to future generations of men, to have a clear understanding of what we mean when we use these words, to remember that while an idea can be absolutely bad, a person can never be, and to defend what we believe to be right, perhaps even at the cost of our lives and those of others.

# FRANZ BOAS

*Franz Boas is one of the greatest of living anthropologists. Many consider him the greatest. A practical fieldworker, a master authority on the American Indian, a rational thinker and researcher in the perilous field of racial differences, a teacher who, almost single-handed, created a brilliant school of American anthropology—in a dozen different ways Franz Boas has altered the face of the social sciences. In the popular mind he is perhaps most readily identified with his devastating refutation of nationalist race theories, such as those produced by the current theorists of Germany, Italy, and Japan. His best-known book is probably the classic 'The Mind of Primitive Man.'*

*Franz Boas was born in Germany in 1858 and attended the Universities of Heidelberg, Bonn, and Kiel. He has received honorary degrees from Oxford, Clark, Howard, Kiel, and Columbia Universities. His early work in Indian ethnology laid the foundation for the present fruitful anthropological investigation into the culture of the American Indian. For many years Franz Boas has been professor of anthropology at Columbia University. In addition to hundreds of specialized shorter studies, his major works include 'Changes in Form of Body of Descendants of Immigrants' (1911); 'The Mind of Primitive Man' (1911, 1938); 'Kultur und Rasse' (1913); 'Primitive Art' (1927); 'Anthropology and Modern Life' (1928, 1932).*

*Martin Vos, New York*

FRANZ BOAS

# *Franz Boas*

I CANNOT describe my general philosophical points of view without saying how, I believe, they came into being. Well aware of the deception that memory may play and uncertain of how much absolute truth there is in a retrospective view of the past, I shall give what, I think, have been the events that determined my present thoughts.

The background of my early thinking is a German home in which the ideals of the Revolution of 1848 were a living force. My father, liberal, but not active in public affairs; my mother, idealistic, with a lively interest in public matters, the founder about 1854 of the kindergarten of my home town, devoted to science. My parents had broken through the shackles of dogma. My father had retained an emotional affection for the ceremonial of his parental home, without allowing it to influence his intellectual freedom. Thus I was spared the struggle against religious dogma that besets the lives of so many young people.

An early intense interest in nature and a burning desire to see everything that I heard or read about dominated my youth. Philosophical questions were, therefore, remote from me during my adolescent period and I lived in the surrounding world without speculation, naïvely enjoying every new impression.

As I remember it now, my first shock came when one of my student friends, a theologian, declared his belief in the authority of tradition and his conviction that he had not the right to doubt what the past had transmitted to us. The shock that this outright abandonment of the freedom of thought gave me is one of the unforgettable moments of my life. I had been taught in home and school that it is our duty to think out our problems according to the best of our ability. The denial of this duty, or rather the claim that what I considered a duty was a wrong, seemed unbelievable to me. A second shock was a series of conversations with an artistically gifted elder sister to whom my materialistic world seemed unendurable. I am inclined to think that these incidents may have had a permanent influence on my life. I am inclined to think so because they stand out so clearly in my memory.

The intellectual shock came in another way. My university studies were a compromise. On account of my intensive, emotional interest in the phenomena of the world I studied geography; on account of my intellectual interest I studied mathematics and physics. In preparing my doctor's thesis I had to use photometric methods to compare intensities of light. In pursuit of the experiments I was led to consider the quantitative values of sensations. In the course of this investigation I learned to recognize that there are domains of our experience in which the concepts of quantity, of measures that can be added or subtracted and with which I was accustomed to operate, are not applicable.

Reading of the writings of philosophers stimulated new lines of thought, so that my previous interests were overshadowed by a desire to understand the relations between the objective and the subjective worlds. Opportunities to continue this line of study by means of psychological investigations did not present themselves, and by a peculiar compromise, presumably largely dictated by the desire to see the world, I decided to make a journey to the Arctic for the purpose of adding to our knowledge of unknown regions and of helping me to understand the reaction of the human mind to natural environment.

A year of life spent as an Eskimo among Eskimos, had a profound influence upon the development of my views, not immediately, but because it led me away from my former interests and toward the desire to understand what determines the behavior of human beings. The first result of my attempts to explain human behavior as a result of geographical environment was a thorough disappointment. The immediate influences are patent, and the results of this study are so shallow that they do not throw any light on the driving forces that mold behavior.

The psychological origin of the implicit belief in the authority of tradition, which was so foreign to my mind and which had shocked me at an earlier time, became a problem that engaged my thoughts for many years. In fact, my whole outlook upon social life is determined by the question: how can we recognize the shackles that tradition has laid upon us? For when we recognize them, we are also able to break them. We cannot hope that everybody will perform this task independently. I consider it the duty of those who are devoted to the study of social problems to become clear in regard to these questions and to see to it that through their influence the intellectual chains in which tradition holds us are gradually broken.

The student of the forms in which human affairs present themselves in different cultures is easily led to a relativistic attitude in which nothing appears as stable. The judgments of men as to what is beautiful or ugly, good or bad, even as to what is useful or harmful, differ so much that there might seem to be no common ground on which to base absolute standards. In this view it is generally overlooked that the *ideas* of good and bad, beautiful and ugly, duty and freedom, praiseworthy and condemnable are ever present and that they persist, however much their forms may vary. If we can discover what is generally human and what is culturally determined we may find those lines of behavior that must guide us, for it is conceivable that those traits of human behavior common to all humanity are biologically determined, while the special traits are due to the particular history of each culture.

The one outstanding fact is that every human society has two distinct ethical standards, the one for the in-group, the other for the out-group. Everybody has close associations with some group, however constituted, and as such has certain duties to other members of the group. The ethical standards in the group, as long as a person is a member of that group, are the same everywhere. Murder, theft, lying find expression in every language. The concepts of "must" and "ought," however clumsily expressed, are probably universal. Co-operation of some sort always exists; so does subjection to a code of behavior that makes living together bearable, because it allows us to predict how individuals will react to our own behavior. Outside of the group the standards are entirely different. Murder, theft, and lying, which are condemned in the in-group, are commendable insofar as they help to protect the interests of one's own group.

We do not observe any progress in the standards of human society. We only recognize a softening of hostility between the conflicting groups, at least in times of peace, though even now the ethical standards that are considered binding differ for the citizen and the alien, for the exploiter and the exploited. War, restrictions of migration, economic barriers, class conflicts are evidences of the persistence of these traits.

The ethical behavior of man is based everywhere on these principles and may be considered as a further development of the herd instinct of higher animals. These animals also hold together as one group, offering protection to one another and showing aggressive hostility to other groups which are potential rivals for food supply or are enemies of the species.

On the whole the tendency has been the enlargement of

the group in which the ethical standards of the in-group are valid. The great ethical leaders of all times have expanded the group to embrace all humanity, because they saw that the primitive concept of specific differences between the in-group and the outsider is not valid.

As indicated before, one of the features of social units is the adoption of a standard of behavior for the whole group that makes it possible for them to live together. This subjection to convention must not be mistaken for stability, for the study of every culture proves it to be the resultant of constant changes which are in part brought about by nonconformists. Discoverers of new devices and new facts, disbelievers, minds given to mysticism are in one way or another nonconformists who for a time may be treated as antisocial, but whose lives, if their ideas are valuable to the community, are liable to work profound changes. The general tendency to conformity must be understood as counterbalanced by the freedom of individuals whose activities result ultimately in cultural changes. We observe in all human societies the struggle of these two tendencies. Conformity keeps tradition alive; nonconformity breaks through tradition and, if directed by reason, helps to free us from the errors of the past.

Thus the study of human cultures should not lead to a relativistic attitude toward ethical standards. The standards within the group are the same everywhere, however much they may differ in form. Groups are formations depending upon the most varied historical developments. They may be genetic, national, occupational, religious. Or they may be very small, consisting of a few individuals who consider themselves the elect. It may even be that a single individual feels himself so distinct from the rest of mankind that he claims for himself superior rights and privileges. In all these cases the ethical demands of the group or in extreme cases of the individual are in conflict with the rights of the outsider.

On the whole in the history of mankind as the size of groups has increased, their solidarity has been weakened in many ways and with that the rights of the outsider have been recognized. There is still a sharp conflict between those who have an intense group feeling and sacrifice their individuality to the group whose life form appears to them superior to all others, and those who feel that the group has a strictly limited cultural function and that those worthy of being preserved must prove their cultural value.

It is my conviction that the fundamental ethical point of view to be taken is that of the in-group which must be expanded over the whole of humanity. This leads naturally to the conclusion that the individual must be valued according to his own worth and not the worth of a class to which we assign him.

The habit of identifying an individual with a class, owing to his bodily appearance, language, or manners, has always seemed to me a survival of barbaric, or rather of primitive, habits of mind. Groups, as they exist among us, are all too often subjective constructions, because those who are assigned to that group do not feel themselves as members of the group and the injustice done them is one of the blots of our civilization. There are too few among us who are willing to forget completely that a particular person is a Negro, a Jew, or a member of some nationality for which we have no sympathy, and to judge him as an individual.

It is pertinent to ask whether any group has a rational basis for a claim to rights not accorded to others. At the present time the national and "racial" groups are the fictions that create most trouble in our world. The hysterical claims of the "Aryan" enthusiasts for the superiority of the "Nordics" have never had any scientific background. It has never been proved that a necessary relation exists between the genetic character of an individual and his mental attitude, solely determined by the local type to which he belongs, not by his individual characteristics. The fact that people of different regions or of different social strata who happen to differ in bodily build behave differently is no proof that these differences are an expression of racial qualities. On the contrary, we see men of the most diverse descent working on the same problems, producing, under proper conditions, similar works of art. We see people of diverse descent taking over parts of the folk poetry, of the literature of others and making them their own. We see immigrants merging in the people among whom they live. The racialists commit the unpardonable error of extending to local types the legitimate concept of inherited qualities, forgetting that every one of these embraces endlessly different heritable qualities. They want to make us believe that a Nordic idiot is worth more than a Chinese genius. We may fairly say that, if we were to select the best third of mankind, according to intellect and personality, every one of the large races would be represented in that group.

The crudest form of "racial consciousness" is at present confined to Germany—although in regard to stronger divergences, such as those between Negroes or Asiatics as against Whites, it is almost equally potent in the United States and in England, mitigated by a hypocritical desire to avoid legal recognition of the facts.

The national group's claims to superiority cannot be substantiated any more than those of "racial" groups. The disease of mutual distrust among nations is widely spread and is the bane of modern civilization. The feeling of cultural unity among people of the same language, united by a political bond, is found among the intellectuals of all nations. By education it is spread as a symbol among the masses. Forcible prevention of attaining national unity is a stimulus to the development of passionate nationalism. There is every reason to wish that the cultural diversity of different groups, generally national groups, should be encouraged and each be given the fullest opportunity to develop along its own lines; but this has nothing to do with modern nationalism which is based on the assumption, often too true, that every nation is the enemy of all others, and therefore in duty bound to protect its members and itself. Thus nationalism becomes concentrated upon the idea of developing power, not national culture; power to defend itself, power to attain national unity, power to break the dangerous neighbor. The cultural mission of nationalism is lost sight of in the desire to be free of the fear of aggression. Nietzsche has well expressed the immorality of this attitude, pointing out how every nation ascribes to itself the highest virtue, to others the basest motives. This type of nationalism is the worst enemy of cultural progress.

The solidarity of the group is presumably founded on certain fundamental traits of mankind and will always remain with us. It must be the object of education to make the individual as free as may be of the automatic adhesion to the group into which he is born or into which he is brought by social pressure.

Where the object of education is to develop the power of a group, its ideals are held up before the young as symbols to which strong emotional value is attached and which prevent clear thinking. In its extreme forms we find this method employed in our modern despotic states—Germany, Italy, Russia. The careful nursing of patriotism in other countries is of similar character. If we want to educate not for power, but for the development of free individuals we must shun symbols. We must arouse enthusiasm by holding up to view the lives of great and free men who devoted their lives to diverse ideals, stressing the cultural state that conditioned these ideals. There is no other way to overcome the herd instinct in man.

It must be admitted that too great an emphasis on individualism would weaken the power of the community. However, the ethical principles of the in-group, when clearly recognized, will prevent individualism from exceeding its legitimate limits and becoming intolerable egotism. It is one of the curious phenomena of our time that intellectual and spiritual freedom is confused with social and economic freedom. There has never been a time or place where the individual was free to follow his own whims. He had to accept certain limitations set by the society in which he lived. Notwithstanding our striving for intellectual and spiritual freedom we must recognize that in our complex society social and economic adjustments are unavoidable. The progress of social legislation over the whole Western world shows that this need makes itself felt more and more. In our communities individuals cannot act according to their own whims without interfering with the freedom of others. It is, however, intolerable that the state should force a person to actions that are against his intellectual or spiritual principles.

Individualism may involve serious dangers for the development of art. When the whole community is swayed by the same ideas, and when these have a high emotional value the same style will appeal to all of them. Its form and symbolism will evoke similar reactions in everyone susceptible to the beauties of art. When the common background is broken, as it is in our times, the artist can appeal only to those who feel with him; and a multiplicity of forms and styles will result that do not call forth that general response that belonged to periods of more uniform culture. Still, who would doubt that the genius may overcome these limitations?

The demand for intellectual and spiritual freedom involves an answer to the question whether we ever can be free. Since we recognize that every happening has a cause it is said that we are not free. Insofar as actions have a purpose we feel free to choose. It seems to me that this is a question of words. We do not doubt that every event follows an antecedent event that is connected with it. Often the connections are so varied and logically unrelated that the result appears to us as an accident, but this does not mean that we deny causality. It merely means that we cannot connect in our minds causes which are independent from one another and that contribute to the same event. A rock falls according to the law of gravity; a man passes under the rock for some reason. The falling of the rock that kills him has no relation to the reasons prompting the man. We cannot dispense with accident. To interpret such an accident as a predestined event requires an imaginative extension of our idea of causation that is beyond our experience. The causal explanation of any observed facts, even given the most intimate knowledge of the governing laws, leads back to some kind of accidental constellation from which our deductions must start.

All our choices are determined partly by our own personalities, partly by our relations to the outer world. They are predictable within narrow limits, namely insofar as personality is the decisive element. By far the greater number of choices are determined by the coincidence of logically disconnected, therefore accidental, elements which are unpredictable. On account of our almost complete ignorance of these accidental elements choice appears to us as free.

The question which troubles so many minds, "What is

the purpose of our existence?" is emotionally intelligible. It transfers the idea of purpose which is so clear in our minds to the outer world. The limits of the domain of the "because" and of the "in order to" depend very much upon the strength of one's imagination. A causal series looked at backwards from its results may become a teleological series.

According to our ways of thinking, the development of the biological series is caused. The great appeal of the evolutionary theories of Lamarck, Darwin, and Wallace was that they suggested causal relations for the development of varied forms. At the same time the regularities of the processes indicate that accident is a minor cause, that inherent forces are at work that control the development of the animate world. It is no more difficult to understand that a species, in the course of untold generations, may undergo changes in a direction inherent in the germ and modified by outer conditions, than that in the individual the germ will develop to a certain type of complex individual. It is equally unilluminating whether we speak of these forces as inherent causes or as teleological tendencies. I should consider the latter expression merely a metaphor borrowed from our own human experience. It is not the purpose of uranium to turn into lead. Neither is it the purpose of an ovum to become a human being or of an apelike creature to become man.

My ideals have developed because I am what I am and lived where I lived; and it is my purpose to work for these ideals, because I am by nature active and because the conditions of our culture that run counter to my ideals stimulate me to action.

# PEARL BUCK

*Pearl Buck is the third American and the first American woman to win the Nobel Prize for Literature. Famous the world over for her magnificent novels of Chinese life, she interprets the Oriental mind to Westerners in such a manner as to bring home to us the truth expressed in the title of her great translation of a Chinese classic—'All Men Are Brothers.'*

*Pearl Buck was born in Hillsboro, West Virginia, in 1892. She attended Randolph-Macon Woman's College and, at a somewhat later date, Cornell University. Her middle years have been largely devoted to China. From 1921 to 1931 she taught at the University of Nanking, and at the Government University of Nanking also. The first fruit of her profound and sympathetic knowledge of her adopted second country was the fine novel 'East Wind—West Wind' (1929), but 'The Good Earth' (1931) was the book that won her a wide international public. 'The Good Earth' was awarded the Pulitzer Prize and has been successfully filmed. Pearl Buck's publications since 1931 include 'Sons' (1932); 'The First Wife and Other Stories' (1933); 'All Men Are Brothers,' a superb translation of the Chinese picaresque classic 'Shui Hu Chuan' (1933); 'The Mother' (1934); 'A House Divided' (1935); 'House of Earth' (1935); the two biographical portraits of her parents, 'The Exile' (1936) and 'Fighting Angel' (1936); 'This Proud Heart' (1938); and 'The Patriot' (1939). Pearl Buck now makes her home permanently in the United States.*

# *Pearl Buck*

IT IS no simple matter to pause in the midst of one's maturity, when life is in full function, to examine what are the principles which control that functioning. That there are principles one knows, of course. No ordered existence is possible without them, and only an ordered existence is productive—of happiness if of nothing else. But the mind is like the body—the less its possessor is aware of it the more easy is its working. To stop the mind, therefore, to examine why it chooses to do what it does, may be the more difficult when long ago that mind deliberately gave up asking why it exists and chose as deliberately to consider for the rest of its conscious time how it would exist.

For a philosophy of living is to the mind what the habit of health is to the body. Both should be taken for granted so long as life goes on happily and fully. Only when malady and unhappiness appear is there reason to examine the philosophy of body or mind. I doubt therefore that any healthy soul can put down the fundamentals of his health. He may make desultory remarks about it, such as giving the fragments of it which he calls his beliefs. But to say I believe in tolerance, or I believe in truth, beauty, goodness, or any other thing, is superficial statement after all, and such stated beliefs may have nothing to do with the actual philosophy of living. The philosophy of any one person is comprehended and expressed in the habit of his being, not in regard to any one thing but toward the whole of life.

This habit has its deepest shape in the primary attitude of the person toward life. We in the West with our traditions of rebellion tend to think that rebellion shows independence, aggressiveness, boldness. But we are wrong, or so I think. The weakest people are often the most rebellious, finding in universal discontent their excuse for no positive and resolute agreement with anything. There are specific times, to be sure, when rebellion is right and necessary. But I am not speaking of specific times, each of which must be judged when it comes. I am speaking of the primary attitude toward life. It is, it must be, acceptance, and this acceptance of life is the most aggressive act of the conscious human mind.

This mind, having made its acceptance, partakes then like everything else in the universe, in its microcosm, of the universe. The universe is in a perpetual motion, and so is the mind. And this motion is constantly between two poles, and the two poles are the two eternal forces of the universe, the positive force of life and the negative force of death. When I say this it may seem that I am arbitrarily assigning these qualities to life and death—life may be negative and death may be positive, for all I know. I do not understand either one enough to ascribe qualities to them. All that I know is that in every thinking individual there are these two forces, life and death, and that they are opposing forces.

When I say life and death in this sense I realize I am putting into these two words more than they ordinarily carry, so that I risk misunderstanding. But there are no other two words to be used. So let me freight them, even if too heavily. By life I mean here that which moves onward, that which is active and vigorous within itself, that which exists and grows by itself and by everything which it touches, which responds positively to any stimulus. By death I mean that which is quiescent and recessive, that which subsides in itself, that which shrinks away from effort, by itself or by anything it touches, which responds negatively to any stimulus.

I do not mean in any sense that life is merely activity.

*Ben Pichot, New York*

PEARL BUCK

Purposeless activity may be a phase of death. What I mean is more nearly expressed when I say life is active being and death is static being. Each has an energy, life the energy of action and death the energy of inertia. I realize again that these two words, energy and inertia, may seem contradictory. But they are not. Inertia is full of recessive energy. Anyone who has lived in the home with a person who chooses death rather than life as a philosophy, will know what I mean. Such a person merely by being inert, by never responding to any stimulus, exercises an energy sufficient to neutralize at least his equal weight of life. There is a tremendous energy in being simply static.

Human beings may then, among all their other classifications, be divided into these two fundamental types, those who choose life and those who choose death. And when an individual chooses between these two he chooses between two parts of himself.

For as soon as a human being is born, perhaps as soon as he is conceived, life and death begin their opposing work in him, and at the same moment he begins the long struggle of his existence, yielding now to one and then to the other. For he is not compounded wholly of the two. He is an entity and he has a will separate from either, or at least a wish separate from either which may develop into a will. But it wavers like a magnetic needle between the two opposing forces.

This dualism in the universe is everywhere recognized, not only in nature but in the minds and spirits of men. Every religion has recognized it in one form or another. But I am not interested in its religious or even in its philosophical expression. I am interested only in how the individual copes with it as he finds it in himself, whether he recognizes it or not, and whether he considers life worth having or not. That, it seems to me, is the primary question which assails each of us—is life worth having? If we decide it is, then the energy of action prevails in us and we fight death, and if it is not worth having, then the energy of inertia prevails and we never really become aware of life, because all of our being is pervaded with death's inertia.

I realize a point to be considered in answering this question of the worth of life. That is, one's answer to it may vary according to mood and circumstance. There are moods which fall upon us all which we cannot explain, or think we cannot explain, a vague illness of the spirit, an unreasoning sadness which has no seeming explanation in any circumstance. We are as rich today in all benefits as we were yesterday; neither accident nor poverty has befallen us. But yesterday we were happy with life and today we are sad with death. Yesterday we knew life was worth having and today we are not sure. We shrink away from it. And yet the external world is the same. It is our mood which has changed.

Of course the external world may or may not be the same. If it is, if the weather is as fine and all as good as it was yesterday, then the cause of inertia is within us. It is obvious to say that it may be caused by some such chemical contention as indigestion, and yet chemistry too is pervaded by this opposition of life and death. And when we have within us the inertia of obstinate chemical properties which refuse to co-operate, that also is the inertia of death and we are pervaded by it and all our being cries out that life is not good, and when we cry that we choose death.

If mood does not confuse us, then circumstance may. There are many people who say, "Certainly the life I now live is not worth having. I am too poor, too unhappy at home, too unsuccessful in achieving the success I crave, and therefore life is not worth having." That is, practically, they choose death since circumstances are unchangeable, or unless they can be changed.

Let me say quickly that of course this choice of death which I have put down so baldly does not mean an actual choice of physical death—that is, suicide. No, in spite of all that one hears said to the contrary, the act of suicide requires a certain courage of conviction of despair of which few persons are capable. When I say death, I return to my own definition. I mean that state in which a person lives when he has ceased to develop any of his abilities or interests, when his existence has become a mere routine of minimum activity, physical or mental, and when so far as the world or himself is concerned, he might as well be dead. That he still continues to eat and sleep and do a little round has no importance. Actually he has already been absorbed into the inertia of death.

The variance of mood is valid, if transient. The person who chooses life will come to recognize mood more and more clearly after he has passed childhood and youth and will take pains to prevent moods by attention to chemistry, or at least he will learn to ascribe mood to its proper causes and not mistake atoms of obdurate matter within him for an obdurate universe without. He will learn to reject the inertia of death in this guise as clearly as he does in any other, though it is true that an individual of less intelligence may never recognize mood for what it is, and, failing in this recognition, will go on repeating the folly of its causes, and so give himself more and more, unwittingly, to the inertia of death.

But the variance of circumstance is much more serious than that of mood because by saying, "The life I now have is not worth living," and by receding from it in spirit while physically it goes on, many persons deprive themselves of any life at all, since their circumstances may not change. The truth is, one who chooses life rather than death will live in any circumstance, pouring life into every cranny, however cramped the space, shaping what is there rather than being shaped by it. I think of gardens I have seen in the Orient where in a few square yards between city walls there was created the illusion of a wide landscape. One could go there and forget the pressing walls and be surrounded with the large atmosphere of trees and mountain streams. For myself, I do not believe that circumstance has anything to do with whether life is worth having or not. In the first place, I have never seen anyone who does not in some important circumstance long to have his life changed. In the second place, those who measure the worth of life itself by the circumstances in which they must live it are already on the side of inertia.

For life is an elemental essence. It may be contained in a vessel of gold or a clay jar, but the essence within both is exactly the same stuff. Gold does not make it more valuable or clay change its quality. It is immutable. If a man says, "Life is so fine that I shall work for a fine vessel to contain it," then he is possessed by life. If he says, "I don't care what the vessel is, gold or clay, so long as it is brimming with the essence," then also he is possessed by life. But if he throws away his clay jar, the only one he has, merely because it is not gold, and so spills the essence within, then he is either a fool or he is already dead in his inertia. In other words, circumstances have nothing to do with the value of life itself. The person who makes this confusion will never find any circumstance good enough for him. He will never value life and he will never be happy in any life. He will be nearest to any happiness possible to him when he has ceased the feeble struggle of his existence and is lost in the inertia which has had its octopus arms around him always.

I suppose there is no one who does not at some point in his philosophy make statements which can be proved by nothing except his own feeling or experience. I make my first one now. I believe that happiness for any individual depends on how clearly he can recognize this dualism in himself and how strongly he can determine that he will consciously choose life and not death. I simply say this, not knowing why I should think life is preferable to death. One of the greatest of human creeds in which millions of people seem to find comfort, is based on the entirely opposite belief, that death is to be sought and life is to be escaped. I do not say it is wrong. All I can say is that I do not believe it.

For myself, I choose life anyhow, anywhere. Whatever my mood or circumstance, I know I choose life. I have at certain times in my life been very poor indeed. There have been times when I surveyed my circumstances and had to acknowledge to myself frankly that every one of them was wrong and that I really had not one thing to make life worth having—and still it was worth having. I have seen too much death to be in the least afraid of it, and yet I do not want any kind of death. I want any kind of life as long as I can have it. Even though I were racked with pain I would find a few free moments between worth having. And I know pain itself may be positively lived.

Is life then merely an attitude of mind toward living? No, it is more than that. The attitude of mind comes as a result of something more primary. And this primary something is the state of being already alive—that is, possessed by the energy of action so that one's being is a positive force in itself, merely by its existence, whatever its circumstance. It means that the being goes out to meet anything and everything new in a spirit of open inquiry and interest, instead of in instant reaction against what is unknown or unaccustomed. It means putting aside circumstances that cannot be changed and living beyond them. It means roving imagination and daring thinking and ready laughter and quick appreciation and intense interests and wide observation. These things have nothing to do with circumstances. A woman tied to a washtub and a man to a machine can possess them all—if they will.

The will is the crux of it, the point at once weakest and strongest in any philosophy. No one knows anything about will, what it is, how to make it, or how it works, or why it works as it does. There is no such thing, of course, as a person without a will. When we say so-and-so has a weak will, we simply mean he wills to do something else—to keep on being drunk or lazy or a slattern. He wills inertia. It is not necessarily the easiest choice. He may suffer a great deal for his will in the loss of affection, public esteem, and such rewards of everyday life which are precious. He may suffer all the inward sorrow of feeling himself a failure and be very lonely. But still he wills the inertia of death because he prefers it.

For I believe, and here is my second statement, that people are what they want most to be. They may not have all they want to have—that is less important, anyway—but they are, in themselves, what they want to be. If they are lazy, they will to be lazy; if they are quarrelsome, they enjoy quarreling, and will to quarrel; if they are despondent and recessive, this is the way they best enjoy being and so they will to be, and nothing can be done about it, unless the will can be changed.

Can the will be changed? It depends on the person who possesses it and on nothing else. If he has sufficient intelligence to see himself whole and is a creature of an order high enough, he may be able alone to change his own will and so change himself into what his new will chooses. But most of us are not so intelligent as this and we go through life without ever knowing ourselves at all. If we saw ourselves on the street, we would not recognize our own faces, and if we could be introduced to ourselves, we would say, "A complete stranger—I never saw him before." So how can a person change his will when he is unaware of himself?

There are various means whereby we do sometimes see ourselves suddenly and unexpectedly, and we receive a shock which has results of one kind or another. Some receive this light upon themselves through religion and they wish they were different, and wish may become will if it persists. Sometimes this light upon the self comes through love of another human creature, and wish stirs again to grow into will. Or time itself may do it, and experience may throw the light on self and the will learns to choose.

But still this presupposes the ability to see, for all of this light falls upon every human creature in one way or another, but not all can see what the light reveals. Some cannot see, for there is not intelligence enough to recognize what is seen, and some seeing, refuse to see, and in that act they choose again the inertia which is death. But some do see.

And why should some be willing to see and others refuse to see? Well, this is the question which men have answered in many ways. They have said inheritance dooms us or environment shapes us or God predestines us. The fatalist says there is no help for us—if we are born to life we will live alive, and if we are born to death, we will live dead. But all this is to deny freedom to the individual since time began.

And so here is my third statement. I believe we are born free—free of inheritance in that we can by our wills determine to be free of it, free of environment because no environment can shape forever one who will not be shaped. We are born free, in other words, of every sort of predestination. In each of us there is a little germ of individual being, compounded, it may be, of everything, inheritance, environment and all else, but the compound itself is new. It is forever unique. This *I* is never *You* or *He*. And this *I* is free, if I only know it and act upon that freedom.

Does this make a philosophy? Such as it is, it is all I have. When we are born, here is the world, composed of life and death. That life or death we must choose, for there is nothing else. We are free, except choose we must, for time compels the choice.

Does this choice persist beyond what we know of time? Who knows? To die is an end, perhaps, but who can tell the end of him who chooses to live?

# STUART CHASE

*Stuart Chase has taken large areas of the social sciences, particularly in the domain of economics, and translated them into vigorous and stirring prose which has captured the popular imagination. As an expositor and social critic he wields a large and justly increasing influence, both through his occasional journalism and the steady stream of books that has flowed from his pen.*

*He was born in Somersworth, New Hampshire, in 1888. He attended Massachusetts Institute of Technology in 1907–08, and graduated,* cum laude, *from Harvard in 1910 (the class of Lippmann, John Reed, etc.). He joined his father's firm of public accountants, the Harvey S. Chase Company of Boston, and served as a partner until 1917. From 1917 through 1921, he investigated the food packing industry, under the Federal Trade Commission and the Food Administration. Since 1922 he has been director of the Labor Bureau, a nonprofit research organization. His home is in Georgetown, Connecticut, where he is one of the community's best tennis players. His books are 'The Tragedy of Waste' (1925); 'Your Money's Worth,' with F. J. Schlink (1927); 'Men and Machines' (1929); 'Prosperity—Fact or Myth?' (1929); 'The Nemesis of American Business' (1931); 'Mexico' (1931); 'A New Deal' (1932); 'The Economy of Abundance' (1934); 'Government in Business' (1935); 'Rich Land, Poor Land' (1936); 'The Tyranny of Words' (1938); 'The New Western Front' (1939).*

# *Stuart Chase*

## I

I TAKE IT one's living philosophy is a somewhat different kettle of fish from one's formal philosophy. I take it a living philosophy is a label for that collection of beliefs and opinions which tends to guide one's conscious decisions.

Perhaps as good a way as any other to formulate my living philosophy is to reconstruct some actual situations, and note how I reacted to them. This is taking a leaf from modern physics. P. W. Bridgman says that physicists now tend to define their concepts in terms of operations or experiments performed. "Length" and "time" are no longer regarded as absolutes; their meaning comes from what one does with clocks and meter sticks. The concept grows out of the experiment.

I will now perform seven operations based on my own experience. I think they will indicate my living philosophy better than an elevating essay about what I think people ought to believe. In most of the stories, I appear to have behaved fairly well. I could tell twice as many stories more damaging to my self-esteem, but besides being painful to the author, these would not illustrate any philosophy at all.

For sixteen hours in the day, I am faced with decisions which determine my behavior as a biological item on this planet. This behavior in turn determines how long I am to survive as a biological item. Happily, many decisions are automatically made for me by a nervous system well adapted to defend the organism from meddling by the conscious mind. Without these sheltered reactions, I should have been dead long ago. Only this morning I escaped a nasty fall from a stone wall by unconsciously thrusting out an arm to regain balance.

Another long list of decisions is made for me by the customs and folkways of my tribe. One does not go to a dinner party in a bathing suit, hot as the evening may be. One does not get up in the middle of a lecture and tell the speaker what a terrible bore he is, truthful as such a remark might be.

Many conscious decisions not inexorably determined by the folkways remain. For these I stop and think. Signs come in from the world outside—light waves, sound waves, tactile pressures. I revolve them somehow in my cortex, then act. If I fail to act, that also is a decision. Why do I act or react *thus,* rather than *so*? Why do I throw *this* letter into the wastebasket, and spend two hours composing an answer to *that* letter, both being on the same subject? Why do I agree to serve on this committee and refuse that one? My living philosophy is manifested in these decisions. Let us now examine seven specific cases.

## II

I am driving along a country road at night. My headlights are tilted for maximum visibility. I see a pair of lights approaching, half a mile away. When the distance between us is halved, I touch a button with my foot, and dim my headlights. Not so in the other car. It sweeps by with a soft, powerful phut, blinding me as it goes. "You poor damned so and so!" I shout to the night air, as I touch the button and extend the lights again.

Hullo, here is another car, blazing down the road. What is this misbegotten troglodyte going to do? I know what *I* am going to do. I am going to give him the works. That last Devonian ape man was the third in a row. Am I to devote my life to protecting hairy anthropoids who should be swinging from limb to limb? Here he is. Going like Halley's comet. I could run over every dog, child, and old lady in Fairfield County in the road shadow cast by that aurora borealis.

*What?* He's dimmed them, although a bulb is missing in his dimmers. A gentleman and a scholar. And here are my lights going at full blast! I reach for the button, but in my haste hit the accelerator instead, and so give my friend not only a hideous glare, but the rudeness, not to say danger, of higher speed while passing him.

I am alone now in the darkness. As a kind of penance, I drive a few miles at 30 with the dimmers on. Of all idiots, I am the world's loftiest. Trying to take the spleen generated by A, B, and C out on D. D is not C; he is not B, he is not A. D is to A, B, and C as Shakespeare is to Elbert Hubbard, Arthur Brisbane, and Dr. Frank Crane.

Just a minute, now. Elbert Hubbard had his moments before big business got him. Perhaps C had a foot button and broke it. Perhaps he was an unemployed carpenter in a 1922 Reo which cost him $15, going to Bridgeport in the forlorn hope of getting a job on the new PWA housing project. Even if he were president of the Stock Exchange, that is no reason I should take out my displeasure on an ornament of civilization like D. I might have killed D. What lesson would that have preached to C or B or A, strung out along Route 58, happy as lightning bugs, burning the eyeballs out of everyone they passed?

What am I going to do now? I am going to press that button for every car I meet, until I get home. I don't care if it is Al Capone breaking out of jail, or Goebbels rushing to a secret meeting of the Bund. Forty thousand dead on the roads last year, and most of them at night.

A trivial decision, true. Yet this nightly intercourse which millions of us experience involves life and death, man as a social animal, the organization of society in the power age, the engineering of roads, automotive design. It involves hospitals and public health, the consumption of alcohol, and the question whether a biological species, geared to four miles an hour on its legs, can adjust itself to twenty times that rate and survive indefinitely.

III

A few years ago I was in Odessa. I spoke no Russian, and English-speaking guides were rare. Finally I was informed at my hotel that just the right man was waiting in the lobby. His English was indeed excellent. He talked like the Prince of Wales. This was the more extraordinary because my guide wore blue overalls, and was a coal-black Negro. As an American, I do not expect Negroes to speak like Oxford graduates. I expect them to speak like Senators from Alabama.

We went to the docks, to rest houses for workers that were once palaces for the rich along the Black Sea Riviera, to factories, stores, beaches, and to the famous stone steps down which the Cossacks had charged and massacred in 1904. My guide asked me to come home to lunch with him. I was born north of the Mason and Dixon line, and therefore I accepted, especially as he said his wife could make the best borsch in Odessa.

We went to his house—very neat, very poor. His wife came out, wiping her hands on an apron, and smiling a welcome. "Hul-lo," she said. That was her only word of English. She was a comely Russian girl, whiter than I am. I steadied myself against the door. The happy pair beamed at each other and at me. I looked apprehensively for children, but none appeared.

While we ate the admirable borsch with tin spoons, my guide explained his household. He came originally from Jamaica. He had been a stoker on a British freighter which sailed from Odessa in a hurry during the civil war, leaving him behind. Negroes were rare in Odessa, and the Soviet authorities made much of him. They got him a job in the local power plant. Then, because he seemed lonely, they found him a wife. The difficulties of mating black with white never seemed to enter anybody's head. His wife was a school teacher. She loved her husband, and was very proud of him. No other girl in Odessa had such a distinctive husband, who could talk beautiful English besides.

I was far from Atlanta, or even from New York. I could only turn a mental somersault, eat the borsch and the butterless gray bread, and accept without comment what a great city of half a million people accepted.

If one intelligent black man and one intelligent white woman can live happily together, proud of each other, in Odessa, why cannot the same thing happen anywhere else? The answer to that is easy: because other places, such as Atlanta, Georgia, are *not* Odessa. Folklore changes in space and in time. Well, suppose folklore about race were unified all over the world. Could black men and white women, or black women and white men, mate as naturally as white and black horses, without ill effects on themselves or on their brown children? Is it *all* a matter of folklore? The answer to that is harder. The deeper the biologists dig into the matter, the more racial differences *which count* seem to recede. Professor Haldane, who contributed to the original *Living Philosophies*, concludes from the evidence that racial differences occurred in superficial characteristics to begin with, such as skin coloring or hair texture, and that so much interbreeding has taken place since that most notions about racial purity are moonshine.

## IV

From Odessa we jump halfway round the globe, to Albuquerque, New Mexico. Not far from that town, the Rio Puerco comes down from the high mountains of the north to join the Rio Grande. I am out with a group of technicians from the United States Soil Conservation Service. They drive me around a 30,000-acre project on the arid plain. They explain that the number of grazing sheep has been limited to the carrying capacity of the grass, and that both mechanical and biological controls are being tried, to hold the soil against wind and water erosion. A wire fence separates the controlled area from the rest of the plain. The difference between the two sides of the fence is striking. On the project side the grama grass grows tall and strong; on the other side it is sparse, brown, and weak, with wide sandy patches between the drooping clumps.

We drive down to the banks of the Rio Puerco, beyond the controlled area. The river was once a clear stream in a shallow, narrow bed. It fed many little irrigation projects of the Pueblo Indians. Look at it now. The water is thick as pea soup, and there is very little of it. The narrow channel has widened in places to half a mile, cut into horrible, quaking clay canyons by the silt. Flash floods come down, tearing out bridges, covering the irrigated lands with gravel, destroying the ancient economy of the pueblos. Grazing lands topple into this loathsome abyss an acre at a time. Between the floods, the river may dry up completely. The underground water table of the whole valley is sinking fast.

What has happened to bring this desolation? Overgrazing on the plain; overcutting and fire on the timbered head waters in the mountains. White men have overturned the balance of natural forces, wrecking in a few years what it took millennia to build. I feel as if smoldering volcanoes were at work, preparing to blast living things out of this land altogether. Against them stand the men of the Conservation Service, but they are still few, and the ruin is great.

I look around the broad valley. The mountain wall is white with snow, for it is early March. The sun is bright and warm. The cloud streamers across the sky are of that indescribable luminosity which only New Mexico knows. This

Stuart Chase

world has been here a long time. This vulture wheeling above us has been here a long time; that antelope we saw through the glasses has been here a long time. Vulture and antelope and Indian accept this world. We palefaces have refused to accept it. We saw a cash return in it. The cash was there for a few years, but the forces of nature are in delicate equilibrium in the arid lands of the Southwest. From a life-giving stream, this river has become a horror. Another generation of neglect, and paleface, Indian, antelope, and bird must go.

Money loss, crop loss, water loss, game loss—these are practical problems, but I do not have to face them, living two thousand miles away. I am facing another problem, a philosophical problem, if you will. I am a creature of this earth, and so a part of these prairies, these mountains, these rivers and clouds. Unless I feel this dependence, I may know all the calculus and all the Talmud, but I have not learned the first lesson of living on this earth.

If there is fire in your house, you fight it. If there is death along the Rio Puerco, you fight that, as these men beside me are fighting. I go back to my hotel and wire that I will accept an invitation to give a talk on conservation, at a place I did not want to go to, and at a time which is very inconvenient.

## V

I am lying on a lonely beach under the Florida sun. The Gulf beyond the breakers is the color of milky jade. A man in a pink silk shirt comes up and sits down on the sand beside me. He is not a prepossessing man. "That's a nice tan you've got," he says. I do not like the way he says it. I do not like the way he looks at me.

"So so," I say.

"Are you married?"

"Yes."

He continues to look at me, more and more strangely.

Suddenly I am filled with rage. I clench my fists under me. I look him in the eye.

"I have two children."

"Oh," says the man. He gets up from the sand, brushes off his not too clean flannels, and walks away.

There is a round stone on the beach by my hand. I have a hot impulse to pick it up and throw it at his retreating pink shirt. I tell myself to wait a minute.

I look at the man again. He is limping. One leg is obviously shorter than the other. His face was plain as a picket fence. Putting these two facts together, I begin to picture a crippled boy who was never asked to parties, at whom the girls turned up their noses, who was a nuisance to overworked parents, who was met at every turn in life with frustration, if not contempt.

The anger goes out of me, though the disgust remains. I begin to reconstruct my scanty scientific knowledge of homosexuals. Some of them are born so. Indeed, all of us are born with both so-called male and female characteristics. When the male predominate, we are boys; when the female, we are girls; when they are equally divided, we balance feebly on the edge. We can no more help it than a moth can help flying into a lantern. Boys who are not strongly male to begin with may be driven over on the other side, by being shunned by girls, by being constantly thwarted or repressed. Or they may be corrupted by older men and boys who in turn have been driven over on the abnormal side. This is not a matter of morals, but a matter of chromosomes or psychological conditioning, or both.

Homosexuals are born so many per hundred thousand, like albinos or left-handed persons. Some borderline cases can be reversed by a good psychiatrist. Perhaps homosexual tendencies are a kind of sickness, a deficiency disease.

I roll over on my back and watch a diving gull making a white streak from blue sky to jade sea. Sick gulls die quickly.

Only the healthy survive. The sick children of men are tolerated and many are restored by medical invention. It is not nature's way, but it is a kind way and worth trying. The pink shirt is far down the beach now. Why throw stones at biology?

## VI

I have written a speech in the course of which I say: "America will never tolerate Fascism; democracy is too deeply imbedded in the national consciousness." I put the manuscript aside, and pick up the day's mail. A correspondent has sent me a quotation: Hegel's definition of love. "Love is the ideality of the relativity of the reality of an infinitesimal portion of the absolute totality of the Infinite Being."

This sounds alarmingly like nonsense, but the reputation of Hegel is profound. Let me see if I can squeeze some meaning from it. "Love" is the name for an emotion which takes many forms—the love of man for woman, of woman for child, of friend for friend, of disciple for master, of man for country. Hegel does not say which kind he is talking about. "Ideality" is an abstraction so high I lose it in the stratosphere. "Relativity" is a useful label in many contexts, but Einstein has warned that the context must be precise. The "relativity of the reality" is anything but precise.

But perhaps Hegel meant something definite. Whatever he meant, he was unable to communicate it to me. I doubt if it has ever been communicated to anyone. The verbal structure itself forbids communication. I could spend my life contemplating this string of symbols and receive no more reward than in contemplating "X is the A of the B of the C of an infinitesimal portion of the D of the E."

So I cease to contemplate it. I pass it up. I pass up all such talk, from Aristotle to Spengler. It saves a lot of time. But the talk of Einstein and Planck I do not pass up. I do not understand all of it, but I know that by diligence I could come to understand it. The symbols connect with real things. The talk checks with observable phenomena. Nobody can do anything but obfuscate himself with Hegel's symbols about love. With the symbols of Maxwell's field equations, one can build 100,000-horsepower generators and send electric power hurtling over the wires from Boulder Dam to Los Angeles. In reading, in listening, I try to separate talk which goes round and round from talk which refers to something definite in the world outside my head.

I return to the manuscript of my speech. With a soft pencil I draw a thick black line through the sentence about Fascism and the national consciousness of America. Perhaps Hegel could understand it, but I cannot.

## VII

The telephone rings. I lift the receiver.

"Yes, this is Mr. Chase. . . ."

"Yes, I wrote that book. . . ."

"That's very flattering. . . ."

"Yes, I am interested in writing other things. . . ."

"That is a lot of money. . . ."

"What kind of copy? . . ."

"Well, I'm damned!"

I jerk the receiver back on the hook. Presently the buzzer rings again, but I do not answer it.

This decision was almost as fast a reaction as the knee jerk. By it I lost a contract for a fabulous sum per week, to write advertising copy for a patent medicine that I had exposed as worthless, on the testimony of the American Medical Association.

Give me no credit for renouncing the fabulous sum. I did not need it. My book was selling very well. But what made me violate the folkways of the telephone, and hang up on a man who was making me a handsome offer? As well as

I could analyze it, it was a feeling of nausea about the integrity of communication among American businessmen. I had made and proved certain statements. These statements, in the form of a book, had produced a financial return. The man on the other end of the telephone—he was a very big shot indeed—saw nothing amiss in asking me to contradict the statements for a larger financial return. He seemed to think that writers sold words as he sold patent medicines, on the basis of all the traffic would bear.

When people are locked together in an interdependent economic machine, the price of tolerable existence is clear communication. Otherwise the machine cannot be operated. What sort of army would it be, where the colonel twisted the words of the general, the major twisted the words of the colonel, the captain those of the major, and the petty officers those of the captain?

Persons who set themselves up as writers and word dealers have a special responsibility in the power age. If they cannot be trusted to talk honestly, who can be trusted? If they can be sold out to the highest bidder like hogs on the hoof, where is an interdependent culture going to land?

This, I think, was the reason that I hung up the receiver. The modern world is confusing enough, even if everyone were quiet. I want to get the truest news I can about the world, from those in a position to report this part of it or that. My survival may depend on it. Per contra I want to give the truest news I can. It is something like driving a car. That unspeakable tycoon wanted to pay me for driving at seventy miles an hour on the wrong side of the road, smashing up other people and smashing myself.

## VIII

He is waiting for me in the lobby of the building where I have an office. His face is haggard. "What is it now?" I ask. For eight years I have listened to his sad stories of a promising mechanical invention and a possible fortune, wrecked by fast-moving patent attorneys, broken contracts, failing friends, and above all, by a deepening business depression.

"Have you five minutes to spare?" he asks.

I hesitate. I know that five minutes means probably an hour, and I am hoping to catch a train. He goes on talking.

"I had to decide Monday whether I would jump out of a window or go on relief."

"I see that you decided right."

"I don't know. The shame of it is killing me."

I can take a later train. If he had brought good news, I would have dodged the interview.

"Come on up," I say. We go silently into the elevator.

I close the door and sit down at my desk. His eyes shift wretchedly about the little room.

"Has it been your fault?" I ask.

"No. I don't think so. Not altogether, anyway. It's this depression. Nobody has any money. People haven't done the things they said they'd do. They couldn't. I couldn't get anywhere without capital. I couldn't manufacture the thing and sell it with my bare hands. I hung on as long as I could. You know that. Mortgaged everything. Since I saw you last, I've tried for any kind of a job. Washing windows, selling insurance, anything. I suppose I'm no good. I was once. Still, I don't see how it's all my fault."

"It isn't your fault. Look at it this way. In 1929, forty-eight million people in the country had jobs. They were making their own way. They were good workers; they couldn't be accused of failure. Today only forty million of them have jobs, many of those at lower pay than in 1929. How could eight million people turn into bums and loafers almost overnight?"

"No. It doesn't make sense."

"Of course it doesn't. You've got plenty of company. There are about twenty million American men, women, and children on relief. The banks are on relief. The railroads are on relief. If it weren't for the RFC, they'd be busted wide open. You aren't up against personal failure. You're up against the failure of a whole economic system. Take your relief money and spend it. You've got it coming to you, and the spending helps the rest of us."

"You really think I have it coming to me?"

"Certainly. On two counts: first, on the ancient principle of group survival; second, on the modern principle that spending is as important as producing, in an economy of abundance. If relief were shut off, a sixth of the American population would starve to death. Not only that, but the loss of their spending, which runs into billions in the aggregate, would finish wrecking an economy geared to making and selling the things they now consume. If you should all jump out of windows, instead of going on relief, the rest of us would have a depression which would make 1932 look like a Vanderbilt garden party."

"That makes me feel a little better. But where's it all going to end? The government can't afford it indefinitely."

"Perhaps the government can't afford it, but the American continent can. By that I mean government bonds may some day cease to be valuable, but there are enough fields, mines, oil wells, factories, power plants, and machines in the United States to give us all a good living. That's what counts in the end. We aren't going to throw up our hands and sink for the third time, with good solid life rafts all around us."

"But how are we going to grab those rafts?"

"Well, you're grabbing one now. We can't 'afford' relief, but we've got it. Germany couldn't afford to rearm, but she did. Italy couldn't afford to conquer Ethiopia, but she conquered it. Russia couldn't afford a Five-Year Plan, but the factories, dams, and schools were built to schedule. England could never leave the gold standard without instant disaster, but she left it and began to prosper. What is impossible for bankers is becoming increasingly possible for engineers. Group survival is more important than a balanced budget."

"So you don't think we're going all to hell?"

"No. We are in for a rough transition period. But I think, if a given community has enough resources, technical skill, man power, and physical plant, the chances are it will find a way to eat what is already on the shelf. If that horrifies the bankers, it's too bad."

"I feel a lot better. I'm going to apply for one of those WPA engineering research jobs. You don't mind shaking hands with a poor bum on relief?"

He held out his hand, with the first real smile I had seen on his face in years. I smiled, too.

"I may be with you any time. No one's job, no one's income, is sure today."

## IX

These are all true stories. They show my reactions and decisions in seven specific situations. The reader is perhaps in a better position to construct my living philosophy from these experiments than I am myself. To me it seems that I tend to be guided in conscious decisions by four criteria:

1. That I am a creature of this earth. (The Rio Puerco case.)

2. That I am a member of a human group. (The headlight case, the telephone case, the relief case.)

3. That it is meaningless to judge other members of the group until the biological and psychological facts are in. (The Florida case, the Odessa case.)

4. That progress depends, not on revealed authority, not on ethics and morals, which shift with the folkways, but on using the scientific attitude in social as well as in physical affairs. (There is more than a hint of this in all the cases. I am not much of a scientist, but I feel myself constantly

groping for the kind of knowledge, the kind of decision, that stays put.)

Every human being is confronted with two major tasks: to establish a relation with the physical environment in which he is rooted as deeply as any oak, and to establish a relation with his fellow creatures.

The physical environment, in the sense of fresh air to breathe, cannot be neglected five minutes. In the sense of the balance of soils and waters, the penalties of neglect are less immediately apparent. But in the end, retribution is sure and terrible. Look at the dust bowl, at the Yellow River, at the blasted lands of Asia Minor.

If people were not members of a group, they would not be human. Stripped of his group, a man becomes as helpless as if he were stripped of his nervous system. If this truism of anthropology were better appreciated, there would be less silly talk about individualism and rugged independence. We cannot get away from other men, and wouldn't if we could. One of the significant things about the explorers of North America is that they made their way through the wilderness, not in splendid isolation, as we like to think, but with the invaluable assistance of one Indian tribe after another.

How large the group should be for healthy survival becomes an increasingly interesting question. The dangers of inbreeding tend to fix a minimum size, while economic interdependence today indicates a much greater maximum than hitherto. Already, a good part of a continent must be integrated, if men are to be supplied with a reasonable budget of necessities and comforts. Even the three million square miles of the United States do not furnish quite all the raw materials for that budget. Some day a Great Society may swing around the whole world. With the planet as the group unit, the only kind of war possible would be civil war. With poverty liquidated through the universal application of the technical arts, civil wars would be rare.

Large or small, if one is perforce a member of a group, it is a good idea to realize it, and play ball. I find the easiest way to play ball is to analyze what makes my fellow players act the way they do. Which of their more infuriating characteristics has been fixed by inheritance; which built in by early conditioning; which determined by custom and the folkways?

Finally, I admit to a deep conviction that progress is attainable through the methods of science. These methods have changed the face of the world since Bruno died at the stake to witness them, three centuries ago. The applications of science have quadrupled the population of Western civilization and greatly improved its health, released twenty billions of man power of energy from coal, falling water and oil, created a vast collectivized, interlocked culture. This is enough to indicate that the scientific method works, and that its laws and techniques are very powerful medicine indeed.

The beginning is auspicious, but the word has not got around. In 1939, most literate persons use the products of science continuously, but have little conception of the discipline. They still cling to revealed authority, and the revelations clash. Their minds are littered with ideological concepts incapable of verification. They subscribe passionately to Nazi dogma, Marxist dogma, Fascist dogma, Christian dogma, Jewish dogma, Mohammedan dogma, racial dogma, laissez-faire dogma, property dogma, money dogma, and even dogma about political democracy. My dogma is eternally right, and your dogma is eternally wrong. As a result, they are constantly in each other's hair, fighting about ghostly matters. The more lettered they are, the tougher the grip on authority, the more agile the logic, the fiercer the dogma.

Once a person acquires a scientific attitude, dogma begins to melt out of his mind, like an ice field melting in the sun. The scientific attitude reverses the older thought channels. Facts come first. Then one employs his reason to draw inferences from the facts. No facts, no useful concepts. The dogmatist uses his reason—and very powerful it often is—to select or torture the facts in support of his ideology. Dogma first, facts second.

The shore line of history, to use the eloquent language of historians, is littered with the wrecks of civilizations. I will not list them, for the recital is getting to be tiresome. Perhaps civilizations are too much for *homo sapiens* altogether. Perhaps we shall have to go back to gathering coconuts and spearing fish. But two observations are in order. When civilizations have fallen in the past, others have sprung up. We keep on trying. This is encouraging. Secondly, there has never been a civilization like the present one, built on inanimate energy and mathematical equations, with stations all over the world. If Europe's civilization is blotted out, America remains. If Europe and America are blotted out, Australasia and South Africa remain.

More cheerful than blotting out is the hope that the members of a culture founded on science will gradually be inculcated with the scientific attitude. For a few hours in the day, a few days in the year, millions of us are already capable of it. Can that small margin be extended, so that we can climb and hold on, and climb again? I do not know. But my hope is strong.

# HAVELOCK ELLIS

*Havelock Ellis's recent death in July, 1939, ended a career of great variety and brilliance. He has been called by H. L. Mencken "the most civilized Englishman living today." His reputation is based largely on his monumental studies in the psychology of sex, but his active and enlightening mind has reached out to encompass a dozen other fields. Notable are his studies in literature and in the character of nations. His most influential book is probably 'The Dance of Life.'*

*Henry Havelock Ellis was born in Croydon, Surrey, in 1859, descended on both sides from seafaring families. He was educated in private schools and at St. Thomas's Hospital. From 1875 to 1879 he taught in New South Wales, Australia. Upon his return to England he qualified as a medical man, but practiced only briefly, soon becoming absorbed in scientific and literary work.*

*The list of his publications, those of which he is sole author and those of which he is editor, is too long for complete recapitulation. Among his more notable works the following should be mentioned: 'The New Spirit' (1890); 'Man and Woman: A Study of Human Secondary Sexual Characters' (1894); 'Affirmations' (1897); 'The Soul of Spain' (1908); 'Impressions and Comments' (1914), Second Series (1921), Third Series (1924); 'Little Essays of Love and Virtue' (1922); 'The Dance of Life' (1923); 'Psychology of Sex: A Manual for Students' (1933); 'From Rousseau to Proust' (1936).*

# *Havelock Ellis*

After the first shock of the demand to state one's philosophical credo the question to put to oneself should be: what *is* a philosophy? It should be, but apparently it seldom is. The victim plunges at random. The professional philosopher is, of course, more cautious. So it is not surprising to find so distinguished a thinker as Professor Dewey, when approached in the matter, pointing out the various senses in which the word "philosophy" may be used.

As I am not a professional in this field, though accustomed to a certain degree of precision in the use of words, I might be tempted to explain what seem to me the various senses in which it may be possible to speak of a "philosophy," thereby indicating in what sense, if any, I myself possess a philosophic credo.

But as that pursuit might lead far I simply assume provisionally the definition, generally assumed by my colleagues in the present task, that one's philosophic credo is the opinions by which a man lives or believes that he lives, though, as may become apparent, I would say, more exactly, that philosophy is the intellectual conception a man forms to himself of the universe. As such it may not directly influence his way of living but it can scarcely fail to affect his attitude to life. But I would not admit that philosophy is one with morality, and while I would agree that even if, for instance, "Honesty is the best policy" makes an admirable rule of life for a tradesman, it cannot properly be regarded as a philosophic creed.

Like many others of my generation, I was brought up in a religious family, and was the eldest child and only son. My mother was not merely conventionally but genuinely religious, belonging to the Evangelical section of the Anglican Church. As a girl she had been considered "volatile" but at the age of seventeen she was "converted" and that event influenced the whole of her subsequent life. Nothing disturbed her firm character which was, however, never harsh, and with increasing years became increasingly tolerant, so that she accepted without protest the varying religious tendencies of her children. My father, a sailor away from home nine months of the year, accepted my mother's religion and decorously went to church with his family every Sunday when at home, but really had no religion of his own. Familiar with many lands and at home with people of all creeds, he was indulgent to all. His own temperament, moreover, was so equable, so free from any tendency to vice or excess, that, liked by everyone, he might be said to be scarcely in need of any religion. I mention these facts because I regard them as of essential importance. A man's philosophy can never be properly apprehended unless we know the foundations for it which he inherited from his parents.

I was mainly my mother's child, whatever tendencies I also inherited from my father. I spontaneously carried a little Testament in my pocket; I read Bunyan's *Pilgrim's Progress* all through. I do not mean that I was a goody-goody boy. I was far too reserved to give any indications of my inner attitude to my schoolfellows, and as my companions were not vicious there was no occasion to reveal my own aspirations. In due course I underwent the Church rite of Confirmation, without any sense of incongruity. But meanwhile my insatiable intellectual appetite was leading me to devour books, especially serious, of all kinds. In this way I was somehow induced to buy a cheap edition of Renan's *Life of Jesus*. It was new to me to see Jesus treated so sympathetically and yet apart from all supernatural ele-

*Adrian Harding*

HAVELOCK ELLIS

ments. I read the book with interest yet critically and I made critical comments on the margins. But Renan's attitude was more congenial to my own temperament than I at first realized. It was not long before books of more or less similar tendency became convincing, and I definitely rejected as intellectually out of court the whole supernatural foundation of Christianity and miraculous theology in general. This led to no active hostility nor to any sense of liberation from restraints. My life remained the same. But I was conscious of loss. The supernatural universe had melted away, and I was without a spiritual home. There were moods of desolation in spite of constant and varied mental activities. This continued from my seventeenth to my nineteenth year. Strauss' *Old Faith and New*, which was to some extent written for the consolation of religious infidels, offered me no comfort at all; it presented a sort of bourgeois spirituality of a completely dull and uninspiring character.

But, about the time when, as a solitary teacher in the Australian bush, I read and threw aside Strauss, I was somehow stimulated to procure James Hinton's *Life in Nature*. I read it and it made no pronounced impression. But it may have touched something in my unconscious mind, for, a few months later, I read it again. This time it produced nothing less than a mental revolution. I still recall the details of that revolution and the day when I walked across the hills, a new being, feeling as light as air, with a new vision, as yet unformulated, of the universe. That moment has influenced the whole of my life.

What had happened to me was what is commonly called "conversion." But that process is usually misunderstood. It is not the sudden acceptance of a new religion, or a change of life, or anything to do with creeds. It is simply, as the word itself may be said to indicate, a complete psychic change, however produced, and the method of production will vary according to the intellectual and emotional caliber of the person experiencing it. "Conversion" in a John Stuart Mill has little in common with conversion in a costermonger. In my own case, as I later realized, what had happened was that the two psychic spheres, intellectual and emotional, which had been divorced, and in constant active or passive friction, were suddenly united in harmony. Hinton's vision of the universe, even though I could not at every point accept it and would never at any time have considered myself his disciple, presented a universal unity of life which was new to me. The world was no longer dead and repellent; there is the same life everywhere; man and "Nature" are fundamentally one. Henceforth I was at home in the universe. With that realization there came a peace which passes all understanding. I never had any more moods of religious depression.

The revolution remained entirely private; I had no impulse to confide it even to intimate friends and still less to preach it to the world. Perhaps I obscurely felt that such experiences are necessarily personal, under the direction of hereditary and constitutional factors which cannot be transmitted.

It was not until thirty years later that I described this experience in an article on Religion in the *Atlantic Monthly,* afterwards embodied in my *Dance of Life,* and rather more elaborately in the Preface to a reprint of *Life in Nature.* It will be seen that I regarded the experience as religious and not as philosophic, and so I still regard it.

In the years of my mentally formative period I was, however, much concerned over philosophy. It seemed to me that one ought to have a philosophic system, and I had none. I bought philosophic books, notably Spinoza's complete works in Latin, as well as the standard histories of philosophy of that time. I was a constant reader of the chief English philosophical journal, *Mind,* and I even wrote a rather lengthy article (a study of Hinton's later thought) and sent it to the editor, Professor Croom Robertson, who welcomed it in a friendly spirit, though from a complete stranger, and published it at once. That was in 1884 when I was twenty-five years of age. Almost immediately afterwards I chanced to become personally acquainted with a genuine philosopher and one of the most remarkable men I have ever known. This was Thomas Davidson. The books he left behind are not of the first importance, nor was he indeed so impressive a writer as speaker. He was above all an original personality, of almost passionate philosophic temperament and that eloquence which sometimes marks the Scotch intellect in its more exalted shapes. He was an outsider in philosophy, without academic associations, though attracted to various lines of thought, ancient and modern, and at this period specially interested in Rosmini. He traveled much, was at home in the United States even more than in England, and was frequently to be found in Rome.

Davidson was at this time collecting around him a small band of young men whom he desired to indoctrinate with his opinions and personally lead in the formation of a sort of quasi-communistic establishment in which to carry them out. My friend, Percival Chubb, afterwards known as an ethical leader in the United States, was prominent among them and by him I was introduced to Davidson and joined the little group who listened to his eloquent speech. He told me later that to me he had been specially drawn, and it was therefore a grievous disappointment for him, after he had expounded his doctrines during a long evening with, as he himself put it, all the unction he could command, to find next day that I, who had seemed to drink in eagerly all his eloquence, had really remained completely unmoved. He had misunderstood my temperament. I willingly and even sympathetically listen to arguments, but that does not mean acceptance or agreement. Davidson was so disgusted at my failure to exhibit the response he desired that a little later in a letter from Rome he broke off relations with me. At a later period, however, when there was no longer any question of my becoming a disciple, occasional friendly relations were resumed. The outcome of this episode doubtless seemed to Davidson entirely negative.

But it was far from being negative for me, or I should not have felt called upon to introduce it here. It had a very positive result, though one that would have been by no means pleasing to Davidson. It convinced me that philosophy is a purely personal matter. A genuine philosopher's credo is the outcome of a single complex personality: it cannot be transferred. No two persons, if sincere, can have the same philosophy.

While I made this discovery for myself, a few years later, when I began to study Nietzsche, I found that he had vaguely suggested a similar viewpoint. It was in my essay on Nietzsche in 1896 that I clearly set forth my attitude: "It is as undignified to think another man's philosophy as to wear another man's cast-off clothes.—Let Brown be a Brownite and Robinson a Robinsonian. It is not good that they should exchange their philosophies, or that either should insist on thrusting his threadbare misfits on Jones, who prefers to be metaphysically naked. When men have generally begun to realize this the world will be a richer and an honester world and a pleasanter one as well."

Though I made the discovery for myself, nowadays of course it is quite taken for granted. It has, for instance, been recently stated clearly by Bertrand Russell: "The logical quality of the cosmos as it appears in each of the great systems is due to the fact that it is one man's cosmos." But even for Bertrand Russell this attitude seems to be recent.

It must have been shortly after the Davidson episode

that I read Lange's *History of Materialism,* and was thereby fortified in my attitude toward philosophy. Lange's book was not only a notable history, fascinating and sympathetic, of the development of the materialist doctrine, but it culminated in the conclusion, for which I was now fully prepared, that metaphysics is a form of poetry. I might not indeed myself put it quite that way. I would draw a distinction between metaphysics and poetry. But I was willing to see the justification of a metaphysical system no longer placed on an abstract pseudo-scientific foundation but on a personal esthetic foundation. I was thus prepared to view later with sympathy and admiration the metaphysical view of the world as a beautiful spectacle put forward by Jules de Gaultier, one of the most notable thinkers of our time, though outside academic circles. So far as I received any stimulus from other thinkers in the foundation of my own philosophic vision, Hinton, Davidson, and Lange are the names I would mention. I had thus, by about the age of twenty-five, at almost the same moment abandoned the active search for a philosophy of my own and yet accepted the functional justification of philosophy on a new intellectual foundation.

While I thus reached the conviction that every man who thinks should have his own philosophy, I do not seem to have shown any anxiety to acquire a philosophy for myself. As I now, long afterwards, look back at this period of my life I am disposed to put this indifference down to a sound instinct. It has come to seem to me that one's philosophical attitude can only be reached by an unconscious process, that it is a spiritual growth as much beyond our control, and often beyond our consciousness, as physical growth.

Not in philosophy alone are the soundest results thus reached. We are probably here faced by a general law. I am interested to see that in the recently published volume of collected essays by the late A. R. Powys, an architect with a sound and penetrating insight into the art of architecture, precisely the same principle is enunciated as I find to hold true in philosophy. Discussing the "Origin of Bad Architecture," he regards dependence on the reasoned theories of others as the source of feeble architecture. We need, he declares, first of all a digested experience. "By 'digested experience' is meant the subconscious result of experience, or in other words the certain feeling and assured knowledge which are in a man without resort to conscious feeling or thought." It has come about, as it were, instinctively. This does not mean that the art product comes solely from within. Powys insisted, on the contrary, that the experience would come from without and include distinctive elements of the age in which the artist lives. But they are unconsciously absorbed and transformed; that is the significance of the term "digested experience." So far as I acquired any philosophy it was the outcome of varied contacts with the world during long years, unconsciously assimilated and transferred into an unrealized personal credo.

It was not until later life when I was contemplating the publication of my book, *The Dance of Life,* largely made up of essays written during the immediately preceding years, that I realized that I had, without directly aiming at it, attained a philosophic attitude and even what may fairly be described as a philosophic creed. I was now sixty years of age but, as I view this matter—though I know that few professional philosophers would agree—that is quite early enough in life for a definitely conscious philosophic credo to be established. Much earlier than this, of course, it must have been slowly constituted and actively operative, but the less consciously the more genuinely. Otherwise it runs the risk of being merely artificial, adopted on grounds that were not the real outcome of personality.

In the determination of my own philosophic outlook it seems evident that there was from the outset the instinctive impulse to embrace the elements of life harmoniously. When I discovered that there was a discordant break between the emotional religious life as I had been experiencing it, and my strong intellectual aptitudes, I was profoundly unhappy. Some of my friends, when they discovered a similar break in their psychic lives, had cheerfully selected the side of intellect and had nothing but contempt to pour on emotional religious demands, while in the mass of mankind, needless to say, neither intellectual nor emotional demands are strong enough to involve any conflict, and the result is an attitude of indifference rather than of serenity. It has been my experience that people of sensitive intelligence have often remarked on my "serenity." This is not the outcome of any conscious intention on my part and I have often enough been far from conscious of any inner serenity. But I can well believe that the conquest of opposing psychic elements into a single harmonious whole naturally results in an attitude of serenity.

During the Great War I came to realize that the harmony I had attained between the two opposing elements was really only a particular application of a deep-lying tendency of my nature. This came about through my contemplation of the disputes between militarists, whether German or English, over the term "conflict," which they confused with "war." I realized that while war was undoubtedly a form of conflict, we must regard conflict as a much wider term, including forms of opposition which were not war and might be of totally different tendency. That brought the disputes between nations into line with that general tendency to opposition which is essential to life and opened out the possibility of superseding war, not in a merely negative manner, but by the fruitful necessity of the presence of opposites. Conflict is in nature but it is a fruitful conflict in which each opposing element may have its essential value. I might have recalled the saying of Heraclitus that "Conflict is the father of all things," since conflict that was violent could hardly be fatherly. I set forth the result I had reached, together with some of its wider implications, in an essay, "The Philosophy of Conflict" (ultimately embodied in a volume with the same title), which I regard as of significance in the presentation of my philosophic outlook.

Those pacifists who supposed that the supersession of war by more civilized methods of adjusting national differences meant the abolition of conflict fell into an error which was fatal, it seemed to me, to a sound conception of life and the world.

Our planetary system, we were taught, must be viewed as carried on harmoniously by the action of opposing forces, centripetal and centrifugal, pulling in opposite ways. The same conflict is even clearer in the vegetable world. We see it in every seed in its vital pressure against the enclosing capsule and every unfolding frond of fern bears witness to a similar opposition of forces. Opposition is not a hindrance to life, it is the necessary condition for the becoming of life. No doubt this realization of opposing forces in the vegetable world came to me as an early suggestion from Hinton's *Life in Nature*. Now I am ever increasingly impressed by the resemblances of vegetable life to animal life. I see how closely akin are the laws that rule in both spheres. I find that the behavior of plants is what my own would be under the same conditions and with the same limitations. That the same law of conflicting forces as the necessary condition of life prevails in the animal world needs no proof, nor that it is most marked in the highest forms of life, and notably in the mammal with its expanding ovum which only develops under the pressure of the firmly constricting womb. I reach out toward a conception of the unity of what we call the universe. What we call life really prevails throughout.

It was not until later that I realized that the vision of

harmonious conflict I had attained in an entirely different direction might be seen perfectly in that sphere of sex the study of which had been my chief life work. I made no clear statement of it until 1931. At that time, in the *Forum Philosophicum,* Professor Del-Negro put forth his view of the problem of sex as one of "antinomies" only to be resolved by compromise. Dr. Schmidt, the editor, invited me to write a reply (which was reprinted in the Second Series of my *Views and Reviews*). I was unable to accept Del-Negro's doctrine of compromise between essential elements of life. Here, as elsewhere, I saw the harmonious conflict of opposite tendencies, each necessary to the other and supporting it, while compromise would merely mean weakness. All the phenomena of sex seemed to illustrate this conflict, from the physical opposites of tumescence and detumescence to the erotic conflict of courtship and the social balance between sex indulgence and sex abstinence. Sex and culture are perfectly balanced. To desire freedom from this balance is to desire annihilation.

Man in his conscious arts illustrates this same conflict. Nowhere is it better revealed than in the primary art of architecture by the device of the arch. Here we see how in the conflict of two opposing forces each supports the other and stability is ensured. If the opposition ceased the arch would collapse in ruin.

In the other primordial art, more ancient even than architecture, that of dancing, we see the same harmonious conflict beautifully illustrated. Every pose of the dancer is the achievement of movement in which the maximum tension of opposing muscular actions is held in the most fluidly harmonious balance.

In other arts, even if this principle is less convincingly illustrated, it is still present. In poetry there is the conflict between the centrifugal impulse of expression and the centripetal restraint of form. From an early period men drawn to poetry seem instinctively to have felt that the impulse to emotionalized expression should be held in check by an impulse to rigid form, and that only when these two opposites were combined could the result be accepted as satisfactory. When, as sometimes happens, a poet rebels against this need for the harmonious opposition and seeks either to concentrate on form or on expression there are but few who enjoy his results.

One could, I believe, detect a similar law in other arts. The demand for the harmonious conflict of opposites rules in nature's operations, and since man is a part of nature it also rules in his operations. He disregards it at his peril and at the sacrifice of that serenity which comes of an even unconscious sense of oneness with our universe.

So much, it seems to me, may serve to indicate all that I have been able to achieve in the general attainment of a philosophic credo. Since, even to myself, it has only been a slow, gradual, and largely unconscious achievement I have naturally made little attempt to preach it to others. But it has been clear to any sympathetic reader of my books, and to some it has been helpful in aiding them to reach their own outlook in the world.

The reward of being simple and sincere with what seem the facts of one's universe is that one sheds abroad an influence that may be incalculable. It is worth while.

# E. M. FORSTER

*E. M. Forster, since the death of D. H. Lawrence, would probably by many critics be ranked as the foremost living English novelist. He has attained his eminence by the production of few books and these have generally reached only a small audience. Mr. Forster is distinguished for the beauty and polish of his style, the subtlety of his understanding, and the rich humanity that underlies the apparently quiet surfaces of his novels.*

*Born in 1879, he was educated at Kings College, Cambridge. His publications include 'Where Angels Fear to Tread' (1905); 'The Longest Journey' (1907); 'A Room With a View' (1908); 'Howards End' (1910); 'The Celestial Omnibus' (1923); 'Alexandria: A History and a Guide' (1923); 'Pharos and Pharillon' (1923); 'A Passage to India,' his most popular and probably his finest novel (1924); 'Aspects of the Novel' (1927); 'The Eternal Moment' (1928); 'Goldsworthy Lowes Dickinson' (1934); and a distinctive collection of essays, 'Abinger Harvest' (1936).*

# *E. M. Forster*

I do not believe in belief. But this is an age of faith, where one is surrounded by so many militant creeds that, in self-defense, one has to formulate a creed of one's own. Tolerance, good temper, and sympathy are no longer enough in a world which is rent by religious and racial persecution, in a world where ignorance rules, and science, who ought to have ruled, plays the subservient pimp. Tolerance, good temper, and sympathy—well, they are what matter really, and if the human race is not to collapse they must come to the front before long. But for the moment they don't seem enough, their action is no stronger than a flower, battered beneath a military jack boot. They want stiffening, even if the process coarsens them. Faith, to my mind, is a stiffening process, a sort of mental starch, which ought to be applied as sparingly as possible. I dislike the stuff. I do not believe in it, for its own sake, at all. Herein I probably differ from most of the contributors to this volume, who believe in belief, and are only sorry they can't swallow even more than they do. My lawgivers are Erasmus and Montaigne, not Moses and St. Paul. My temple stands not upon Mount Moriah but in that Elysian Field where even the immoral are admitted. My motto is "Lord, I disbelieve—help thou my unbelief."

I have, however, to live in an Age of Faith—the sort of thing I used to hear praised and recommended when I was a boy. It is damned unpleasant, really. It is bloody in every sense of the word. And I have to keep my end up in it. Where do I start?

With personal relationships. Here is something comparatively solid in a world full of violence and cruelty. Not absolutely solid, for psychology has split and shattered the idea of a "person," and has shown that there is something incalculable in each of us, which may at any moment rise to the surface and destroy our normal balance. We don't know what we're like. We can't know what other people are like. How then can we put any trust in personal relationships, or cling to them in the gathering political storm? In theory we can't. But in practice we can and do. Though A isn't unchangeably A or B unchangeably B, there can still be love and loyalty between the two. For the purpose of living one has to assume that the personality is solid, and the "self" is an entity, and to ignore all contrary evidence. And since to ignore evidence is one of the characteristics of faith, I certainly can proclaim that I believe in personal relationships.

Starting from them, I get a little order into the contemporary chaos. One must be fond of people and trust them if one isn't to make a mess of life, and it is therefore essential that they shouldn't let one down. They often do. The moral of which is that I must myself be as reliable as possible, and this I try to be. But reliability isn't a matter of contract—that is the main difference between the world of personal relationships and the world of business relationships. It is a matter for the heart, which signs no documents. In other words, reliability is impossible unless there is a natural warmth. Most men possess this warmth, though they often have bad luck and get chilled. Most of them, even when they are politicians, *want* to keep faith. And one can, at all events, show one's own little light here, one's own poor little trembling flame, with the knowledge that it's not the only light that is shining in the darkness, and not the only one which the darkness doesn't comprehend. Personal relations are despised today. They are regarded as bourgeois luxuries, as products of a time of fair weather which has now passed, and we are urged to get rid of them, and to dedicate ourselves to some movement or cause instead. I hate the idea of dying for a cause, and if I had to choose between betraying my country and betraying my friend, I hope I should have the guts to betray my country. Such a choice may scandalize the modern reader, and he may stretch out his patriotic hand to the telephone at once, and ring up the police. It wouldn't have shocked Dante, though. Dante places Brutus and Cassius in the lowest circle of Hell because they had chosen to betray their friend Julius Caesar rather than their country Rome. Probably one won't be asked to make such an agonizing choice. Still there lies at the back of every creed something terrible and hard for which the worshiper may one day be required to suffer, and there is even a terror and a hardness in this creed of personal relationships, urbane and mild though it sounds. Love and loyalty to an individual can run counter to the claims of the state. When they do—down with the state, say I, which means that the state will down me.

This brings me along to democracy, "even Love, the Beloved Republic, which feeds upon Freedom and lives." Democracy isn't a beloved republic really, and never will be. But it is less hateful than other contemporary forms of government, and to that extent it deserves our support. It does start from the assumption that the individual is important, and that all types are needed to make a civilization. It doesn't divide its citizens into the bossers and the bossed, as an efficiency regime tends to do. The people I admire most are those who are sensitive and want to create something or discover something, and don't see life in terms of power, and such people get more of a chance under a democracy than elsewhere. They found religions, great or small, or they produce literature and art, or they do disinterested scientific research, or they may be what is called "ordinary people," who are creative in their private lives, bring up their children decently, for instance, or help their neighbors. All these people need to express themselves, they can't do so unless society allows them liberty to do so, and the society which allows them most liberty is a democracy.

Democracy has another merit. It allows criticism, and if there isn't public criticism there are bound to be hushed-up scandals. That is why I believe in the press, despite all its lies and vulgarity, and why I believe in Parliament. The British Parliament is often sneered at because it's a talking shop. Well, I believe in it because it is a talking shop. I believe in the private member who makes himself a nuisance. He gets snubbed and is told that he is cranky or ill-informed, but he exposes abuses which would otherwise never have been mentioned, and very often an abuse gets put right just by being mentioned. Occasionally, too, in my country, a well-meaning public official loses his head in the cause of efficiency, and thinks himself God Almighty. Such officials are particularly frequent in the Home Office. Well, there will be questions about them in Parliament sooner or later, and then they'll have to mend their steps. Whether Parliament is either a representative body or an efficient one is very doubtful, but I value it because it criticizes and talks, and because its chatter gets widely reported.

So two cheers for democracy: one because it admits variety and two because it permits criticism. Two cheers are quite enough: there is no occasion to give three. Only Love, the Beloved Republic deserves that.

What about force, though? While we are trying to be sensitive and advanced and affectionate and tolerant, an unpleasant question pops up: Doesn't all society rest upon force? If a government can't count upon the police and the army, how can it hope to rule? And if an individual gets knocked on the head or sent to a labor camp, of what significance are his opinions?

E. M. Forster

This dilemma doesn't worry me as much as it does some. I realize that all society rests upon force. But all the great creative actions, all the decent human relations, occur during the intervals when force has not managed to come to the front. These intervals are what matter. I want them to be as frequent and as lengthy as possible and I call them "civilization." Some people idealize force and pull it into the foreground and worship it, instead of keeping it in the background as long as possible. I think they make a mistake, and I think that their opposites, the mystics, err even more when they declare that force doesn't exist. I believe that it does exist, and that one of our jobs is to prevent it from getting out of its box. It gets out sooner or later, and then it destroys us and all the lovely things which we have made. But it isn't out all the time, for the fortunate reason that the strong are so stupid. Consider their conduct for a moment in the Nibelung's *Ring*. The giants there have the guns, or in other words the gold; but they do nothing with it, they do not realize that they are all-powerful, with the result that the catastrophe is delayed and the castle of Walhalla, insecure but glorious, fronts the storms for generations. Fafnir, coiled around his hoard, grumbles and grunts; we can hear him under Europe today; the leaves of the wood already tremble, and the Bird calls its warnings uselessly. Fafnir will destroy us, but by a blessed dispensation he is stupid and slow, and creation goes on just outside the poisonous blast of his breath. The Nietzschean would hurry the monster up, the mystic would say he didn't exist, but Wotan, wiser than either, hastens to create warriors before doom declares itself. The Valkyries are symbols not only of courage but of intelligence; they represent the human spirit snatching its opportunity while the going is good, and one of them even finds time to love. Brunhilde's last song hymns the recurrence of love, and since it is the privilege of art to exaggerate she goes even further, and proclaims the love which is eternally triumphant and feeds upon freedom, and lives.

So that is what I feel about force and violence. It is, alas! the ultimate reality, on this earth, but—hooray!—it doesn't always get to the front. Some people call its absences "decadence"; I call them "civilization" and find in such interludes the chief justification for the human experiment. I look the other way until fate strikes me. Whether this is due to courage or to cowardice in my own case I cannot be sure. But I know that if men hadn't looked the other way in the past nothing of any value would survive. The people I respect most behave as if they were immortal and as if society were eternal. Both assumptions are false: both of them must be accepted as true if we are to go on eating and working and loving, and are to keep open a few breathing holes for the human spirit. No millennium seems likely to descend upon humanity; no better and stronger League of Nations will be instituted; no form of Christianity and no alternative to Christianity will bring peace to the world or integrity to the individual; no "change of heart" will occur. And yet we needn't despair, indeed we cannot despair; the evidence of history shows us that men have always insisted on behaving creatively under the shadow of the sword; that they have done their artistic and scientific and domestic stuff for the sake of doing it, and that we had better follow their example under the shadow of the airplanes. Others, with more vision or courage than myself, see the salvation of humanity ahead, and will dismiss my conception of civilization as paltry, a sort of tip-and-run game. Certainly it is presumptuous to say that we *can't* improve, and that man, who has only been in power for a few thousand years, will never learn to make use of his power. All I mean is that, if people continue to kill one another at the rate they do, the world cannot get better than it is, and that since there are more people than formerly, and their means for destroying one another more diabolic, the world may well get worse. What's good in people—and consequently in the world—is their insistence on creation, their belief in friendship, in loyalty, for its own sake; and though violence remains and is indeed the major partner in this muddled establishment, I believe that creativeness remains too, and will always assume direction when violence sleeps. So, though I am not an optimist, I cannot agree with Sophocles that it were better never to have been born. And although I see no evidence that each batch of births is superior to the last, I leave the field open for this happier view. This is such a difficult time to live in, especially for a European, one can't help getting gloomy and also a bit rattled.

There is of course hero worship, fervently recommended as a panacea in some quarters. But here we shall get no help. Hero worship is a dangerous vice, and one of the minor merits of a democracy is that it does not encourage it, or produce that unmanageable type of citizen known as the Great Man. It produces instead different kinds of small men, and that's a much finer achievement. But people who can't get interested in the variety of life and can't make up their own minds get discontented over this, and they long for a hero to bow down before and to follow blindly. It's significant that a hero is an integral part of the authoritarian stock in trade today. An efficiency regime can't be run without a few heroes stuck about to carry off the dullness—much as plums have to be put into a bad pudding to make it palatable. One hero at the top and a smaller one each side of him is a favorite arrangement, and the timid and the bored are comforted by such a trinity, and, bowing down, feel exalted by it.

No, I distrust Great Men. They produce a desert of uniformity around them and often a pool of blood too, and I always feel a little man's pleasure when they come a cropper. Every now and then one reads in the newspapers some such statement as, "The *coup d'état* appears to have failed, and Admiral Boga's whereabouts is at present unknown." Admiral Boga had probably every qualification for being a great man—an iron will, personal magnetism, dash, flair—but fate was against him, so he retires to unknown whereabouts instead of parading history with his peers. He fails with a completeness that no artist and no lover can experience, because with them the process of creation is itself an achievement, whereas with him the only possible achievement is success. I believe in aristocracy though—if that's the right word, and if a democrat may use it. Not an aristocracy of power, based upon rank and influence, but an aristocracy of the sensitive, the considerate, and the plucky. Its members are to be found in all nations and classes, and all through the ages, and there is a secret understanding between them when they meet. They represent the true human tradition, the one permanent victory of our queer race over cruelty and chaos. Thousands of them perish in obscurity; a few are great names. They are sensitive for others as well as for themselves, they are considerate without being fussy, their pluck is not swankiness but the power to endure, and they can take a joke. I give no examples—it is risky to do that—but the reader may as well consider whether this is the type of person he would like to meet and to be, and whether (going further with me) he would prefer that the type should *not* be an ascetic one. I'm against asceticism myself. I'm with the old Scotchman who wanted less chastity and more delicacy. I don't feel that my aristocrats are a real aristocracy if they thwart their bodies, since bodies are the instruments through which we register and enjoy the world. Still, I don't insist here. This isn't a major point. It's clearly possible to be sensitive, considerate, and plucky and yet be an ascetic too, and if anyone possesses the first three qualities, I'll let him in! On they go—an invincible army, yet not a victorious one. The aristocrats, the elect, the chosen, the best people—all the words that describe them are false, and all attempts to organize them fail. Again and again authority, seeing their value, has tried to net them and to utilize them as the Egyptian priesthood or the Christian Church or the Chinese civil service or the Group Movement, or some other worthy stunt. But they slip through the net and are gone; when the door is shut they are no longer in the room; their temple, as one of them remarked, is the holiness of the heart's imagination, and their kingdom, though they never possess it, is the wide open world.

With this type of person knocking about, and constantly crossing one's path if one has eyes to see or hands to feel, the experiment of earthly life cannot be dismissed as a failure. But it may well be hailed as a tragedy, the tragedy being that no device has been found by which these private decencies can be transferred to public affairs. As soon as people have power they go crooked and sometimes dotty, too, because the possession of power lifts them into a region where normal honesty never pays. For instance, the man who is selling newspapers outside the Houses of Parliament can safely leave his papers to go for a drink, and his cap beside them: anyone who takes a paper is sure to drop a copper into the cap. But the men who are inside the Houses of Parliament—they can't trust one another like that; still less can the government they compose trust other governments. No caps upon the pavement here, but suspicion, treachery, and armaments. The more highly public life is organized the lower does its morality sink; the nations of today behave to each other worse than they ever did in the past, they cheat, rob, bully, and bluff, make war without notice, and kill as many women and children as possible; whereas primitive tribes were at all events restrained by taboos. It's a humiliating outlook—though the greater the darkness, the brighter shine the little lights, reassuring one another, signaling, "Well, at all events I'm still here. I don't like it very much, but how are you?" Unquenchable lights of my aristocracy! Signals of the invincible army! "Come along—anyway let's have a good time while we can." I think they signal that too.

The savior of the future—if ever he comes—will not preach a new gospel. He will merely utilize my aristocracy; he will make effective the good will and the good temper which are already existing. In other words he will introduce a new technique. In economics, we are told that if there was a new technique of distribution, there need be no poverty, and people would not starve in one place while crops were dug under in another. A similar change is needed in the sphere of morals and politics. The desire for it is by no means new; it was expressed, for example, in theological terms by Jacopone da Todi over six hundred years ago. *"Ordina questo amore, O tu che m'ami,"* he said. "O thou who lovest me—set this love in order." His prayer was not granted and I do not myself believe that it ever will be, but here, and not through a change of heart, is our probable route. Not by becoming better, but by ordering and distributing his native goodness, will man shut up force into its box, and so gain time to explore the universe and to set his mark upon it worthily. At present he only explores it at odd moments, when force is looking the other way, and his divine creativeness appears as a trivial by-product, to be scrapped as soon as the drums beat and the bombers hum.

Such a change, claim the orthodox, can only be made by Christianity, and will be made by it in God's good time: man always has failed and always will fail to organize his own goodness, and it is presumptuous of him to try. This claim—solemn as it is—leaves me cold. I cannot believe that Christianity will ever cope with the present world-wide mess, and I think that such influence as it retains in modern society is due to its financial backing rather than to its spiritual appeal. It was a spiritual force once, but the indwelling spirit will have to be restated if it is to calm the waters again, and probably restated in a non-Christian form. Naturally a great many people, and people who are not only good but able and intelligent, will disagree with me here; they will vehemently deny that Christianity has failed, or they will argue that its failure proceeds from the wickedness of men, and really proves its ultimate success. They have Faith, with a large F. My faith has a very small one, and I only bring it into the open because these are strenuous and serious days, and one likes to say what one thinks while speech is still free: it may not be free much longer.

These are the reflections of an individualist and a liberal who has found his liberalism crumbling beneath him and at first felt ashamed. Then, looking around, he decided there was no special reason for shame, since other people, whatever they felt, were equally insecure. And as for individualism—there seems no way out of this, even if one wants to find one. The dictator-hero can grind down his citizens till they are all alike, but he can't melt them into a single man. That is beyond his power. He can order them to merge, he can incite them to mass antics, but they are obliged to be born separately and to die separately and, owing to these unavoidable termini, will always be running off the totalitarian rails. The memory of birth and the expectation of death always lurk within the human being, making him separate from his fellows and consequently capable of intercourse with them. Naked I came into the world, naked I shall go out of it! And a very good thing too, for it reminds me that I am naked under my shirt. Until psychologists and biologists have done much more tinkering than seems likely, the individual remains firm and each of us must consent to be one, and to make the best of the difficult job.

ELLEN GLASGOW

*Ellen Glasgow is perhaps the sanest and intellectually most mature of the many talented writers of fiction produced by the South since the turn of the century. She is also extraordinary among American writers for the consistency of her development: her books continually improve in wisdom without losing in wit. To her long series of novels, beginning as far back as 1897 with 'The Descendant,' Americans owe a clear picture of the post-bellum South, drawn by a novelist who, though she writes out of a long family tradition, is not blinded by provincial partisanship. It is a minor but still somewhat remarkable fact that though she is clearly among the best half dozen of American novelists, she has never received the Pulitzer Prize.*

*Ellen Glasgow was born in Richmond, Virginia, and makes her home there. She was privately, and obviously well, educated. Among a score of books that have come from her pen during the past forty years may be mentioned 'The Voice of the People' (1900); 'The Battle-Ground' (1902); 'The Deliverance' (1904); 'Virginia' (1913); 'Barren Ground' (1925); 'The Romantic Comedians' (1926); 'They Stooped to Folly' (1929); 'The Sheltered Life' (1932); 'Vein of Iron' (1935).*

# *Ellen Glasgow*

Few of us, I imagine, would regard our unimportant theories of life and death as a philosophy; and concerning my own private opinions I cherish no such delusion. Nevertheless, even those of us who think in symbols as concrete as facts, and scarcely more flexible, continue to be governed by rules of custom and doctrine which embody in essence the highly concentrated philosophy of the ages. Whenever and wherever we may speculate upon the mysteries of nature or upon the mortality of man, we are, in our humble degree, invoking some august metaphysical system. Although it is true that speculation represents only a single branch of philosophy, still it contains within itself the whole substance of root and flower. So long as one lives at all, one must, of necessity, hold by some fixed principle, if it is merely the common assumption that it is safer to be good than bad, or that the sun will rise again after it has gone down, or that, in any event, there is always tomorrow. But even these few certainties must have arisen in response to some elementary conjectures.

As a very small child, I was a believing animal. I believed in fairies; I believed in witches; I believed in white and gray and black magic; I believed in Santa Claus and in Original Sin; I believed in souls—not only in the souls of men and women and children and animals, but in the souls, too, of trees and plants, and of winds and clouds. I believed that, by some miraculous performance, all this countless multitude of souls would be taken care of, through a Sabbath day without ending, in an infinite Heaven. But in one thing, I cannot recall that I ever believed; and that was in the kind of God who had once savored the smoke of burnt offerings, and to whose ghost, in churches everywhere, good people were still chanting hymns of immelodious praise. From the paternal stock, I had inherited the single-minded Scottish creed of generations. On the distaff side, I derived my free and easy faith from the gentler piety of the Episcopal Church. Yet I have no recollection that I ever truly believed either in the God of the Shorter Catechism or in the God of the Thirty-nine Articles. I could not trust an Everlasting Mercy, whether stern or mild, which was omnipotent, but permitted pain to exist, and the Prince of Darkness to roam the earth in search of whom he might devour.

Had my parents been alike in mental and physical characteristics it is possible that I should have continued a united family tradition. The longer I observe experience, the greater emphasis I place upon determinism both in our beliefs and in our bodies. Regarding the freedom of the will, and regarding that doctrine alone, I suppose I may call myself more or less of a pragmatist. Indefensible in theory, no doubt, that exalted error—if it be an error—appears necessary to the order of civilized man, and seems to justify, on higher grounds, its long record of service as a moral utility. But certainly every consequence, whether material or immaterial, must follow a cause; and so, it then seemed to me that I had inherited not only my inquiring mind and sensitive nerves, but, less directly perhaps, some tragic conflict of types. My father, a man of sterling integrity and unshakable fortitude, accepted literally the most barbaric texts in the Scriptures, and was equally sound on doctrine, from the fall of Adam to infant damnation. My mother, magnanimous to a fault, would have divided her last hope of Heaven with any spiritual beggar. Defying modern theories of heredity, I was always, in sympathy at least, a mother's child, endowed, I liked to imagine, with some generous prenatal influence. When I think of her, after forty years of absence, I see her eternally poised in an attitude of giving or blessing, as if time, or the past, or merely an illusion of memory, had crystallized around her lovely and beneficent image.

It is because of her that, in looking back, I seem never to have been too young to side with the helpless. And it is still because of her that I have fought against cruelty and intolerance as my arch-antagonists. For I was barely more than a child—or so it seems to me now—when I found myself first confronting the knowledge of good and evil in the things my elders believed. By this time, I had seen not only the joys and sorrows of human life, but the joys and sorrows of that vast and imperfectly understood animal world; and, for me, the fate of animals in a hostile universe had demolished all the airy towers of theological dogma. I worried, too, at that early age, for I was a child who dreamed dreams and saw visions, over the unhappy end of the heathen. Suppose, I would ask myself when I awoke in the night, that, after all, damnation should turn out to be true at the Last Judgment? So many things were true that I could not believe in! I was only ten, I remember, when I told myself, with a kind of cheerful desperation, "If I am damned, I am damned, and there is nothing to be done about it." Whatever happened to the larger unredeemed part of creation, I would stand, with my mother, on the side of the heathen, and on the side, too, of our lesser brethren, the animals; for none of these disinherited tribes, I was assured, could expect so much as a crust or crumb of divine grace in the exclusive plan of salvation. Then gradually, as I grew up, these questions dissolved and evaporated, and at last ceased to disturb me. While I groped my way toward an unattainable meaning in life, I found that orthodox Christianity, in company with orthodox Judaism, retreated to a position among yet older mythologies, beside other impressive but inadequate symbols of man's communion with that Unknown Power he has called God. As time flows on, and creeds soften, the immaterial, if not the material, rights of the heathen are coming slowly to be recognized; and as time moves still nearer its end and softened creeds disappear, our elastic sense of justice may extend even into the animal kingdom.

But if I could not worship my father's God, I could, and did with all my mind and heart, adore my mother's goodness of soul. This faith I have never lost, since it is rooted, not in the mind alone, but in the deepest sources of personality. As the image of a revealed Deity faded beyond the vanishing point in the perspective, my vague religious instinct leaned toward a distant trust in some spirit, or divine essence, which many poets and a few philosophers have called the Good. Although the Good was only a part of the whole (was there not proof of this all around us?), it was nevertheless the most pure and the highest part. In a universe such as ours, the existence of an all-powerful Providence, concerned with the intimate hopes and the special fate of mankind alone, was, for me at least, then and always incredible. Yet was it not even more unreasonable to assume that there existed no consciousness superior to ours in an infinity of universes? To this question, I could find no answer; but I knew, or thought I knew, that wherever we looked in nature or in civilization, we could not fail to perceive the signs, explicit or implicit, of an actual presence we had named goodness. We might observe also, if we persevered with an open mind, that during our life on this planet, the Good, though always struggling and refusing to surrender, was seldom wholly triumphant outside the pictorial fantasies of the saints.

Like Mr. Santayana, whose work I came to know only in later years, I had been repelled in youth by that "moral equivocation" which seemed to pervade the best-thought-of philosophers. This was "the survival of a sort of forced optimism and pulpit unction, by which a cruel and nasty world, painted by them in the most lurid colors, was nevertheless set up as the model and standard of what ought to be. The duty of an honest moralist would have been rather to distinguish, in this bad or mixed reality, the part, however small, that could be loved and chosen from the remainder, however large, which was to be rejected and renounced. Certainly the universe was in flux and dynamically single; but this fatal flux could very well take care of itself; and it was not so fluid that no islands of a relative permanence and beauty might not be formed in it."

In this pronouncement I might have found comfort had I stumbled upon it at the exact right moment in youth. Unlike Mr. Santayana, however, since I am no philosopher, I was repelled also by his early idol, Spinoza, whose system appeared to my youthful mind as a pure anatomy of the intellect. Compared with Schopenhauer, indeed, who seemed to me essentially human, I felt that Spinoza's philosophy needed a covering of flesh and blood over its bare structure. Yet, even then, I was beginning slowly to understand that a man's religion or philosophy is as natural an expression of his identity as the color of his eyes or the tones of his voice. When he has not accepted an inherited and traditional way of living and thinking, he obeys the special compulsion of his education and of his environment.

But to return. Was this Good, I then asked myself, a spirit or an immanence, indwelling and all-pervading, though not all-powerful? Or was it merely one of those inevitable results of biological expediency which have accompanied the slow processes of evolution? Certainly I could not believe that goodness was rewarded either in the present world or in some problematical Heaven. In a state of nature, goodness had too often gone down before the cannibal necessities; nor had it appeared constantly victorious among the utilitarian morals of civilization. Yet, in spite of these weaknesses—for I was compelled to recognize the limitations of the Good, just as I recognized the more obvious limitations of the True—I continued to revere this power as the one and only principle deserving of worship. Not, I thought, because the Good is omnipotent, but because, though lacking in omnipotence, it has endured and survived in the struggle with evil, whether or not that evil is inseparable from the nature of life on the earth.

So far I have dealt only with my early search for a faith—or at least for a stable conviction. In this youthful pursuit feeling was naturally more active than reason; for religion is, after all, an affair of the heart, and we have not forgotten that "the heart has its reasons which reason does not comprehend." We worship a personal God, not a First Principle. We worship him the more passionately because we know nothing about him, not even that we know nothing. We have created our idea of him in our own image, and he embodies the wish fulfillment of an ego we believe immortal. Twenty-five centuries ago Xenophanes first remarked: "Men have always made their gods in their own images—the Greeks like the Greeks, the Ethiopians like the Ethiopians." And so it has continued down to our distracted epoch. The god of astronomers is an astronomer, the god of mathematicians is a mathematician, the god of geologists is a geologist, the god of poets is a poet, the god of dictators is a dictator, the god of democrats is a democrat, and, incredible as it may appear, the god of politicians is, no doubt, a politician. This practice has never varied, notwithstanding the commandment, "God is a spirit: and they that worship him must worship him in spirit and in truth."

Thus it was in the beginning that my heart more than my mind was left unsatisfied by theological dogma. Years afterwards, when I began a comparative study of religious beliefs, this yearning was still unappeased; but it was my intelligence now, not my emotions, that demanded a reason.

*Foster Studio, Richmond, Va.*

Ellen Glasgow

Few religious figures, and fewer religious creeds, appealed to my individual blend of inherited and acquired characteristics. It is true that the ineffable dim figures of the Christ and the Buddha affected me deeply. Still, I could not deny that the last place to search for them, either in spirit or in truth, would be the imposing systems of theology which had borrowed their names and so frequently rejected their natures. My sense no less than my sensibilities revolted from the primitive myth, confirmed in bloodguiltiness, of a murdered god, whose body must be partaken of, whether by consubstantiation or transubstantiation. Yet the image of St. Francis of Assisi, who has been called the only Christian since Christ, almost persuaded me in one of "the dark nights of the soul." There was a summer many years ago when I followed the footsteps of the saint over Italy, and that journey moved me as poetry moves me—or the poetry in religion. Here indeed was the way of the heart as well as the way of the cross! Then, as I came down the hill from Assisi, I met one of the wretched "little brothers" of St. Francis, a small skeleton of a horse, staggering under a lash as it dragged several robust Franciscan friars up to the church. And I saw then, as I saw again and again throughout my Italian pilgrimage, that St. Francis was one alone, but the Franciscan friars are a multitude.

It was not long after this that I studied the Sacred Books of the East, and found inspiration, however fleeting, in the *Upanishads,* but more especially in the Buddhist *Sutras.* The figure of the Compassionate One, whose mercy embraced all living things, regardless of race or tribe or species, seemed to fulfill that ancient Hindu invocation, which Schopenhauer considered the noblest of prayers, "May all that have life be delivered from suffering." Moreover, the appeal of Buddha was not to the heart alone. I agree with Mr. H. G. Wells when he says: "The fundamental teaching of Gautama, as it is now being made plain to us by the study of original sources, is clear and simple, and in the closest harmony with modern ideas. It is beyond all dispute the achievement of one of the most penetrating intelligences the world has ever known."

But even more than the religion of Jesus, since Buddhism is many centuries older, the Eightfold Path has been buried beneath the parasitic growths of human greed, stupidity, and ignorance. No, my mind could not rest there. My mind could not rest anywhere, since neither of the world's greatest religions held the right message for me. I was young; I was groping my way; and I was impeded by that serious obstacle to contentment, the certainty that one may grasp and hold, not only facts, but even truth itself, if one seeks it very earnestly.

There was a period, following grief and illness, when I turned to the philosophy of mysticism, and endeavored to reach, through intuition alone, that absolute truth which is denied to the intellect. For several years I read widely in the writings of the mystics, both pagan and Christian; and I drew strength from Krishna in the *Bhagavad-Gita,* from the Alone of Plotinus, from Pascal's God known of the heart. I remember an August afternoon high up in the Alps, when I persuaded myself that I had felt, if only for an infinitesimal point of time, that inward light which shone for Jakob Böhme when he looked through it into "the essences" of the waving grass and herbs on the hillside. For an instant only this light shone; then it passed on with the wind in the grass; and I was never, in all the years that came afterwards, to know it again. The world and the time spirit together bore down on me. In the end, I recalled that moment of vision merely as a lost endeavor to escape from physical boundaries.

So it was that I passed, briefly and safely, through a perilous metaphysical stage; and if my search taught me nothing else, at least it left me with a broader tolerance of the unseen and the unknown, and with a knowledge, drawn directly from experience, of the urgent needs of the spirit. In the fresh enthusiasm with which I turned toward the material aspects of nature and the immediate testimony of science, I could still rejoice that I had once inhabited both the visible and the invisible worlds. After all, what I wanted from life was to live, to feel, and to know as completely as the circumscribed scope of my being allowed. It was inevitable, no doubt, that I should move on to another angle of vision; yet I have never lost a consuming interest in the origin of ideas, and in philosophy as an expression of man's relation to the mystery around him. For I believe matter to be only a single aspect or manifestation of that mystery, though I doubt whether we shall ever know, through our perceptions alone, a world far other than the world of matter—or the sensations we assume to be matter. If life has a deeper meaning, it must forever elude us. Neither science nor philosophy can do more than illumine or enkindle the senses through which impressions or what we call knowledge must come. Yet it is of these vague impressions and of this uncertain knowledge that the scholar, as well as the creative artist, must assemble and build up the very substance, the feeling, sight, taste, touch, scents and sounds, of reality.

It is true, nevertheless, that even in my efforts and my failures, in my belief and my skepticism, I had arrived at the basis of what I may call a determining point of view, if not a philosophy. In my endless curiosity about life, I had fallen by a happy accident (how else could this occur in my special environment?) upon a strayed copy of *The Origin of Species*; and this single book had led me back, through biology, to the older philosophic theory of evolution. The Darwinian hypothesis did not especially concern me, nor was I greatly interested in the scientific question of its survival. In any case, it was well able, I felt, to take care of itself and fight its own battles. What did interest me, supremely, was the broader synthesis of implications and inferences. On this foundation of probability, if not of certainty, I have found—or so it still seems to me—a permanent resting place; and in the many years that have come and gone, I have seen no reason, by and large, to reject this cornerstone of my creed.

All this, precipitate as it appears in print, was by no means within the nature of a revelation, though it is true that my discovery of the vast province of ideas was not without the startled wonder, and the eager awakening, of a religious conversion. When I came upon them, in the beginning, all philosophies were new, exhilarating, and bathed in a mental climate that was like the freshness of dawn. It was as if my intelligence, eager and undisciplined, had escaped suddenly into some new republic of the mind. The charming social culture in which I had lived and moved regarded all abstract ideas as dangerously contagious; and in our incessant sprightly talk we had confined our topics to light gossip of persons or food or clothes, or occasionally to the blunted malice of anonymous scandal. I had known in my younger years only two persons with whom I had ever discussed books or intellectual ideas. Such subjects were not only avoided, as they are nowadays in many circles both in New York and London, but they were, in some strange fashion, classed as socially untouchable. When I look back upon this Southern ostracism of the abstract, it appears amusing. Yet only a year or two ago I was warned by a literary Frenchman that I must never speak of books if I wished to find a welcome in "the best circles" of London. My problem was simplified, however, because I wanted, above all things, to know the truth of life, and I cared nothing whatever for the best circles anywhere. In my eagerness to test experience, to be many-minded, as well as many-sided, I had often lost my ground and grasped vainly at shadows. Still, in that eagerness there was a vital impulse;

there was energy; there was intensity of purpose. Almost every phase of thought, indeed, I seem to have shared, or at least recognized, except the state of vegetable calm which is usually mistaken for resignation.

It is far indeed from Plotinus to Locke or Hume or Darwin; yet I traveled that journey through the ether to what I feel to be the solid ground under my feet. And all the while, though I had never suspected this, I was revolving in a circular course, which would lead me back to the nature of self in the end. While I imagined that I traveled into space, I was, in fact, merely turning round and round within the area of my own consciousness. In seeking alike the known and the unknowable, I was trying to discover the laws of my own being, and to establish my own inner harmony. This, for a novelist of reality, remains, I think, the source of all indispensable knowledge; to order one's internal sphere, until the conflict of outward forms with the substance of personality may deepen the tone without impairing the design and proportion of a world the imagination reflects. If my growth had been slow, and my apprenticeship long, this was partly because life, the enemy of reflection, was constantly—or so it then seemed to me—thrusting its more vital activities into the necessary mood of reverie or contemplation. There is mystery in the abstract, and mystery never loses its fascination for the inquiring mind, but there are possibilities and fulfillments to be found upon the shifting surface of experience. I had tried both, I told myself, however inaccurately, and I had won, if not wisdom, at least the quick and nimble exercise of intelligence. It is well, no doubt, that an artist should hold by a rational code; but it is even better, I believe, that he should have charted the obscure seas of his own consciousness, and that he should perceive clearly the distance that divides the subject within from the nearer objects, as well as from the far perspective, of the external world.

Side by side with the inquiring faculty, that other half of my mind, the creative faculty, had been perpetually at work spinning an imaginary universe of earth, sun, and moon. Sometimes these two factors of the intelligence would labor together in harmony. At other times, they seemed to break apart, and there would follow long intervals when one or the other of these powers would lie dormant for months or even a year. Because, both by temperament and outlook, I share the artist's prepossession with nuances rather than the scientist's preoccupation with analysis, everything that has ever happened to me, whether in the material or the immaterial sphere, has become in time the property of my imagination, and has passed on into my work as a novelist.

When I turn now and look back over the past, I can discern, however dimly, that, beneath the ambiguous maze of ideas, a protective barrier was forming between my identity as a human being and a scheme of things which would always appear hostile. Even when I was unaware of the impulse, or especially when I was unaware of the impulse, this subconscious wall was slowly expanding. Pain I feared, but not truth; and even had I feared truth, something stronger than volition, that deep instinct for reality, would still have sought after it. The dual conscience within me, that union of the Calvinist with the Episcopal, was mortally stricken, but dying slowly. Although it survived merely as a double-edged instinct, still it survived. There were moments when I suffered again from the feeling, so familiar in early youth, that a moral being has no right to seek happiness in a world where many fellow mortals are enduring on earth the extreme tortures of hell. Yet as I wandered farther away from the older horizon, I discovered a more steadfast serenity in fortitude than in any dubious faith.

I could not put in any doctrine my entire trust. Nor would everlasting identity possess, for me, an allurement. But mortal existence, here, now, in the immediate present, would impose its own obligation.

In late years, while we were engaged in our most recent war to end war, many fine words were scattered lavishly among throngs that demanded phrases with blood. Some of us liked then to speak of "the conscience of mankind," and of "breaking the heart of the world." Well, whatever delusions I may have picked up in that moment of exaltation or hysteria, I mislaid them some twenty years ago among a forgotten generation. Nowadays, in a state of what appears to be recovered sanity, I distrust not only rhetoric, but the heart of the world; and I believe, moreover, that a conscience may have evolved, by and through biological necessity, in some men and women, but not yet in mankind. I believe that the masses of men continue to live not by bread alone, but by bread and circuses; and that no circus can compare in thrills with a national conflict or a world crusade. I do not believe that nations are driven to war as patient beasts to the slaughter. On the contrary, I believe that there survives in the human race a deep destructive instinct; and that this unconscious energy, whenever it is inflamed by hatred, and yet unassuaged by war, will find an outlet in vicarious cruelties, and in those racial and religious animosities which still exist below the surface of a state we have agreed to call peace. Nobody wants war, we hear everywhere. What we do not hear is that many people, the vast majority, in some place and time, will presently be in need of something that war, and war alone, can accomplish. And war, when it comes at last, will seem again, as always, to be an inevitable choice between a greater and a lesser evil. But under the semblance of right or justice or liberty, psychologists assure us that the old Adam of our primary function will still discharge its repressed sadistic tendency in its natural outbreak of violence. Having lived through one world war, I can remember that the worst of such hostilities was not the thought of death in battle; it was not even the thought of the young and the best who were sacrificed: but it was the pleasurable excitement with which so many men, and more especially so many women, responded to the shock and the hatred and even the horror. For I still think, as I thought then: the worst part of war is that so many people enjoy it. In my childhood I was accustomed to hearing decorous Southern pillars of society declare that the happiest years of their lives were the four years in which they marched and fought and starved with the Army of Northern Virginia. Only yesterday, I recalled this when a mild-mannered woman confided to me that, though she hated war and worked in peace to avert it, the most interesting part in her life was the time that she had spent with the Red Cross in France. Certainly no impartial and unsentimental observer could have missed, in the attitude of the noncombatant nations, an involuntary recoil from enthusiasm to disappointment or even disgust, when the recent crisis in Europe postponed, for a breathing space, yet another world war to end war. So it would seem that the only effective way to end war forever would be to make all our ideas of war as unromantic and unheroic as is the average man's daily struggle for his drab-colored existence. Meanwhile, "If war were called mass murder," remarks an eminent psychiatrist, "the term mass murder would soon lose its horror and in time become even a designation of honor." There remains, it is needless to point out, a minority that dissents; but this dissenting minority can expect only the painful fate of all civilized minorities wherever we find them. For it is true that the most tragic figure in our modern society is not the semi-barbarian; it is not even the sophisticated barbarian; it is the truly civilized man who has been thrust back upon the level of Neanderthal impulses.

I believe in evolution, though I do not believe that evolution must, of necessity, mean progress. All change is not growth; all movement is not forward. Yet I believe that life on this planet has groped its way up from primeval darkness; and I believe likewise that, in this bloodstained pilgrimage from a lower to a higher form, humanity has collected a few sublime virtues, or ideas of sublime virtue, which are called truth, justice, courage, loyalty, compassion. I believe, therefore, in a moral order; and I believe that this order was not imposed by a supernatural decree, but throughout the ages has been slowly evolving from the mind of man.

I believe in the scientific spirit, but I dislike the scientific manner when it forsakes the ponderable for the imponderable values. Although noble in motive, no doubt, science too often appears Janus-faced in behavior. Confronting us, it wears the bland features of a ministering angel; but turn the mask, and we have the grim countenance of a war goddess preparing weapons of destruction to kill or maim her children. And I dislike, too, the fetish that science has made of natural law, as if all things natural were excellent. It is not that I deny the ordinances of Heaven; but I find it a negligible distinction whether humankind suffers under the reign of natural law or under the rule of universal anarchy. Nevertheless, it is more agreeable, I confess, to regard oneself, not as a biological accident, but either as a thought in the mind of God or as a unit with an appointed harmonious place in the vast rhythm of creation.

I believe in social justice, as I believe in peace on earth, good will toward men, as an ideal to be pursued, though scarcely to be attained this side of Paradise. I believe, as I have said elsewhere, that the approach to a fairer order lies, not without, but within; and that the only way to make a civilized world is to begin and end with the civilizing of man. "Blessedness," Spinoza has said in one of my favorite passages, "is not the reward of virtue, but virtue itself." Though I feel an active interest in social philosophies, I am wholly indifferent to the labels we inaccurately assign to social systems. All forms of government, miscall them as we will, have been invented, cherished, debased, and finally demolished by that erratic quantity we know as human nature. And one cannot fail to observe how frequently in the pages of history this same human nature, as Karl Marx might have warned us, "has sown dragons' teeth and reaped —fleas." Yet we must have observed also that men are enslaved by names, and that they will fight for a word more readily than for an idea or a fact. Nowadays, as in the past, they will rally to defend a name among other names; they will battle for the term "democracy" more zealously than they will safeguard those living principles upon which all stable democracies must rest. Freedom is won, not by counting noses, but by keeping alight the inward watch fires of liberty; and true liberty of conscience is as remote from license as it is from moral surrender.

There are honest souls in our midst who warn us, with increasing vehemence, that the Western civilization we have known and admired is already westering toward an abrupt decline. Yet it is only the valiant heart of the pessimist that would dare even to prophesy. For it is at least possible that, whenever the threatened decline and fall of our culture overtake us in fact, those who are alive at the time will not know of the catastrophe, and would not care if they did. It is more plausible, on the whole, to assume that they will have something they like better to put in its place, and that, following our example, they will continue to miscall this something "civilization."

I believe that there are two equal and enduring satisfactions in life: the association with one's fellow beings in friendship, in love, or in a community of interest, and the faithful pursuit of an art, a profession, or an esthetic enjoyment, not for outward advantage, but in obedience to a permanent and self-renewing inner compulsion. I believe, moreover, in the now discredited faculty of good taste, which means discrimination in all things; and I treasure the pregnant saying of Goethe: "The assassination of Julius Cæsar was not in good taste." Even cruelty and intolerance, one imagines, might be banished, with ugliness, from a society which had cultivated good taste in such matters. I prefer, among other things, victory to defeat, fortitude to futility, and consideration to rudeness, especially toward the weak, the defenseless, and all those who are placed in positions we think of as inferior. I believe that there are many evils, but that the only sin is inhumanity; and I believe, too, that benign laughter is the best tonic for life. If life is sad, it is also a laughing matter, and it has its moments of rapture.

I believe that the greatest need of the modern world is not for a multitude of machines, but for a new and a higher conception of God. Yet I believe likewise that any god of the modern temper would necessarily manifest himself as a spiritual sans-culotte; and as such could not ever divide the light from the darkness or bring order into the new chaos. For it would seem that the road to God Eternal is strewn with the earth-gods man has made in His name; and although a purer knowledge of Divinity would be the greatest human achievement, it is true, nevertheless, that the Ages of Faith were the Dark Ages of the Inquisition and the auto-da-fé. Around us nowadays we hear prophetic whispers of a "spiritual awakening," but before we welcome it too earnestly we should examine not only the spirit but the immediate process of the awakening. It is not easy, on the surface, to distinguish between spiritual and emotional vehemence. There is danger in any too sudden conversion of the unthinking mind; and the mob that would die for a belief seldom hesitates to inflict death upon any opposing heretical group. I believe, therefore, that faith has its victories, but that skepticism remains the only permanent basis of tolerance.

These things I believe; and I believe not less firmly in that Good which has been seldom recognized, and never apprehended completely. I believe not in the Good alone, but in the good life which Spinoza has called blessedness. I believe in the challenging mind, in the unreconciled heart, and in the will toward perfection. When, in spite of all the miracles of science and religion, we seem, for the moment, to sink into deeper despair of humanity, we are reminded, it may be, that somewhere a saint has given his life for mankind, or a hero has given his life for strangers, or a lover has given his life for his friends; and then at last we comprehend that the true value of life can be measured only, as it borrows meaning, from the things that are valued above and beyond life.

LANCELOT HOGBEN

*Lancelot Hogben bids fair to become the Thomas Henry Huxley of this generation. His researches in endocrinology and human genetics have won for him a high place in the technical scientific world. His reputation has of late years been enlarged by the publication of two monumental works of popular science: 'Mathematics for the Million' and 'Science for the Citizen,' both of them extremely (and surprisingly) successful. His little book 'The Retreat from Reason' is also worth any serious reader's perusal. Mr. Hogben's contribution to this volume was solicited because he is among the most articulate and intelligent of those first-rate younger scientists who have recognized at last that a bridge must be constructed between the laboratory and the world of common men.*

*Lancelot Hogben was born in Southsea, England, in 1895, and educated at Trinity College, Cambridge. He has been in turn lecturer in zoology, Imperial College of Science; assistant director of the Animal-Breeding Research Department; lecturer in experimental physiology at Edinburgh; assistant professor of zoology at McGill University; professor of zoology at the University of Cape Town; professor of social biology in the University of London. At present he is Regius Professor of natural history at the University of Aberdeen, Scotland. He has been married for twenty years to Dr. Enid Charles, the well-known authority on population statistics, and has four children. In 1936 he became a Fellow of the Royal Society. In addition to his two well-known popular works, his publications include many books and monographs in the fields of mathematical genetics, endocrinology, general physiology, and biology.*

## *Lancelot Hogben*

If I had been asked to give a label to my creed, when I was starting in my profession as a scientific worker, I should have called it socialism. That was over twenty years ago. Today I prefer to call it scientific humanism. Scientific humanism is the creed I profess and the profession I try to practice.

This does not mean that the socialist creed of my adolescence was contrary to the scientific outlook, or that I have renounced it. It means that when I was younger my political left hand did not bother about what my professional right hand was doing. I did not yet realize how the pursuit of science is bound up with the responsibilities of citizenship in a society which has been transformed by scientific knowledge. When I began to do so, I saw that socialism can mean two different ways of using scientific discoveries.

In prewar days few except socialists clearly recognized that cyclical depression is an inherent characteristic of competitive industry conducted for private gain. During the period which elapsed between the end of the Great War and the beginning of the great depression most of the older generation of political leaders still believed that capitalism has a self-regulating capacity for promoting progress in knowledge and general well-being, except insofar as it is embarrassed by wars and strikes. Meanwhile a new generation had grown accustomed to state control over war industries and large relief schemes for a permanent army of unemployed. In these circumstances all that socialists had preached seemed vindicated by events. The last generation which believed in laissez-faire was passing away, and the success of socialism seemed to be assured.

In Germany and Britain nothing of the sort happened. From the moment when all hope of return to prewar conditions was officially abandoned by Conservative politicians the official socialist parties entered an eclipse which has lasted ever since. How it so happened is a question which admits of many answers. One is that the only things about which all socialists could agree were now generally accepted. To all but themselves the new situation exposed differences which cut across the sectarian strategies of Social Democrat and Communist or of Stalinist and Trotskyist. While laissez-faire was in the ascendant, socialism meant having some plan in contradistinction to having *none*. The collapse of liberalism meant that socialism could no longer survive by asserting the need for planning in the abstract. What socialists had long forgotten was now clear to their competitors. From its inception there had been two sorts of socialism, each with a plan of its own.

One socialism starts where orthodox free trade leaves off. It embraces or assumes the liberal doctrine that prosperity is measured by the number and variety of salable commodities which the consumer is "free" to purchase. Its chief quarrel with liberalism is that inequalities of spending power and recurrent unemployment restrict the choice of a large section of the population. To remedy this it proposes to redistribute spending power more profitably by fixing prices, by restricting income to services (past, present, or future) and by statutory limitation of working hours adjusted under public ownership. In short it does not criticize the way in which capitalist society uses scientific knowledge. It is primarily a protest against how it distributes its products, and the change at which it aims is primarily a change in the *administrative* machinery of industry. Its success does not entail any radical change in the creative policy

Lancelot Hogben

of industry. Under a socialist regime conceived in such terms industry will continue to produce much the same things as before. As a corollary, the intellectual leadership of socialism will be recruited from lawyers and journalists. The success of socialism so defined therefore demands no far-reaching educational reforms.

The other socialism, that of Robert Owen, of Charles Kingsley, of Edward Carpenter, and of William Morris, began as a protest against the dreary squalor which was effacing the common wealth of the countryside during the earlier stages of steam power production. It denounced the worldly wisdom which chose an ever-increasing multiplicity of gewgaws and passive distractions as the goal of co-operative endeavor. In opposition to the liberal doctrine that prosperity is being able to choose the greatest variety of goods, it asserted the need to decide whether the dark satanic mills were making things which are good for men to choose. There was at first no clear recognition that science could create the prospect of a new heaven for uncongested traffic and a new earth for spacious living. The Utopians—as they are usually called—anticipated scientific humanism because they saw clearly that human needs cannot be assessed in terms of "consumers' choice" and because they saw the hypertrophied metropolitanism of capitalist evolution creating psychological strains for which redistribution of spending power furnishes no sufficient remedy.

Throughout the period which begins with the inspired prose of Owen and ends with the uninspired verse of Morris, steam was still the only source of power for factory production, electrolytic processes of chemical manufacture were in their infancy, and motor transport was unknown. Inescapably a higher level of productivity had been achieved at the price of urban congestion, and no radical departure from the fundamental plan of capitalism could be accomplished without lowering the available potential of leisure and creature comforts. So the term Utopian became a term of abuse. Wise in the wisdom of the world as it then was, socialists made it their chief business to convince the clerk that the municipal milkman will wake him as punctually as the boy from the shop at the end of the street, or that a nationally owned railway service will get him to the office as early as the company which now owns the trains.

Today scientific knowledge offers us the possibility of a new plan of social living more akin to the Utopia of a William Morris or an Edward Carpenter. Mobile power, aviation, and electrical communications make it possible to distribute population at a high level of productive capacity without the disabilities of cultural isolation. A high potential of leisure and creature comforts no longer demands the beehive pattern of social living. Co-operative organization in the age of hydro-electric power, of light metals, of artificial fertilizers, and applied genetics offer us new instruments of manufacture, new means of transport, and new means of communications, both to restore the serenity of small community life and to promote a lively sympathy with folk in other lands. Broadcasting has now brought the cultural benefits of travel to the bedside, and scientific horticulture offers us a program of bio-esthetic planning which may prove more congenial to basic human needs than the spectacle of a five-and-ten-cent store building.

The straphanging multitudes of our great cities need circuses as well as bread. It is no longer Utopian to ask what sort of circus human nature demands. The Third Reich has given its answer. The answer is Jew-baiting, war, and neopagan weddings. The revolt against the beehive city of competitive industrialism has already become a retreat into barbarism. The retreat will continue unless science can foster a lively recognition of the positive achievements of civilization by reinstating faith in a future of constructive effort. It will not be arrested by old-school-tie socialists fresh from the exploits of the Oxford Union.

Seventy years ago it was still possible to discuss whether poverty is morally tolerable or materially inevitable. It was still possible to discuss whether war was spiritually edifying or socially escapable. All this is changed. Poverty in the sense in which it was then defined, the sense in which the word is intelligible to the social biologist, is not materially inevitable. The only obstacle to removing it is lack of social initiative. War is not a moral picnic. It threatens to destroy the entire fabric of our civilization, if we do not eradicate it with as much promptitude and ruthlessness as we have eradicated or are eradicating smallpox, malaria, and yellow fever.

Thus the civilized world of today vacillates between deep disillusionments and great expectations of imminent possibilities. Mass unemployment has destroyed confidence in progress and prosperity through private enterprise, while abundant intimations of available plenty dazzle us with new potentials of social achievement made possible by advancing scientific knowledge. In the day-to-day drama of politics partisans of the progressive movements are preoccupied with eleemosynary makeshifts and have done little to show how public enterprise can take creative initiative from production for private gain. So it is becoming daily obvious that education for political leadership in democratic countries was not devised to take advantage of our new opportunities, and it is becoming equally obvious that the machinery of democratic government was not devised to exploit expert knowledge for general well-being.

Advancing scientific knowledge has swept away many beliefs which sustained popular aspirations in the formative stages of modern democracy. The providential dispensation which endorsed the same plan of governance for Church and State, the mythology of the Beautiful Savage, and metaphysical libertarianism with its hypertrophied insistence on diversity of personal preference do not belong to the century in which we are living. In their place modern science now offers us a *New Social Contract.* The social contract of scientific humanism is the recognition that the sufficient basis for rational co-operation between citizens is scientific investigation of the common needs of mankind, a scientific inventory of resources available for satisfying them, and a realistic survey of how modern social institutions contribute to or militate against the use of such resources for the satisfaction of fundamental human needs.

Power to shape the future course of events so as to extend the benefits of advancing scientific knowledge for the satisfaction of common human needs must be guided by an understanding of the impact of science on human society. So the New Social Contract demands a new orientation of educational values and new qualifications for civic responsibilities. While others call for change in the methods of education and rightly demand removal of restrictions to educational opportunities, scientific humanism also asserts the need for a far-reaching reformation in the *content* of education to endow the pursuit of knowledge with a *new sense of social relevance.* The scientific humanist believes that an educational reformation so conceived is an indispensable prerequisite to genuine social advance.

Herein lies an essential difference between the standpoint of scientific humanism and current views of political partisans who aspire to a progressive outlook. Those who now call themselves progressives generally adopt one of two attitudes to education. Insofar as liberals and moderate socialists deign to trouble themselves about educational issues their concern is to utilize a more ample reservoir of talent in the service of the community. Socialists of the extreme Left are chiefly concerned with propagating a creed which is partly based on the teaching of the Prussian mystic Hegel and partly on a shrewd analysis of the impact of early nineteenth-century technology on mid-nineteenth-century social institutions. In practice such differences are trivial, because so many people now believe that a war against the dictator countries is inevitable. Education is therefore an effeminate topic.

For several reasons I cannot share this conviction. There are three possibilities ahead of us. The first is another world war, resulting in the complete destruction of civilization as depicted in Cicely Hamilton's novel, *Lest Ye Die*. The second is that another world war will stop before civilization is completely destroyed. The third is that hell will not be let loose, because the warlike temper of the dictator countries will exhaust itself or because an effective policy of constructive pacification will mature in the so-called democratic countries. If the first, or most likely, happens, no social effort is worth while. So the rational alternative to suicide for parents is to take a chance on the second or third.

Either way it is important to base social action on correct views about how new scientific knowledge affects the potential of social change. I believe that this must force us to conclusions which are not palatable to die-hard progressives of the nineteenth century. I believe also that the eclipse of the progressive outlook is specially due to wrong views about the impact of new scientific knowledge on contemporary social change. To illustrate this I shall cite two examples. One is the fact that most progressives believed in the early collapse of Hitler's power, when he announced the policy of autarchy. The other is that most socialists have believed that the relative increase of the employed section of the community is necessarily propitious to their aims.

The belief that increasing scientific knowledge makes for closer economic interdependence, and, what was often stated as a corollary to this, the belief that this interdependence provides a guarantee of world peace, were dogmas almost universally held by progressive thinkers in the nineteenth century. This was not unnatural in the first flush of surprise which followed the introduction of steam navigation, transcontinental railways, and oceanic telegraphy. Our own perspective should be different. We need only recall that Chilean saltpeter can now be made anywhere, that hospitals are using radioactive sodium prepared from ordinary salt instead of having to import the rare radioactive minerals, that the Channel Islands are no longer regarded as a sufficient guarantee of the genetic credentials of cattle, that we may soon be making most of our machinery of aluminum from the clay of our soils or of magnesium from sea salt, that we are already beginning to feed our pigs on the disintegration products of wood pulp, to grow several crops of tomatoes a year by tank gardening, and to produce sugar by the agency of bacteria from vegetable waste matter.

Without committing ourselves to any dogmatic assertions about how far this will go on, what we can at least say is this: The effect of scientific discovery during the past two centuries has been mainly to increase the potential of local self-sufficiency consistent with the satisfaction of fundamental human needs. One result is that we can now entertain the possibility of a less centralized, and therefore less bureaucratic and less congested, type of world organization as a goal for rationally guided effort. The warmongers of Central Europe and elsewhere know too well that free trade is no longer part of the ideological temper of the age in which we live, and that the appeal for national self-sufficiency canalizes discontent with the dreary futilities of planless mechanization in congested modern communities. It is therefore a tragic fact that those who have the will to peace too often resist propaganda for promoting a greater measure of local self-sufficiency with arguments which antedate the synthetic manufacture of nitrate fertilizers.

Of itself the appeal for local self-sufficiency is neither good nor bad. In Fascist states social policy is dominated by the death wish, and self-sufficiency is advocated as a means of warmaking without regard for the social welfare of the citizen. Where social policy becomes alert to the new powers and inventions available for human well-being, the satisfaction of basic human needs will take precedence over the multiplication of useless commodities to distract neurotic urban populations, and the merits of more or less industrial specialization will be examined with proper regard to the distribution of population in congenial and healthful surroundings. Because the doctrine of free trade was sustained by the moral conviction that the greatest good of the greatest number is the same as the greatest number of goods available to the greatest number of people, its apostles accepted the urban squalor of a coal economy as the inevitable price of their own definition of prosperity. For privacy and serenity of life, the satisfactions of parenthood and the graces of human fellowship in modest communities they offered mankind the compensation of the department store and labor-saving flats in flowerless streets. Some of the more distasteful features of Fascism are the reaction of outraged human nature endowed with enough intelligence to be exasperated, and too demoralized to explore an alternative constructive use for the new powers at hand.

One feature of the impact of new technical resources during the first phase of steam-power production was a steady reduction in the demand for skilled handicraftsmen. This encouraged socialists to believe that society was splitting up into a small parasitic class of owners and an ever-growing, increasingly militant class of employees with common political aspirations. A skyscraper of social tactic was built on this foundation of *a priori* psychology which was in essence legalistic like the political theories of the orthodox parties. The implicit assumption is that the physical character of a man's work, the surroundings in which it is carried out, monotony, initiative, solitude, propinquity to home environment, accessibility to outdoor exercise are all negligible in their effect upon his political affiliations in comparison with the legal contract regulating his employment. This is bad human biology. The reaction of a human being to the contents of books or to the sound of the human voice is affected by his work in many ways. It depends among other things upon whether he is physically weary or merely bored, upon whether he does work that is fatiguing or work that is monotonous. Consequently we should not expect that a miner will necessarily react to the same type of political propaganda in the same way as the clerk in a department store.

Even before the introduction of electricity as a source of power, the conduct of a mechanized and more highly urbanized society had initiated changes which counteracted the cultural process of leveling down. Universal schooling, a popular press, free libraries succeeded one another in countries with a democratic constitution. With the coming of electricity as a source of power industry came under the impact of new problems of costing and new technical advantages of mobility. Where it has been introduced into the factory, it has created a new demand for a new type of skill and special training, while dispensing with a large volume of unskilled and casual labor which can be replaced by machinery. To see the impact of the new technical forces most clearly we need to examine the statistics of a country which is in a more advanced state of technical development than Britain. In his recent book *Insurgent America,* Alfred Bingham's analysis of the growth of social classes during recent years shows that the new type of skilled administrative employee has steadily increased in proportion to laborers performing heavy unskilled work in the United States.

Thus modern technology has brought into being a social group with social aspirations and a social status of its own. Its social aspirations for further opportunity of employment can be realized only by the further extension of technical improvements which have encouraged its growth. For the time being at least, it is still growing and at present, politically inarticulate. It may therefore play a decisive role in the success of any social movement which can claim its allegiance. In a period of social crisis its importance should not be judged by its numerical strength, because its personnel commands resources against which mere man power is helpless and barricades are literary illusions. If it can be enlisted in a task which will offer far greater opportunities of creative service than it now enjoys, the transition from a discredited and demoralized competitive to a rationally planned industrial system is assured. If it is driven by hysterical fear to support any dictator movement which offers the prospect of a breathing space, it may become the instrument for destroying democracy and freedom of discourse.

# JULIAN HUXLEY

*Julian Huxley, brother of Aldous Huxley, grandson of Thomas Henry Huxley, has added luster to a distinguished name. Like Lancelot Hogben, he represents the forward-looking viewpoint of the younger British scientists. Like him, also, he is eminent both as a research scientist and as a brilliant popularizer. He commands an expository style of superb ease, clarity, and dignity. The general reader may be particularly directed to Mr. Huxley's 'Essays of a Biologist' and to the fascinating and monumental 'Science of Life,' written in collaboration with H. G. Wells and G. P. Wells. The influence of his writings has been enlarged through his many radio talks, lectures, etc.*

*Julian Huxley was born in 1887 and educated at Eton and Oxford. He has taught in Oxford University; the Rice Institute at Houston, Texas; King's College, London; and in the Royal Institution, where he held the chair of Fullerian Professor of Physiology. He was biological editor of the Encyclopedia Britannica, 14th edition, and since 1935 has been Secretary of the Zoological Society of London.*

*Some of his major publications, in addition to those noted above, include 'The Stream of Life' (1926); 'Animal Biology,' with J. B. S. Haldane (1927); 'Africa View' (1931); 'Problems of Relative Growth' (1932); 'Scientific Research and Social Needs' (1934); 'We Europeans,' with A. C. Haddon (1935).*

# *Julian Huxley*

I BELIEVE that life can be worth living. I believe this in spite of pain, squalor, cruelty, unhappiness, and death. I do not believe that it is necessarily worth living, but only that for most people it can be.

I also believe that man, as individual, as group, and collectively as mankind, can achieve a satisfying purpose in existence. I believe this in spite of frustration, aimlessness, frivolity, boredom, sloth, and failure. Again I do not believe that a purpose inevitably inheres in the universe or in our existence, or that mankind is bound to achieve a satisfying purpose, but only that such a purpose can be found.

I believe that there exists a scale or hierarchy of values, ranging from simple physical comforts up to the highest satisfactions of love, esthetic enjoyment, intellect, creative achievement, virtue. I do not believe that these are absolute, or transcendental in the sense of being vouchsafed by some external power or divinity: they are the product of human nature interacting with the outer world. Nor do I suppose that we can grade every valuable experience into an accepted order, any more than I can say whether a beetle is a higher organism than a cuttlefish or a herring. But just as it can unhesitatingly be stated that there are general grades of biological organization, and that a beetle *is* a higher organism than a sponge, or a human being than a frog, so I can assert, with the general consensus of civilized human beings, that there is a higher value in Dante's *Divine Comedy* than in a popular hymn, in the scientific activity of Newton or Darwin than in solving a crossword puzzle, in the fullness of love than in sexual gratification, in selfless than in purely self-regarding activities—although each and all can have their value of a sort.

I do not believe that there is any absolute of truth, beauty, morality, or virtue, whether emanating from an external power or imposed by an internal standard. But this does not drive me to the curious conclusion, fashionable in certain quarters, that truth and beauty and goodness do not exist, or that there is no force or value in them.

I believe that there are a number of questions that it is no use our asking, because they can never be answered. Nothing but waste, worry, or unhappiness is caused by trying to solve insoluble problems. Yet some people seem determined to try. I recall the story of the philosopher and the theologian. The two were engaged in disputation and the theologian used the old quip about a philosopher resembling a blind man, in a dark room, looking for a black cat—which wasn't there. "That may be," said the philosopher: "but a theologian would have found it."

Even in matters of science, we must learn to ask the right questions. It seemed an obvious question to ask how animals inherit the result of their parents' experience, and enormous amounts of time and energy have been spent on trying to give an answer to it. It is, however, no good asking the question, for the simple reason that no such inheritance of acquired characters exists. The chemists of the eighteenth century, because they asked themselves the question, "What substance is involved in the process of burning?" became involved in the mazes of the phlogiston theory; they had to ask, "What sort of process is burning?" before they could see that it did not involve a special substance, but was merely a particular case of chemical combination.

When we come to what are usually referred to as fundamentals, the difficulty of not asking the wrong kind of question is much increased. Among most African tribes, if a person dies, the only question asked is, "Who caused his death, and by what form of magic?" The idea of death from natural causes is unknown. Indeed, the life of the less civilized half of mankind is largely based on trying to find an answer to a wrong question, "What magical forces or powers are responsible for good or bad fortune, and how can they be circumvented or propitiated?"

I do not believe in the existence of a god or gods. The conception of divinity seems to me, though built up out of a number of real elements of experience, to be a false one, based on the quite unjustifiable postulate that there must be some more or less personal power in control of the world. We are confronted with forces beyond our control, with incomprehensible disasters, with death; and also with ecstasy, with a mystical sense of union with something greater than our ordinary selves, with sudden conversion to a new way of life, with the burden of guilt and sin and of ways in which these burdens may be lifted. In theistic religions, all these elements of actual experience have been woven into a unified body of belief and practice, in relation to the fundamental postulate of the existence of a god or gods.

I believe this fundamental postulate to be nothing more than the result of asking a wrong question, "Who or what rules the universe?" So far as we can see, it rules itself, and indeed the whole analogy with a country and its ruler is false. Even if a god does exist behind or above the universe as we experience it, we can have no knowledge of such a power: the actual gods of historical religions are only the personifications of impersonal facts of nature and of facts of our inner mental life. Though we can answer the question, "What are the Gods of actual religions?" we can only do so by dissecting them into their components and showing their divinity to be a figment of human imagination, emotion, and rationalization. The question, "What is the nature of God?" we cannot answer, since we have no means of knowing whether such a being exists or not.

Similarly with immortality. With our present faculties, we have no means of giving a categorical answer to the question whether we survive death, much less the question of what any such life after death will be like. That being so, it is a waste of time and energy to devote ourselves to the problem of achieving salvation in the life to come. However, just as the idea of God is built out of bricks of real experience, so too is the idea of salvation. If we translate salvation into terms of this world, we find that it means achieving harmony between different parts of our nature, including its subconscious depths and its rarely touched heights, and also achieving some satisfactory relation of adjustment between ourselves and the outer world, including not only the world of nature, but the social world of man. I believe it to be possible to "achieve salvation" in this sense, and right to aim at doing so, just as I believe it possible and valuable to achieve a sense of union with something bigger than our ordinary selves, even if that something be not a god but an extension of our narrow core to include in a single grasp ranges of outer experience and inner nature on which we do not ordinarily draw.

But if God and immortality be repudiated, what is left? That is the question usually thrown at the atheist's head. The orthodox believer likes to think that nothing is left. That, however, is because he has only been accustomed to think in terms of his orthodoxy.

In point of fact, a great deal is left.

That is immediately obvious from the fact that many men and women have led active, or self-sacrificing, or noble, or devoted lives without any belief in God or immortality. Buddhism in its uncorrupted form has no such

*Bassano, London*

JULIAN HUXLEY

belief, nor did the great nineteenth-century agnostics, nor do the orthodox Russian Communists, nor did the Stoics. Of course, the unbelievers have often been guilty of selfish or wicked actions; but so have the believers. And in any case that is not the fundamental point. The point is that without these beliefs men and women may yet possess the mainspring of full and purposive living, and just as strong a sense that existence can be worth while as is possible to the most devout believers.

I would say that this is much more readily possible today than in any previous age. The reason lies in the advances of science.

No longer are we forced to accept the external catastrophes and miseries of existence as inevitable or mysterious; no longer are we obliged to live in a world without history, where change is only meaningless. Our ancestors saw an epidemic as an act of divine punishment: to us it is a challenge to be overcome, since we know its causes and that it could be controlled or prevented. The understanding of infectious disease is entirely due to scientific advance. So, to take a very recent happening, is our understanding of the basis of nutrition, which holds out new possibilities of health and energy to the human race. So is our understanding of earthquakes and storms: if we cannot control them, we at least do not have to fear them as evidence of God's anger.

Some, at least, of our internal miseries can be lightened in the same way. Through knowledge derived from psychology, children can be prevented from growing up with an abnormal sense of guilt, and so making life a burden both to themselves and to those with whom they come into contact. We are beginning to understand the psychological roots of irrational fear and irrational cruelty: some day we shall be able to make the world a brighter place by preventing their appearance.

The ancients had no history worth mentioning. Human existence in the present was regarded as a degradation from that of the original Golden Age. Down even to the nineteenth century, what was known of human history was regarded by the nations of the West as an essentially meaningless series of episodes sandwiched into the brief space between the Creation and the Fall, a few thousand years ago, and the Second Coming and the Last Judgment, which might be on us at any moment, and in any case could not be pushed back for more than a few thousand years into the future. In this perspective, a millennium was almost an eternity. With such an outlook, no wonder life seemed, to the great mass of humanity, "nasty, brutish and short," its miseries and shortcomings merely bewildering unless illuminated by the illusory light of religion.

Today, human history merges back into prehistory, and prehistory again into biological evolution. Our time-scale is profoundly altered. A thousand years is a short time for prehistory, which thinks in terms of hundreds of thousands of years, and an insignificant time for evolution, which deals in ten-million-year periods. The future is extended equally with the past: if it took over a thousand million years for primeval life to generate man, man and his descendants have at least an equal allowance of time before them.

Most important of all, the new history has a basis of hope. Biological evolution has been appallingly slow and appallingly wasteful. It has been cruel, it has generated the parasites and the pests as well as the more agreeable types. It has led life up innumerable blind alleys. But in spite of this, it has achieved progress. In a few lines, whose number has steadily diminished with time, it has avoided the cul-de-sac of mere specialization and arrived at a new level of organization, more harmonious and more efficient, from which it could again launch out toward greater control, greater knowledge, and greater independence. Progress is, if you will, all-round specialization. Finally, but one line was left which was able to achieve further progress: all the others had led up blind alleys. This was the line leading to the evolution of the human brain.

This at one bound altered the perspective of evolution. Experience could now be handed down from generation to generation; deliberate purpose could be substituted for the blind sifting of selection; change could be speeded up ten-thousandfold. In man evolution could become conscious. Admittedly it is far from conscious yet, but the possibility is there, and it has at least been consciously envisaged.

Seen in this perspective, human history represents but the tiniest portion of the time man has before him; it is only the first ignorant and clumsy gropings of the new type, born heir to so much biological history. Attempts at a general philosophy of history are seen in all their futility—as if someone whose acquaintance with man as a species were limited to a baby one year old should attempt a general account of the human mind and soul. The constant setbacks, the lack of improvement in certain respects for over two thousand years, are seen to be phenomena as natural as the tumbles of a child learning to walk, or the deflection of a sensitive boy's attention by the need of making a living.

The broad facts remain. Life had progressed, even before man was first evolved. Life progressed further by evolving man. Man has progressed during the half million or so years from the first Hominidae, even during the ten thousand years since the final amelioration of climate after the Ice Age. And the potentialities of progress which are revealed, once his eyes have been opened to the evolutionary vista, are unlimited.

At last we have an optimistic, instead of a pessimistic, theory of this world and our life upon it. Admittedly the optimism cannot be facile, and must be tempered with reflection on the length of time involved, on the hard work that will be necessary, on the inevitable residuum of accident and unhappiness that will remain. Perhaps we had better call it a melioristic rather than an optimistic view: but at least it preaches hope and inspires to action.

I believe very definitely that it is among human personalities that there exist the highest and most valuable achievements of the universe—or at least the highest and most valuable achievements of which we have or, apparently, can have knowledge. That means that I believe that the State exists for the development of individual lives, not individuals for the development of the State.

But I also believe that the individual is not an isolated, separate thing. An individual is a transformer of matter and experience: it is a system of relations between its own basis and the universe, including other individuals. An individual may believe that he should devote himself entirely to a cause, even sacrifice himself to it—his country, truth, art, love. It is in the devotion or the sacrifice that he becomes most himself, it is because of the devotion or sacrifice of individuals that causes become of value. But of course the individual must in many ways subordinate himself to the community—only not to the extent of believing that in the community resides any virtue higher than that of the individuals which compose it.

The community provides the machinery for the existence and development of individuals. There are those who deny the importance of social machinery, who assert that the only important thing is a change of heart, and that the right machinery is merely a natural consequence of the right inner attitude. This appears to me mere solipsism. Different kinds of social machinery predispose to different inner attitudes. The most admirable machinery is useless if the inner life is unchanged: but social machinery *can* affect the fullness and quality of life. Social machinery can be devised to make war more difficult, to promote health, to add interest to life. Let us not despise machinery in our zeal for fullness of life, any more than we should dream that machinery can ever automatically grind out perfection of living.

I believe in diversity. Every biologist knows that human beings differ in their hereditary outfits, and therefore in the possibilities that they can realize. Psychology is showing us how different are the types that jostle each other on the world's streets. No amount of persuasion or education can make the extravert really understand the introvert, the verbalist understand the lover of handicraft, the nonmathematical or nonmusical person understand the passion of the mathematician or the musician. We can try to forbid certain attitudes of mind. We could theoretically breed out much of human variety. But this would be a sacrifice. Diversity is not only the salt of life, but the basis of collective achievement. And the complement of diversity is tolerance and understanding. This does not mean rating all values alike. We must protect society against criminals: we must struggle against what we think wrong. But just as in our handling of the criminal we should try to reform rather than merely to punish, so we must try to understand why we judge others' actions as wrong, which implies trying to understand the workings of our own minds, and discounting our own prejudices.

Finally, I believe that we can never reduce our principles to any few simple terms. Existence is always too various and too complicated. We must supplement principles with faith. And the only faith that is both concrete and comprehensive is in life, its abundance and its progress. My final belief is in life.

# HAROLD J. LASKI

*Harold Laski is generally ranked as one of the outstanding political thinkers, educators, and debaters of the English-speaking world. He has influenced a whole generation of students on both sides of the Atlantic. His career represents a successful merger of writing, teaching, and practical public service.*

*Harold Laski was born in Manchester, England, in 1893, and was educated at the Manchester Grammar School and at New College, Oxford. He has taught at McGill University, Harvard, Yale, Amherst, Trinity College (Dublin), and Cambridge. Since 1920 he has been connected with the London School of Economics. His present title is professor of political science in the University of London. He has served on numerous educational and legislative boards and committees and is widely known for his contributions to the English and American journals of scholarship and opinion.*

*Some of his major publications: 'The Problem of Sovereignty' (1917); 'Authority in the Modern State' (1919); 'Political Thought from Locke to Bentham' (1920); 'Foundations of Sovereignty' (1921); 'Liberty in the Modern State' (1930); 'An Introduction to Politics' (1931); 'Democracy in Crisis' (1933); 'The State in Theory and Practice' (1935); 'The Rise of European Liberalism' (1936).*

# *Harold J. Laski*

I HAVE, I suppose, been a socialist in some degree ever since the last years of my schooldays. When I try to think out the sources of a faith that has been the central conviction of my life, I find that the difficulties of sorting them out are immense. Something was due to the influence of a great schoolmaster who made us feel the sickness of an acquisitive society. Something, too, was the outcome of a Jewish upbringing, the sense it conferred of being treated differently from other people and for no obviously assignable cause. I learned a good deal from books, especially from those of Sidney and Beatrice Webb. They made me realize that a whole class of human beings was overlooked in the traditional liberalism of the family to which I belonged. And there stays in my mind a speech I heard in Manchester as a boy on the threshold of a university career from Keir Hardie, whose account of the effort of the Scottish miners to form a trade-union made me begin, at least dimly, to understand the price the workers have to pay for the social reform they achieve.

I went up to Oxford with radical views, and my years there confirmed me in them. It was the first experience I had of the intensity of class division in England. It was the first experience I had, also, of the resistance atmosphere can impose upon the admission of new ideas, which are dismissed less because they have been examined than because their premises are outside the environment they seek to penetrate. My debt to Oxford is immeasurable. Contact there with the late Professor Dicey, with Mr. Herbert Fisher and Professor Ernest Barker, was, on the purely academic plane, a superb experience. But they were all, if I may so phrase it, aloof from life. Oxford generally, so far as its teachers were concerned, thought about social problems in a way which suggested interest in them but not responsibility for their solution. It told you, as it were, that correct analysis was important. It did not suggest that, when the analysis was made, any obligation emerged to act upon the principles it suggested.

I devoted a good deal of time at Oxford to the Fabian Society and to propaganda in behalf of woman suffrage. These brought me into contact with two of the greatest men I have ever known—George Lansbury and H. W. Nevinson. From the first I learned the meaning and importance of equality, and from the second the meaning and importance of liberty. George Lansbury, too, gave me my first job. He was then editing *The Daily Herald*, and when I left Oxford, in the summer of 1914, he asked me to write editorials for his paper. That was a significant experience for me. It brought me into contact with a good deal of what was most radical in the prewar socialist movement, and it made me formulate to myself, in a coherent way, some of the lessons I learned at Oxford. Contact with Lansbury was a great education. He was absolutely straightforward, absolutely democratic, and entirely fearless. He always meant every word he said, and it never occurred to him to say less than he meant. Through him, I got my first chance of seeing the inside of the socialist movement at first hand, and that at a critical time. Within six weeks of my going to the *Herald* Great Britain was at war. I sought to enlist on the first day. I did not believe in the war. But I did believe that, on the whole, the victory of Germany would mean more evil than its defeat. I was rejected on physical grounds, mainly a weak heart. That rejection altered the whole course of my life. For I was asked, through the influence of Herbert Fisher, to take a lectureship in history at McGill University, to replace an Oxford don who was anxious to serve. I did not believe that the war would last long. The life of a university teacher was my main ambition; and I was anxious for the leisure to write a book on sovereignty—an issue which seemed to me to lie at the root of the war. I accepted the invitation, expecting to stay a year on the American continent. Instead, I remained there, first at McGill and then, for four years, at Harvard, until 1920.

There is, I think, a sense in which my years on the American continent were the most fundamental experience of my life. I learned there that it was my vocation to be a teacher, that, in whatever other fields I might wander, this was the activity, above all, to which I should devote my energies. I learned, secondly, that to teach political science, it was not enough to read books; one had to learn politics from actual experience of their working, and to seek to make of one's lectures an intimate marriage of theory and practice. I learned, thirdly, that the university scene in America was vitally related to the social environment. One could speculate freely, but one must not question the basic assumptions of the system. When I was at McGill, I made a speech attacking the "bitter-endism" of Mr. Lloyd George, that was immediately followed by urgent demands for my dismissal. When I was at Harvard, the famous Boston police strike occurred. President Lowell at once offered the services of the University to the city. It seemed to me that one ought to know why the police were striking before one accepted the view that the city was right. Accordingly, I took great pains to discover what had led to the strike, and found that it was the outcome of long-accumulated grievances met without sympathy or insight. I ventured to say so; and there broke about my head a storm of indignation in which I was described as almost everything from a villain who seduced youth to a Bolshevik who preached revolution. I was solemnly investigated by the Overseers of the university; and though it was decided that I was not to be dismissed, President Lowell explained to me with emphasis that a teacher limited his utility when he spoke on matters of current controversy. I was not, I inferred, to say my say on the living issues of the time if what I said was inconvenient to the rulers of Harvard. Mr. Lowell spoke with kindness, but his implication was clear. Thus though I loved Harvard, and found there friendships that have been of inestimable value to me, I was not sorry when, in the next year, the London School of Economics and Political Science invited me to join its faculty. There I have remained since 1920; and there I hope to remain during my life as a teacher.

But it was not only that I learned in America what I believe to be my vocation. I saw there, more nakedly than I had seen in Europe, the significance of the struggle between capital and labor. I learned how little meaning there can be in an abstract political liberty which is subdued to the control of an economic plutocracy. I saw, too, in strikes like those of Ludlow and Lowell, how the vast machinery of the state is used to crush any movement that questions the authority of those who own economic power. I learned from the imprisonment of Debs and the attacks on La Follette how immense are the pressures to conformity, how fragile the claims of tolerance, whenever the security of a social order is threatened. Not least, I began to perceive, in the difference in the average American attitude to the February and October revolutions in Russia, how profound is the influence of the property relation in shaping opinion. I came back from America convinced that liberty has no meaning save in the context of equality, and I had begun to understand that equality, also, has no meaning unless the instruments of production are socially owned. But I was still academic enough in experience to believe that this could be proved on rational grounds, and that its proof would be sufficient to win acceptance for it as a principle of social organization. I had associated in America mostly with progressive or academic people who were accustomed to give argument its due weight; and even when, like Mr. Justice Holmes, they were fundamentally conservative in outlook, they were prepared to change their views in the light of discussion. Up to 1920, I think, as I look back, that my socialism was above all the outcome of a sense of the injustice of things as they were. It had not become an insight into the processes of history.

That, I believe, is the main burden of my experience in the eighteen years since I returned to England. They have been full years. From the outset I have been an active member of the Labour Party. I have served on government committees. I have "deviled" for ministers during the two periods when a Labour government was in power. I have done a good deal of industrial arbitration. I have helped the trade-unions in every important strike, especially the general strike of 1926. Teaching and the writing of books apart, most of my leisure has gone into work for socialism. I learned a great deal from five years as an alderman of a London borough. I have seen, too, a good deal of political journalism from within, not least in those four last brilliant years in which H. W. Massingham edited the London *Nation*. I have been closely concerned with the adult-education movement. Invitations to lecture abroad have given me first-hand acquaintance with the politics and the universities of France and Spain, pre-Hitler Germany, and the Soviet Union; and I have returned constantly to America, latterly almost year by year, as a fairly close observer of its political powers.

Out of it all, the great lesson I have learned is the broad truth of the Marxian philosophy. What I have seen at firsthand, no less than what I have read, has left me no alternative. I came back to England in 1920 hopeful that I was going to watch the slow permeation of economic relationships by the democratic principle. I have been driven to the conclusion that no class voluntarily abdicates from the possession of power. I have come to learn that the private ownership of the means of production makes it impossible for the democratic idea to transcend the barriers of class without the capture of the state power by the working class. The experience of Russia, the advent of Fascism in central and southeastern Europe, the attitude of the owning class in Spain and France and the United States to all serious attempts at social reform, the general strike of 1926 and the betrayal of 1931 in England, the new imperialisms of Japan and Italy, have all convinced me that, in large outline, there is no answer to the philosophy of Marx. Men, broadly, think in terms of an experience made and unmade by their class position. Their conceptions of right action are born of the inferences they draw from the experience of that class position. Individuals may transcend it. But taken generally, all our institutions and their working are conditioned by the property relations of any given society. The dominant ideas and principles of that society will be set by the way in which, in any moment, its property relations are working. If they are working well, there will be a period of concession to the multitude which can live only by the sale of its labor power. If they are working badly, the policy of concession will halt. A system which lives by profit must make profit. If its power to do so is challenged, the owners of the system will seek to destroy the men and the movements which challenge that power.

This is the reason for the decline of liberalism in the postwar epoch. Ours is that age, the coming of which was foreseen by Marx, in which the relations of production are in contradiction with the essential forces of production. Our time is comparable to that of the Reformation, when a similar contradiction appeared. Then as now a new property relation was essential, and then as now those who lived by the privileges inherent in the old were ready to fight for them rather than find the terms of a new accommodation. For when such a contradiction reaches its maturity, the price of continuing concession means the erosion of the privileges associated with private ownership. It means a scale of taxation fatal to the making of profit in international competition. It compels that examination of social foundations which, because it disturbs traditional routines, destroys men's ability to be tolerant in matters of social constitution. For those who have been taught by long use to regard privilege as right are rarely able to adjust themselves to the admission that their right may be built upon what other men have come to experience as wrong.

It is, as I think, in this background that all the central problems of our time have to be set. That it makes the future of capitalist democracy dubious is clear. That the inference from it, in the international sphere, is the necessary relation between capitalism and war is clear also. For, given the present distribution of economic power, the owning class is driven into the search for markets abroad in order to win profit. Thence comes the need for armament. Thence comes also the politics of imperialism, concession hunting, spheres of influence—that whole gamut of power politics to which the world since 1919 has so grimly accustomed us. The failure of the League of Nations is built upon the fact that it demands from its members the surrender of the policy to which the whole inherent logic of their economic system impels them. We have either to find the way to a resumption of the economic expansion of the Victorian age or enter upon—we have already entered—a period of war and revolution. But we cannot resume that expansion unless we adjust the relations of production in our society to the potential forces of production. Unless we do so, we are bound to have poverty in the midst of potential plenty, restrictionism, that economic nationalism which, all over the world, is lowering the standard of life. Since the state power is directed by men who live by the vested interests represented by these policies, it is at least difficult, and probably impossible, to transcend them within the limits of existing class relations.

I know no other way of explaining adequately the position in which our generation finds itself. The conclusion I draw from it is the necessity of a unified working-class party able either to win political power or, if it meets the challenge of Fascism, to emerge victorious from the conflict. The lesson of Germany and Italy is the clear one that division of the working class means its defeat. The lesson of France is the equally clear one that the attainment of unity at the least enables the working class to give a good account of itself when the challenge comes. And the evidence makes it plain that capitalism in its phase of contraction will respect no principle, however venerable, in its effort to retain the power of the state in its hands. That has been the experience of M. Blum in France; it has been, also, the experience of Mr. Roosevelt in the United States. Each had a great popular majority behind him. Each found that the power of his majority was largely nullified by the refusal of the propertied class to co-operate with his purposes. At the historical stage we have reached, the will of the people is unable to use the institutions of

Harold J. Laski

capitalist democracy for democratic purposes. For at this stage democracy needs to transform class relations in order to affirm itself; and it will not be allowed to do so by the owning class if it is able to prevent that achievement.

This attitude seems to me the explicit result of postwar experience, and it is, as I have said, the vindication of the analysis Marx made of social phenomena now nearly a century ago. Certain modes of behavior that I profoundly respect are, I think, ruled out of court by the inferences it involves. It is incompatible with the pacifist doctrine of nonresistance. It rules out, also, the Fabian method of gradualism. That principle was the natural method to recommend in an age of capitalist expansion. In the period of capitalism's decline, its result would, I think, be to give to the owning class a supreme opportunity to organize itself for counterattack. The real lesson of postwar Germany is the futility of trying to reorganize the economic foundations of capitalism by half measures. That, again, is the inference I would draw from the experience of the two Labour governments in Great Britain. Each was more anxious to prove its orthodox respectability to its opponents than it was to get on with the work of socialism to which it was committed by public profession. The result was to discourage its friends and to persuade its enemies that the price of social reform was greater than capitalism could afford. The time has come for a central attack on the structure of capitalism. Nothing less than wholesale socialization can remedy the position. The alternative in all Western civilization outside the Soviet Union is, I believe, a rapid drift to Fascism, in which the working class will be at a definite disadvantage by reason of the division of its forces. That division has already cost it Italy and Germany. It may one day cost it England and the United States as well. In that event, we shall see a new iron age descend upon mankind in which the very memory of civilized living may well become no more than a traditional legend.

I have spoken so far of a framework of experience out of which my social philosophy has been formed. Of religious conviction, for almost as long as I can remember, I have had none. I was brought up in an orthodox Jewish household; but I cannot even remember a period in which either ritual or dogma had meaning for me. Nor has experience of the living religions led me to doubt my doubts. George Lansbury apart, I have rarely met men whose behavior seems to me to have been influenced by religious principles; and both in England and America I have never been able to see in any of the organized churches a faith in its principles sufficient to make it do serious battle for justice. That is particularly true of England. The history of the Established Church is, predominantly, one of either indifference or antagonism to the main social demands of my time. Its real influence has been to persuade its votaries that the acceptance of the established order is a religious obligation. The problems of historical evidence apart, it has been increasingly clear to me that the main religions, as such, are simply not interested in the problems of social justice. The test, surely, of a creed is not the ability of those who accept it to announce their faith; its test is its ability to change their behavior in the ordinary round of daily life. Judged by that test, I know no religion that has a moral claim upon the allegiance of men. I can see in few individual lives the effect of belief. I cannot see, in the historic process, that the churches have been other than the enemies of reason in thought and of justice in social arrangements. Their concentration upon the life to come—for the reality of which I see no evidence—has, it seems to me, done more than most factors in history to deflect the attention of men from the realities of our life here and now. The result of that deflection has always been to the interest of those who live by privilege.

One whose vocation is teaching can hardly help reflection upon the conditions under which he should practice it. I have never tried to be what it is popular to call an "impartial" teacher. First of all, in my own experience, "impartiality" is an impossible ideal. Either it means the complete erosion of the teacher's personality; or, as is more usual, it means that he suppresses the main premises of his thinking and equates his results with universal truth. I have therefore always sought to do two things: I have tried to present the truth to my students as I see it; and I have sought, as best I can, to make them see all the difficulties inherent in my position. I have never, that is to say, consciously sought to proselytize. It has not been my concern whether students have accepted or no my own particular brand of thought. My business has been to make them see what the problems are, and the way in which one person arrives at his conclusions. But I have never thought it consistent with honesty to be one person in the lecture room and another person outside it. So long as I make my students aware of difficulties to be faced, so long, also, as I try myself honestly to face those difficulties, I have, as I think, done my duty by them.

It has been intensely interesting to me to note the indignation this attitude has aroused. When, for instance, I lectured in Moscow in 1934, and outlined the difficulties a Socialist government might encounter in England, Conservative protests in the House of Commons at once led to a threat by the University that I should be investigated. The threat, indeed, came to nothing, largely because some of the more distinguished of my colleagues, together with Mr. Bernard Shaw and Mr. J. M. Keynes, entered the lists on my side. But it has been significant that colleagues of mine could speak fiercely on the side of the existing order, both within and without the classroom, without even a hint from authority that they were going beyond due bounds. There has been protest because I wrote in socialist newspapers, or because I have been a member of the Labour Party executive. No such protest has been aroused when my colleagues have written in capitalist newspapers, or sat, as one eminent political scientist sits, on the executive of the Liberal Party. Practically all my colleagues in the Department of Economics are strongly opposed to interventionism. But no one has ever suggested that the University should deliberately seek to redress the balance or to interfere with the public expression of their views.

The truth, I think, is the simple one that the limits of academic freedom are set by the social tensions of the society. If these are great, then the frame of reference within which they operate will tend to inhibit free expression in those fields about which men feel keenly. In one age it is religion; in another it is science; in another, again, it is politics or economics. And because universities so largely depend upon public or private generosity for their existence, they will tend to frown upon the teacher whose views are a hindrance to their development. The pressure to conformity is great; it is not easy to feel that one stands in the way of gifts that might make possible growth that is of decisive importance to learning. But I do not think that one is entitled to escape by silence the obligations of citizenship. "It makes all the difference in the world," said Coleridge, "whether one puts truth in the first place or in the second." A university that proposes to study matters of social constitution must expect to find true controversy within its halls in an age when these are a matter of profound dispute. If it is not prepared for the free competition of ideas, it is not, in the true sense, a university.

I think, of course, that it is important for the teacher to be capable of detachment about his ideas. He must be ready to surrender beliefs no longer tenable, with the honesty that characterized John Stuart Mill when he gave up the doctrine of the wages fund. But I have not found, in nearly a quarter of a century of academic life, any greater self-criticism in my colleagues who think it a duty to dwell in the ivory tower than in those who, like myself, have been immersed in practical life. Perhaps rather the contrary. For those who have dwelt in the ivory tower have, only too often, thereby cut themselves off from the healthy experience of criticism. Their tendency is to refuse to examine the consequences of their beliefs lest this commit them to some action in the world of life. They devote a large part of their energy to technical minutiae. They avoid the basic problems of valuation. They refuse to admit that, as Plato said, true knowledge compels to action. They pursue a discipline of conduct that enables them to evade the obligation to act as citizens. They reprehend the teachers who are active in the battle. But they do not realize that their own refusal to choose is itself a choice. More than that: their refusal is only too often a part of that inertia which, perhaps more than any other quality in life, helps those who perpetrate injustice to live by their wrongdoing.

I am, at least, certain of this: that no one can teach politics seriously who does not know politics at firsthand. It was, I think, Bacon who pointed out that most books on politics that count are the books of men who have been active in the political battle. There is a quality of experience in the exercise of actual responsibility which is of vital importance to the analysis of experience. Certainly I have learned more about the problem of administration from actual work in local government than from all the textbooks I ever read. Certainly, also, my effort, however humble, to assist in shaping the policy of the Labour Party has taught me more about how political parties really work than I have learned from Ostrogorski and Michels and the other classic authorities. I think it is a reasonable criticism of a good deal of academic work in politics that, because the writer has not seen things from the inside, he tends to mistake the formal appearance for the living reality. The way to know men is to mingle with them; and a university that consciously separates itself from life is, I suspect, unlikely to influence its quality. The captaincy in the Hampshire grenadiers was not entirely useless to the historian of the Roman empire; long years in the service of Shaftesbury were vital to the thought of Locke, and the election campaigns for the London County Council taught Graham Wallas a good deal he could not have learned in books about human nature in politics. The professor's business, so far as he can fulfill it, is to be a whole man; and without what I may call clinical experience of politics in action I do not think he is likely to get a full perspective of the nature of things.

As I look back on the dead years, two things stand out for me as of inestimable value. I grant freely that, beside the measure of desire, the things one achieves seem, in retrospect, pitifully small. I grant, also, that the defeats one encounters are often so bitter as to make one doubt, at times, the worth of the whole adventure. A teacher, above all, who knows how little education can do, who sees the academic generations pass with such stark swiftness, is not tempted easily to exaggerate the influence of any save the outstanding personalities of history. The brief procession of human life seems, to the historian's gaze, little more than the flicker of a dying candle against eternity.

Yet there are, I think, two goods which make the adventure endlessly worth while. The first is the sense that every active socialist has of being what Heine called a "soldier in the liberation war of humanity." Certain memories that come back: a handshake and a brief word from Arthur Henderson after the election of 1929; the eager faces of a score of miners at a day school on politics in a northern village in which there was little save hope upon which to feed; the set determination of a thousand trade-union officials when they decided upon the general strike in May of 1926, men who risked all for the sake of solidarity; the moment when, in 1934, we took over the government of London into socialist hands; or when I have sat in Madrid and heard the defenders of Spanish democracy count life as nothing beside the defense of their cause; or when, in Moscow, I heard some of the leaders of the November Revolution describe the magic of that day when Lenin inaugurated the victory of the first socialist revolution in the world; these, after all, give one the sense that, at bottom, there is reality in the dream.

And there is the glory of love and friendship. Of the first I do not speak; its beauty defies the written word. Of the second, I will say only that to have known men like Mr. Justice Holmes, like Lansbury and Henry Nevinson, like J. L. Hammond and Graham Wallas, like the Webbs and Stafford Cripps, is to have warmed one's hands at the central fire of life. What I have had, too, in affection from Felix Frankfurter is greater even than he has given me in insights; more than that I could not say. From it all, despite its pain and disappointments, I emerge, so far, with the sense that I have lived near great events and known men and women intimately who have served great causes greatly. As I look back, I would not ask for wealth or power; I would ask only for the supreme gift of friends. That I have had in full measure. It has given me a sense of fellowship that has given to life a happiness beyond the power of sorrow to destroy.

# LIN YUTANG

*Lin Yutang's mellow and humane interpretations of Chinese life and culture have proved of inestimable service to curious Western readers. His knowledge of Eastern civilization is matched by his sensitive appreciation of Occidental culture.*

*He was born in 1895, in Chang Chow, Fukien Province, China. He has an A.M. from Harvard and a doctor of philosophy degree from Leipzig. From 1923 to 1926 he held a professorship at Peking National University. In his native land he has won a reputation for his literary criticism and edited a number of literary periodicals. His books in Chinese are numerous and influential. He is also master of a charming English style. Americans know him through his 'My Country and My People' (1935) and 'The Importance of Living' (1937). He has edited 'The Wisdom of Confucius' (Modern Library, 1938).*

# *Lin Yutang*

## I

LIKE all other common men, I have a common philosophy of life. Curiously I have always been repelled by idle philosophical speculations; terms like Plato's "idea," Spinoza's "essence," "substance," and "attribute," and Kant's "categorical imperative" have always aroused in me a sense of suspicion that the philosopher was getting too much involved in his own thought. A thing may sound so logical you are convinced it must be wrong. The moment a philosophical system becomes too impressive or logically beautiful, I become suspicious. The more complacent, self-satisfied, and foolishly logical systems, like Hegel's philosophy of history and Calvin's doctrine of total depravity, arouse in me only a smile. On a still lower level, the political ideologies, like Fascism and Communism as they are actually represented today, seem to me but caricatures of thought itself. For Communism I have a much higher respect than for Fascism, because the former is based on an idealistic love, while the latter is based on a cynical contempt, for the common man; but as they are practiced today, both are to me products of Western intellectualism and show to me a curious lack of self-restraint. More and more I am impressed by the wisdom of Confucius: "I know now why the moral life is not practiced. The wise mistake the moral law for something higher than it really is; and the foolish do not know enough what moral law is. I know now why the moral law is not understood. The noble natures want to live too high, high above their ordinary self; and the ignoble natures do not live high enough, i.e., not up to their moral ordinary true self. There is no one who does not eat and drink, but few there are who really know flavor."

And so while I have the utmost patience for science, when it is discussing or bisecting the small minutiae of life, I have no patience for hair-splitting philosophy. Yet in their simplest terms, science, religion, and philosophy have always fascinated me from childhood on. Stated in the simplest terms, science is but a sense of curiosity about life, religion is a sense of reverence for life, literature is a sense of wonder at life, art is a taste for life, while philosophy is an attitude toward life, based on a greater or lesser, but always limited, comprehension of the universe as far as we happen to know it. I regret profoundly that I was presented with the choice of enrolling in the school of arts or the school of science as a freshman when I did not know anything about either, and always feel that perhaps I made a wrong choice by choosing arts. But my love for science has never ceased, and I have tried to make up for it by constant reading of popular summaries. If by science is meant an eternal curiosity about life and the universe, then I may still claim to be a scientist. Also I am so profoundly religious by nature that the religions often make me furious. My being a pastor's son does not explain it all.

In saying that I have a common philosophy of life, therefore, I merely mean that, as an ordinary educated man, I have tried to adopt a reasonable and, as far as possible, harmonious attitude toward life, toward living, toward human society and the universe and God. The fact that I am naturally predisposed to suspect philosophical systems does not mean that I disbelieve in the possibility of a more or less unified and harmonious view of life, issuing in a harmonious attitude toward the business of living—money, marriage, success, the family, patriotism, and politics. I believe rather that the distrust of involved and airtight systems makes the adoption of a reasonable, unified view of life fairly simple and easy.

I know science's limitations, but with my worship of science, I always let the scientist do the spadework, having complete confidence in him, knowing that he is thoroughly conscientious. I let him discover the physical universe for me—the physical universe that I desire so much to know. Then, after getting as much as possible of the scientist's knowledge of the physical universe, I remember that the man is greater than the scientist, that the latter cannot tell us everything, cannot tell us about the most important things, the things that make for happiness. Then I have to rely on *bon sens*—that eighteenth-century word which deserves reviving a little. Call it *bon sens*, or common sense, or intuition, or intuitive thinking, it is that type of thinking which alone can help us attain the truth and wisdom of living. True thinking is always that type of thinking, a sort of warm, emotional, half-humorous, and half-whimsical thinking, mixed with a grain of idealism and a grain of delightful nonsense. Give imagination a little play, and then restrain it by a little hard cynicism, like the kite and its string. The history of mankind seems like kiteflying: sometimes, when the wind is favorable, we let go the string a little and the kite soars a little higher; sometimes the wind is too rough and we have to lower it a little, and sometimes it gets caught among tree branches; but to reach the upper strata of pure bliss—ah, perhaps never!

For the world is both a good and a bad world, and man is both a noble and a wicked creature. Life is often so happy and often so sad, and human society is often so cruel, and yet often not lacking in true kindness. Knowing that this is the case, how shall we proceed except by eminently kind, tolerant, and ironic thinking? Great wisdom consists in not demanding too much of human nature, and yet not altogether spoiling it by indulgence. One must try to do one's best, and at the same time, one must, when rewarded by partial success or confronted by partial failure, say to himself, "I have done my best." That is about all the philosophy of living that one needs.

The fact that human society and human nature are so imperfect is what makes life exciting to me. It makes me grateful to have been born a man, of which I am very proud. Interested as I am in the physical universe, it is in man, in his loves and hatreds, his noble achievements and ludicrous failures, that I am interested. I am interested in man because the way he loves and hates and behaves in general is so funny. That is to say, I am fundamentally sympathetic to man, which is only natural, as he is my own species. Take, for instance, some of the Fascist nations. How I despise their chiefs and their slobbering patriotism! How I see in them images of beasts filled with greed and cunning and egotism; and how they delude themselves! How I shudder when they proceed from action to speech to defend themselves, and offend the very words "peace," "justice," "self-determination" by their contamination! How infinitely ridiculous seem to me their propaganda chiefs; and I wonder what they think of their own people and of themselves, these small men! How they destroy the statue of Heine and rape the Universities of Göttingen and Heidelberg, and how they join in the mad dance around their golden calf, the pagan gods! Yet in these very nations, I see the great common people. In the most "warlike" nations, I refuse to admit that more than one per cent of the people, down in their hearts, welcome another war. Is not life still beautiful in those countries—beautiful in its marrying and giving births and scientific researches?

This is typical of the attitude we ought to take toward life in general, an attitude of tolerant irony. It is the attitude of expecting something finer and nobler of human nature than what it often appears to be; and, in expecting, not forgetting to forgive; an attitude of forgiving human nature for its shortcomings, and, in forgiving, not forgetting to chide it for not doing better. In some such fashion, we, the human species, shall always proceed further and higher. That is the warm, emotional, sympathetic thinking that I mean. Here the intellect is going to help us very little. After science has done its spadework, religion, art, literature, and philosophy must take their rightful place in human life. These things seem poorly correlated in the modern world; the specialist has usurped the man. For science can never replace art, religion, literature, and philosophy. Besides knowledge, we must retain, and never lose, a taste for life, a reverence for life, a sense of wonder at life, and a proper and reasonable attitude toward life. The taste for life must be unspoiled, the reverence for life must be truly profound, the sense of wonder must be fully alive, and the attitude toward life must be harmonious and reasonable.

## II

But let us first examine what the spadework of science has done for us, for science represents to us sound knowledge as far as it is perceivable by our intelligence. While science cannot tell us everything, yet in those things that science tells us about, there is no sense in setting oneself against the light of knowledge. As we are both flesh and spirit inextricably compounded, what we know about the flesh must influence our views of the spirit. And whatever else science may do, it certainly does not destroy, but rather increases, our sense of wonder at and reverence for life.

I am not speaking about the influence of science on the external conditions of our life, which is extensive enough, but rather of its unconscious influence on our views of things. Since Galileo's time, this influence has been so vast and deep that it has enveloped all of us. Say what you will, the modern man's views of God, of the universe, of the atom, of the basis and nature and constitution of matter, of man's creation and past history, of his goodness or badness, of his soul and its possible survival, of what to do with his body, of sin, punishment, the character of God's vengeance and forgiveness, of man's relationship with the animal kingdom—all these notions have undergone definite changes and are not those of the man of Galileo's times. On the whole, I may sum it up by saying that, in our minds, God has become bigger and man smaller, while on the other hand, the body has become cleaner and immortality vaguer. Thus all the most important notions involved in the practice of religion—God, man, sin, and immortality (or salvation)—have been, or should be, overhauled. All these things seem to me interrelated with each other and related to the teachings of science.

It is not because I am irreligious, but rather because I am supremely interested in religion, that I cannot help tracing how the progress of scientific knowledge impinges on the externals of religious belief. While the Sermon on the Mount is left practically intact, as is also the beauty of the moral realm and of noble living, we must bravely admit that science has played havoc with the paraphernalia of religion, or the stock notions with which the religions have always worked, like the notion of sin. What I want to point out is that these notions have changed very gradually and imperceptibly, almost without our knowing it, and that this influence has been an *unconscious* influence. Take the most obvious and superficial notion of hell in religion. I think not one in a hundred college freshmen or seniors today, perhaps not one in a thousand, believes in a literal hell. No one explicitly argues for or against the existence of hell; everyone assumes it is not worth arguing about. And while such stock notions (hell, sin, origin of evil, punishment, heaven, vicarious suffering) have undergone a profound

*Photo by Carl Van Vechten*

LIN YUTANG

change, religion, or at least organized religion, certainly must be affected.

When I say that in our minds God has become bigger and man smaller, I mean *bigger* and *smaller physically.* These things simply cannot be helped. Since we cannot but conceive of God as being at least commensurate with His universe, we naturally become, or I did become, awe-struck and spellbound as modern astronomy steadily revealed a wider and wider physical universe to us. The greatest enemy to old religions and all anthropocentric faiths is the two-hundred-inch diameter telescope. When I took up a New York paper a few weeks ago and read that some astronomer had discovered a new star cluster 250,000 light-years away from the earth, my notion of man's place in nature became downright ridiculous. These things are not unimportant in their bearings on our belief; they are highly important. I long ago reached the point where I realized how small and puny and humble I looked in God's, or the universe's, eyes, until the idea of a complicated system of downfall, punishment, and redemption seemed as absurd and preposterous to me as if I were to imagine myself evolving a system of punishment and redemption for a being less than the size of an ant's feeler, or even of a fair-sized maggot. We are individually not worth God's anger. We are not worth a damn, literally.

Science, or modern knowledge in general, has changed our idea of good and evil, of retribution, and of the worth or necessity of vicarious suffering. The idealized contrast of sin and perfection is no longer tenable. A better knowledge of man's heritage of animal instincts or savage instincts, products of a natural course of evolution, has rendered meaningless the age-old debate over the original goodness or badness of human nature. The fighting instinct, the hunger instinct, the sex instinct, the herd instinct, and in general the superior power of instinct over that of reason, all become readily understandable. You cannot blame man for having the sex instinct any more than you can blame the beaver for having the same; consequently, the whole mysticism about the evil of the flesh, upon which religion was built, seems singularly devoid of meaning. The medieval, or monastic, or typical "religious" attitude toward the body and toward this material life is therefore gone, and in its place has come a healthier and more sensible view of man himself and of his earthly occupations. I believe this attitude is the attitude of the average thinking man of today. In other words, the modern man's feeling is that this earthly life is not "damned." To say, therefore, that God was angry with man for being made imperfect, or for being merely halfway on the road of evolution, does not quite make sense, and to say that He would punish man for the same is equally unconvincing. But to imagine that God could not forgive without making somebody suffer for it is a travesty. It is to impute to God the savage notion of vicarious suffering, which we ourselves are not willing to practice in civilized life today. In one of Somerset Maugham's plays, the missionary lady who is enraged by an act of human sacrifice among the savages and tries to prevent it does not realize that her own religion is based on that same savage notion of human sacrifice to appease a God. My general position is that, God being so great and man being so small, God simply would not have bothered. The whole idea seems too artificial and complicated. As in physics we discard a theory when it becomes too artificial and complicated in the light of new facts, so we must discard this theory of redemption for something simpler.

What repels me particularly today in religion is its emphasis on sin. I have no consciousness of sin and no feeling of being damned. I think many men, looking at the problem coldly and sensibly, have come to take the same position. While not living a saint's life, I believe I have lived a fairly decent human life. Legally I am perfect, while morally I have imperfections. But all these moral imperfections or delinquencies, like occasional lying and neglect of duty, all added up together and placed before my mother as the judge, would probably make me deserve a three years' imprisonment at the most, but certainly not the damnation of hell-fire. This is not boasting; most of my friends do not deserve five years at the worst. And if I can face the memory of my mother, I can face God. She could not condemn me to eternal hell-fire. This I know. And I believe God is reasonable and understanding. Because the modern church is still determined to contemplate sin exclusively, and because missionaries in making converts always start out by injecting the consciousness of sin, I am unable to accept it.

At the other end of the Christian teaching is the notion of perfection. Perfection was the state of man in the Garden of Eden, and perfection is also the state aimed at in the future heaven. Why perfection? I cannot understand it. It does not even spring from the artistic instinct. The idea developed by the logic of Asia Minor of the first centuries was that we wanted to live in heaven in the company of God, and that consequently unless we were perfect, we could not do so. This perfection is therefore of a mystical character, having no logical basis except the desire of man to live in a heaven of perfect bliss. I doubt whether, if the Christian were not promised a heaven of perfect bliss to live in, he would care to be perfect. In actual daily life, this notion has no import whatsoever. I therefore repudiate also for myself the ideal of the perfect man. The ideal man is one who has tried honestly to do his best to live a decent life and to see the truth according to his lights. The ideal man for me is merely a reasonable man, willing to admit his mistakes and correct them. I don't ask for better creatures on this earth.

## III

Such a revelation of belief must be profoundly disturbing to many sincere Christians. Yet unless we are ruthlessly honest, we are not worthy to know the truth. In this matter we ought to behave as the scientists do. It is generally as painful for us to discard old beliefs as for the scientists to discard the old laws of physics and accept new theories. In fact, even the scientists always struggle against new theories, but somehow they are a fair-minded lot and accept or discard theories as their scientific conscience dictates. Truth is always disturbing, as the sudden impact of light is painful to the eye. Yet after the mental or physical eye is adjusted to the new light, the situation is not so bad after all. It is the children of little faith who are easily scared.

What then have we left? A great deal. The contours of old religions have been changed and their outlines blurred, but religion remains and always will remain. I am speaking of religion as belief colored with emotion, an elemental sense of piety or reverence for life, summing up man's certainty as to what is right and noble. One might think that by analyzing the spectrums of the rainbow or creating artificial rainbows at fountains in squares, our belief in Noah's pact with God would be destroyed and we would therefore be left in a world of satanic skepticism. But no, the rainbow is just as beautiful to look at, if one will only look. Not a bit of the beauty and mystery of the rainbow and the river breeze is destroyed.

There is a world of simpler beliefs left for us. I like them because they are simpler and perfectly natural. What I call the old "machinery" of salvation is gone; in fact the very object of that salvation for me is gone. The paternal God whom the old Salvation Army lady preached while brandishing her black umbrella, the God who takes an almost inquisitive interest in our trivial personal affairs, is also gone. The perfect logical chain of original perfection, downfall, damnation, vicarious suffering, and back to perfection again is definitely broken. Hell is gone, and after it heaven. In this philosophy of living, I believe we simply have to leave heaven out; we can't be too sure about it. It may frighten us, but it should not. For we still have a marvelous universe, physical in its aspects and almost spiritual in its workings, moved as it were by forces unseen. The wonders of the heavenly bodies and life on earth are still there, rich, overwhelmingly rich. Not just barely nice and useful for living, but intoxicating us with their beauty and their mystery. Back of it all we feel a Great Force—some call it God—so overwhelmingly great as to compel in us the greatest reverence. And while God is there, it is surely enough that life with all its intoxicating beauty and variety and mystery is before us. Forget the unknown and uncertain heaven, and live close to the rocks and the trees, and after watching the sunset watch the twinkling stars. This earth, this visible universe, I say, is enough! It is, in fact, spiritual, visibly so. We ought to be contented with it. And sometimes mixed with a sense of reverence for the great author of things, we ought also to feel a sense of gratitude.

The spirituality of man, too, is untouched. The moral realm is untouched and untouchable by the realm of physics. Understanding the rainbow is physics, but delight at the rainbow is morality. Understanding does not, and should not, and cannot, destroy the delight. This is the world of simple beliefs, requiring no theology and no hypothetical rewards and punishments. It is enough that man's heart is still touched by beauty and goodness and justice and kindness. Knowing that God who is the author of all things is ever so high above us, how can we live except by the highest and best in us? We should be ashamed to live otherwise. To live the good life, to act according to our highest and noblest instincts is merely the right thing to do. It is in fact to be religious, to have reverence for this life. Granted that we have the animal heritage, that we have instincts that are survivals of our savage and animal ancestry—the "sin," if you like, that we carry with us in our history of development—it is only common sense to say and believe that we have a higher and a lower self. There are instincts noble and instincts ignoble. Without believing that the ignoble instincts are attributable to a Satan working in us, it still does not follow that we have to follow the ignoble instincts at the expense of the noble instincts. As Mencius says, "The sense of mercy is found in all men; the sense of shame is found in all men; the sense of respect is found in all men; the sense of right and wrong is found in all men." Again as Mencius, the advocate of the higher life and the greater self, puts it, "He who attends to his greater self becomes a great man, and he who attends to his smaller self becomes a small man."

But though materialism does not logically follow the disappearance of the old religious point of view, morally it does follow, so curiously are we human beings made up. The modern world is on the whole increasingly materialistic as it becomes increasingly less religious. Religion has always meant to man a unified body of valid beliefs with a divine sanction back of it. It is something which man feels instinctively and emotionally rather than believes intellectually. The loss of religion would therefore be a loss to mankind. Cold rationalistic beliefs cannot take the place of religion. Furthermore, it has the sanctity of age, carrying with it or in it the force of an old tradition. It is not good that this tradition be lost; but this has happened. The modern age is moreover not the kind of age to produce new founders of religion. We are too critical for it. And the force of an individual's private belief about rational conduct compared with the force of a great religion is like a gutter pool compared with a great river. This private belief is good enough, and I believe fully adequate, for the superior man, but not enough for the inferior man, in Confucian terms. We have really landed in a modern dilemma.

It testifies to the wisdom of Moses and Confucius that they both tried to give the laws of civil life a religious sanction. We cannot produce a Moses or a Confucius in the modern age. I believe that the only kind of religious belief left for the modern man is a kind of mysticism in the broadest sense of the word, such as preached by Laotse. Broadly speaking, it is a kind of reverence and respect for the moral order of the universe, philosophic resignation to the moral order, and the effort to live our life in harmony with this moral order. The *tao* in Taoism exactly means this thing. It is broad enough to cover the most advanced present and future theories of the universe. It is both mystical and practical. For it breeds the philosophic temper. It is, for me, the only antidote against modern materialism.

The antidote against modern materialism lies obviously in the contemplative life, in man becoming philosophic. I do not know whether I am a Taoist. I simply have not thought of the question. But I do know that Taoism is a powerful deterrent against the excesses of the external life. Without calling oneself a Taoist—since I heartily dislike all isms—an educated man must come to have a unified and philosophic view of himself, of his fellowmen, of life, and the universe. The process of education mainly consists in clearing oneself of a number of foolish presumptions, humbugs, and prejudices that beset the common man's mind. Some of the commonest assumptions and presumptions that are dangerous to a man's spiritual life are our worship of wealth and power and success, and beliefs in luck, adversity, and triumph over others, and the reality of the material world. For all these illusions of the material world, Taoism has rather specific antidotes. Above all, it enables us to have a unified view of ourselves, our fellow beings, of God, and the universe. It teaches the spirituality of things. It teaches us to see the material phenomena as spiritual phenomena and life as manifestation of the laws of continuous growth and decay. It also teaches eternal justice. Thus man is fortified with a mysticism which is all-embracing. Then he may call this conception Tao or Truth or God or the Laws of the Universe, as he likes, and he does not have even to go to a church to worship it. You can't even pray to Tao. But emotionally it satisfies.

I can even be quite specific. Against the materialism of success, the Taoist has a kindly, indulgent smile. Materialism looks foolish rather than evil in the light of Taoism. Hatred and envy are diluted with laughter. Against the excesses of luxurious living, it teaches the simple life and, against the urban life, it teaches the love of nature. Against ruthless competition and struggle, it teaches the emptiness of the prize, the defeat of the conqueror, and the victory of the humiliated. Against the foolish desire for individual immortality, it teaches the immortality of the universe and of life itself. Against overaction it teaches inaction and contemplation. Against achievement, it teaches being. Against strength, it teaches softness. Against the most sinister force of modern life, the belief in brute force as exemplified by the Fascist nations, it teaches the important doctrine that you are not the only clever guy in the world, that you get nowhere by trying to push ahead, that nobody is a damn fool all the time, and that the law of action and reaction works eternally, bringing vengeance upon those who violate it. It works toward world peace by breeding the fundamental peaceful temper. All these things, while somewhat mystical, can be put in plain words that the common man can understand. The Taoist does not make mystical deductions; he merely teaches you to observe life carefully by the long view. If you look at life as carefully as the Taoist, you will agree with him.

In the reconstruction of religion in other respects, I do not think we shall be so successful. I have defined religion as an elemental sense of reverence for life, summing up man's beliefs as to what is right and noble, in a unified view of God and life and man. The body of valid beliefs naturally changes from age to age. These valid beliefs form the content of religion and the content must change from time to time. "Remember to keep holy the Sabbath" was, for instance, an important tenet of religion, but it is entirely unimportant today for the modern man. Probably "Remember to keep holy the international treaties," if it could receive the emotional color of a religious belief, would contribute more to our happiness in the present age. "Thou shalt not covet thy neighbor's goods" can be liberally interpreted, but it would certainly be better if man today could believe religiously, "Thou shalt not covet thy neighbor's territory." It would have much more real force. "Thou shalt not kill" can be considerably improved by adding these phrases "not even people of a different country." These beliefs should be religiously valid, but they are not. These are what I call the content of religious belief. Their importance entitles them to a place among religious beliefs in the new unified view of God and life and man, but it takes time for a newly knighted baronet to grow a halo of aristocracy. Living in a truly international community, we lack an international religion. About racial prejudices, for instance, we should all be taught to believe that the difference between peoples of any two countries is much smaller than that between the gentlemen and the gangsters of any particular country. Let us try to believe that the gentleman is international, even as gangsters are international. Today, however, the gangsters are internationally-minded, but the gentlemen are still "patriots."

We are living in a cynical age. Man is less optimistic about himself, or has less faith in humanity than the French encyclopedists of a century and half ago. Less than ever do we as a whole believe in liberty, equality, and fraternity. Diderot and D'Alembert might really be ashamed of us as their intellectual descendants. International morality has never sunk so low. The Spanish War, as a piece of extraordinary human chicanery and shamelessness, is about the lowest kind of war the creatures of this earth, birds, beasts, and men included, ever started. It is the most immoral war in all history. "For sheer shamelessness we have to hand it to the people of the nineteen-thirties," some future historian will write. As far as killing each other is concerned, and all that slobbering patriotism of the Fascist countries, we are living in the age of superbarbarism. Mechanized barbarism is barbarism none the less. In such a cynical age, only the supreme cynicism of a Taoist is not cynical. The law of action and reaction again. The world will right itself. Take a long view and you are comforted.

# EMIL LUDWIG

*Emil Ludwig began his career as a writer of plays in verse. Only at the end of his thirties did he begin the creation of the psychological essays and biographies that have won him world-wide fame. His best books are noted for their dramatic power and vividness. Some of them have been translated into twenty-six languages, notably his book on the outbreak of the war, 'July 14.' While it would be hard to choose among them, perhaps his most enduring work will prove his magnificent biography of a river, 'The Nile.'*

*Emil Ludwig was born in Germany in 1881 but has for many years been a Swiss citizen. He was educated at Breslau and Heidelberg. Some of his best-known publications include his lives of Jesus, Goethe, Bismarck, Napoleon, William II, and Lincoln; 'Three Titans' (1930); 'Schliemann of Troy' (1931); 'The Nile' (1936). He has also written several novels and many plays.*

*The essay that follows is translated from the German by Grace McConnaughey.*

# *Emil Ludwig*

I BELIEVE in the wisdom and beneficence of nature; but she does not give everything to all. I believe in the power of the gods; but they give the main chance to the strong. I believe in the dictatorship of fate; but fate favors the creative man and is justifiable, therefore, in the long run.

To make this statement clear, I must first sketch the path by which I arrived at this belief. Son of a naturalist and humanist, I was brought up in the precepts of neither Moses nor Jesus. Moral values were self-evident. I learned the Ten Commandments, indeed, but the foundation for a respectable way of life was laid by the example of my parents. The widest tolerance toward all forms of belief was exemplified in my father, who as physician devoted himself to his fellowmen and as scholar trusted nature. He showed his children that over us rules a power which is always the same, though called by many names. Brought up to distrust force and to reverence the spiritual and beautiful, I learned to venerate, besides the Greeks, two prophets—Goethe and Beethoven. In the half century that has followed I have come to know none greater.

At the same time I learned responsibility. We did not acquire the habit of taking refuge behind the fatherland or behind our race, least of all behind the suffering of a prophet said to have died for us all. The whole structure of my world would break down were I to believe that another than myself could give me salvation.

And why salvation? From what? The thought of man's fall and his original sin as the medium between God and myself, as well as the whole conception of a transfigured

Son of God who will save me from the hell burning beneath paradise: this is alien to me. I have never disturbed this belief in others, nor have I envied them for it. To me Jesus—whom I was later to represent as a fighter and prophet—was as worthy of reverence as Socrates, because he died for truth, as men are doing again today.

At an early age there grew in me a striving to be as God intended me. This was to be attained not by prayer and ecstasies but only by a laborious development of those inborn capacities which I regard as the gifts of nature, namely, my health and vigor, my spirit and imagination.

All my development since my youth I owe to one alone. Goethe has served as my leader not only in all realms of thought and deed but throughout the different decades of my life. Goethe and Nietzsche remain the only philosophers whom I have read; none among my contemporaries is known to me. My philosophical studies, thus limited, set my feet in the right path and left my mind free to approach God through contemplation of his works as found in nature, in music, and in great characters.

Problems of guilt and expiation have no meaning in my life. My point of view is that we sin in falling short of such efficiency as nature may expect, according to her gifts to us. On this account I do not believe that there is such a thing as thwarted genius, or that a man may die before his time. Nature soon recalled great creative geniuses like Mozart, Schubert, Byron, and Giorgione when they had given all that lay within them. Goethe, Beethoven, Shakespeare, and Leonardo were given a longer time, in order that they might complete their work according to the more measured tempo of their lives. I have no sympathy for the baffled poet or statesman who blames his failure on the misunderstanding of the rest of the world.

In fact, my sympathy for the higher forms of mankind steadily wanes, while my sympathy for the animal world increases. I cannot feel for a vanquished dictator, but my sympathy goes out to any dog struck down by an automobile. However, I do not hold the exercise of sympathy to be a service for which anyone may recommend his soul to God. Nature puts upon no man an unbearable burden; if her limits be exceeded, man responds by suicide. I have always respected suicide as a regulator of nature. But a believing or philosophic man who has pondered upon God should call upon the sympathy of man, or upon that of God, only when in the direst extremity. When I do this, I am unable to determine whether my prayer may still be termed monotheistic.

But it is of little importance, for whether I pray to a single power or to the many manifestations of it, whether I worship the πολγ or the παυ, in which dwells the same single power, the difference is not great enough to warrant the war of words or weapons that men have waged. What I worship is the creative power, and that alone. Goethe called it *Gott-Natur,* seeking a way out by this compound expression. In the prime of his life, Goethe voiced this concept in an ode. For twenty years it has hung on the wall beside my bed.

> Nature! By whom we are surrounded and enfolded, powerless to step without her limits, impotent to sink deeper within her. Unbidden, she takes us up and carries us along in the cycle of her dance, until we weary and fall from her arms. . . . Although we continually influence her, we have no power over her. She is manifest in her countless children—this mother. . . . She is pleased with illusion; she punishes, like a harsh tyrant, him who destroys it in himself or in others. But him who follows her trustfully she presses close to her heart. Her children are without number. She is miserly toward none, but she has favorites on whom she spends lavishly and for whom much is sacrificed. Her protection is given to the great. Her drama is ever new, because she continually provides new spectators.

> Life is her most wonderful invention, and death a master stroke whereby she may have much life. She envelops man in darkness and spurs him eternally toward the light. She makes him dependent upon the earth, slow and heavy, yet always is stirring him up. . . . She is generous; praise be to her and all her works. She is wise and calm. . . . She has brought me thus far; she will lead me out. I place myself in her hands without reserve. Do with me as she may, she will not spite her own creation. All lies at her door. She alone is culpable, and she alone is deserving of credit.

Since I have not the systems of the philosophers and lack the commentaries of the theologians (nor do I miss them), I can reconstruct my faith only from the feelings which possess me when I contemplate God's works. It seems possible, indeed, to draw near to him without a systematized belief or form of thought. Goethe has said it in the cold sentence: "Let us seek nothing behind the phenomena; they themselves are the lesson."

This acceptance of the world through the sensuous apperception of it is possible and bearable only to one who is daily conscious of the reality of death but nevertheless makes out his program for days and years to come, as if he were immortal. This paradox is similar to that in which we stubbornly postulate freedom of the will and at the same time believe, perforce, in a fate which must someday cross its path. It was only by virtue of these paradoxes that Goethe justified to himself his constant activity as an escape from destructive powers. Belief and accomplishment were so closely allied in him that at eighty years of age he spoke the daring words, "The conviction of my continuation after death springs from my belief in action. For if I continue to work ceaselessly until my death, then nature is obliged to give me another form of existence when the present one can no longer house my spirit."

The force of this argument impressed me even in my

Emil Ludwig

youth, and I have arrived at similar sources of a faith which rests, fundamentally, upon realistic forms. On this account my belief is all the more easily associated with a pantheism which sees God in all manifestations of nature, whether peopled with discrete gods or seen as one all-inherent spirit. In our romantic youth, we were prone to see dryads and nymphs, satyrs and hippocampi in the woods and streams, as I have so represented them in choruses and drama. Today, nature seems to me filled with a universal rustling which I need not personify. I feel this before an open geological atlas, or while walking, or when looking up into the evening sky.

From so deep a feeling of the animate quality of all things there comes of itself a belief in the symbolism of all being. The symbolic character of every happening shines with overwhelming power into the heart of him who sees each creature as the representative of others and to whom all appearances are but the varied play of the same creative will. Instead of isolated fates which concern his personal grief or joy, he sees tributaries of life which issue, perhaps by winding ways, but inevitably, in the open sea. There, in the great ocean, all the streams unite, later to change into clouds and rain and, finally, to become streams again. Here, for me, ends every question as to the future. "Toying with ideas of immortality," said the aged Goethe, "is for the genteel classes and for women, especially, who have nothing else to do. But a capable man who has something to think about, here and now, and who must daily struggle, fight, and act lets the future world take care of itself and is active and useful in this one."

Goethe's final wisdom, "All mortality is but a symbol," gives me a similar feeling of peace, for it takes the shock from occurrences without destroying their illusory charm. When I have learned to see the negative and unsuccessful aspects of my work, my environment, or my country as symbolic, then I have learned to bear them.

When we look upon the events of our life, in their rise and fall, their ripening and withering, their success and failure, as among the experiments of one and the same creator with millions of his creations, we cannot but feel ourselves encompassed by a circle of circumstance which neither we nor our more fortunate rivals can break through. "Everything," wrote Goethe, "in which man seriously interests himself stretches out to infinity; against this his only weapon is unremitting industry."

From such realization of the relativity of each individual happiness, I have built myself a harmonious labyrinth whose blueprint I have never seen and cannot, therefore, describe. It is the labyrinth in every man's soul. Only faith in a guiding Ariadne can give us confidence as we thread its mazes. Ariadne is faith in the logic of all happenings or, more simply, the goodness of God.

The more definitely a belief in the wisdom of nature took shape in me the less I admired the ascendance of one man over another and the more I admired man's victories over the elements, which I attempted to portray in writing. Not only my excursions into history but those through the woods and mountains have essentially changed in character. The thirty years of my life spent in the country brought this about. Long past is the romanticism of youth, when the Latin name of a moss or the sight of a telegraph wire disturbed me. Trees and animals, stones and clouds, affect me much more strongly since I have begun to know something of their sources and their life.

Out of such feelings I have come, in the historical world also, to be conscious of an unseen destiny, of a necessity. It is this that I have tried to express in my biographical studies. Never studying history but always the human heart, I transferred my knowledge from the present into the past, and sought there to construe the great characters in their immediate manifestation, first of all, and then according to the circumstances. One should never represent a man simply as an individual but always as the symbol of a human type, an aspiring child of the gods in battle with himself. To me, at least, individual destinies are interesting only as such symbols. For character is nothing other than the Biblical pound which the master gave to his servant that he might invest it. The amount of the gift is less important than the purpose and strength to make something of it. It is in the crossways of genius and character, therefore, that I see the critical region whence arise the significant figures of yesterday and today. In my researches, whether in the immediate present or in the past, I have always found more talent rusting through lack of character than strong characters failing to advance through lack of talent. Out of this has developed my *moral* concept of history as opposed to the modern "dynamic" or economic interpretation.

Never, however, have I taken the way of the psychoanalysts, who, it seems to me, overshadow the colorful abundance of life with their systematized doctrines until it becomes a sorry figment indeed. Contradictions are to be found in every human soul, beyond question, and whoever attempts to unravel them by some abracadabra only destroys their fascinating configurations. That childhood and sex are fundamental experiences of mankind was known and shown by Plutarch, but in no one attribute or stage of development have I found the key to character. Sex and ambition are important motives of action, but the play instinct is just as vital, whether in men of action or in men of reflection.

It is the interplay of motives that is decisive; from this springs the morality of a person.

A man's contribution to human welfare is important in

the light of history, the forum of humanity, but before God the greatest is he who has brought his abilities to their highest point, he whose personality has penetrated most deeply the lives of others. Out of this contradiction there has arisen for me a problem which I have been unable to solve completely.

While honoring the man who, through ingenuity, healing, and helping, adds to the happiness of mankind, and while the conquest of cities and countries seems to me to be unimportant for the land of my birth or for any other country known to history, nevertheless, I am most strongly attracted to powerful creative natures, not only in the platonic sense, but creative as men of action are creative, men who know how to enforce their will upon others and so raise themselves a step nearer to divinity. The creative power of conquering heroes is not negated by a thousand deaths for which they may have been responsible upon their way, for such men, as Goethe says, "step beyond morality; they are elemental forces like water and fire." So it is that I am ever more drawn to those who are heroes in the old sense of the word, and that my interest in the saints lessens, although the latter, not the former, contribute to human progress. Even today I should have nothing against hero-worship; but where are the heroes? I realize, however, that sometimes a patina lends charm to a bronze that would not have pleased us when new.

But neither by this romantic preference for the great adventurers nor by a recognition of the symbolic am I led to approve the adulation of force in our times, which clothes itself in new names and forms. The era contradicts itself. Conquest of lands and peoples has lost its beauty. The mastery of time and space accomplished by technical advances has made the subjugation of one people by another absurd. Mechanized warfare and conscription have similarly rendered absurd the pathos of classical heroism.

I grew up in the land of inborn obedience, but even as a youngster I could not but recognize the madness of modern war. I saw the union of peoples, of all Europe, as a necessity demanded by the interdependence of all upon all, just as the radio, bringing us news of the most distant occurrences, instantaneously unites our minds.

It was the war that really brought home to me the decadence of our social system. What I saw in Germany of the shallow vanity, arrogance, and self-interest of the ruling classes fostered mistrust of everything supported by the inheritance of rank or money. For me the only hero to emerge from this war was the Unknown Soldier. Yet here, too, arises an undeniable contradiction. An individualist, anarchical by nature, feels himself in opposition to the friend of man who is always working for justice. This contradiction, familiar to Nietzsche, allows me to feel the power and beauty of masterful, highly gifted characters who dominate in the world of men just as there are certain outstanding individuals among animals and plants. But I feel that there are limits to an esthetic view of the world, and so I am dedicated to the destruction of all false privilege based on inheritance or cunning, until society be so completely reconstructed that everyone has the opportunity to reach the goal to which he is entitled by talent and character.

For the sake of this reconstruction, this equalization of classes, a portion of personal freedom must, from time to time, be sacrificed, but never at the arbitrary command of a state. With world commerce making neighbors of the chief cities of rival peoples, the epoch of the national state enters its decline. The sacrifice of the life and peace of a people to so-called national honor or greatness is absurd today, for no people disputes the honor of another, and "great powers" no longer exist, in the higher sense of the term. Since culture has become accessible to all peoples, a flowing medium miscible with all, the question of what flag waves over a government building is far less important than what is being done in that building toward the equable distribution of goods. One hopes that a world once made free will afford the spirit more room and peace in which to spread its wings.

But I do not perceive in this struggle the essence of the age, nor would I in any sense sacrifice my life to it. Necessary as it is, and much as I agree in principle, yet I know that only the material fortunes of men will be improved as a result of this battle of the classes. The chance which we would give the poor and lowly to learn and to become what they will is bound to raise the average, but it cannot advance the highest achievements, which in all times have had their source in gifted and creative characters without distinction of birth or possession. No more than any one race has any one class a monopoly of the finest exploits of mankind. For among the creative and enlightened figures of history, the great prophets and artists, philosophers and inventors, popes and emperors, there are those who were born slaves, bastards, sons of peasants and the people. The spirit is always autochthonous and not to be brought into being by breeding or by the elevation of a class.

And only the spirit matters, for it is that alone which connects us with God. The smallest discovery in nature is of more importance than a shifting of the balance of power in Europe. Biologists, physicians, and engineers, the true builders of our age, compete to outlaw sickness, to master the elements, and to lengthen life, ever striving toward, and in some degree achieving, the very opposite of that effected by the statesmen preparing for war. And even when nothing practical is accomplished, when only new knowledge of the nature of the stars, or of the ocean depths, or of the atom is won, we are approaching God.

Therefore, I do not believe in an ideal state, since the ideal can never be sought in the state. I do not believe in salvation through an idea, because every idea must perish as it succeeds. But I do believe that the imagination and the thirst after knowledge have the power to bring me closer to the wonders of the world as symbols of the Godhead.

I recognize God in the logical construction of a crystal no less than in that of a Bach fugue. I see God in the pleading look of a dog as well as in the lovely bosom of a woman. I find him in the iridescent wings of a butterfly, and in the early-morning frost which means its death. He appears to me in the hairy covering of the magnolia bud, and in the hand of the child who plucks it before it can blossom. I see him in the revolution of our times which seeks to wipe out old injustices and in the end achieves a modicum of justice. I see him in the smoldering eyes of a man who vows revenge upon his rival in love, and in the poised hand of the surgeon who removes a bullet from the eye, after the duel. I see him in the master hand of Leonardo, as he fixed an unearthly smile upon the lips of his divine creation, and in the caricatures which he made of men's features. I see him in a playful kitten which seeks its playfellow in the mirror, and in the murderous eyes with which it follows the movements of a robin. I recognize God in the inspiration which he sends me as if in a dream, and in the long labor by which I must carry it out.

# THOMAS MANN

*Thomas Mann is ranked by many thoughtful critics as the finest of living imaginative writers. There are some rasher spirits—the editor of this book is one—who believe he will eventually take his place among the very greatest novelists the race has produced. Artistically he has progressed from the masterly naturalism of 'Buddenbrooks' to the rich symbolism of the great Joseph story. Politically he has moved from his original position of detachment to one of absorption in the struggle for true democratic and humanistic values. Self-exiled from his native land, he is at this writing looking forward to becoming a citizen of our country.*

*He was born in 1875, in Lübeck, of a solid bourgeois family. His creative gift matured early: at twenty-five he had published 'Buddenbrooks.' His middle years were spent mainly in Munich, in an environment well suited to assist his creative impulses. In 1929 he was awarded the Nobel prize for literature. In 1933 he left Germany, voluntarily. His books have since been banned by the Nazis.*

*The following is a list of his major works in translation, with the dates of their American publications: 'Buddenbrooks' (1924); 'The Magic Mountain' (1927); 'Three Essays' (1929); 'Joseph and His Brothers' (1934 —) ('Joseph and His Brothers,' 'Young Joseph,' 'Joseph in Egypt'); 'Stories of Three Decades,' (1936); 'Freud, Goethe, Wagner' (1937).*

*The essay which follows is translated from the German by Helen Lowe-Porter.*

# *Thomas Mann*

I FIND it singularly difficult to formulate, either briefly or in a more extended pronouncement, my philosophical ideas or convictions—shall I say my views, or, even better, my feelings?—about life and the world. The habit of expressing indirectly, through the media of picture and rhythm, my attitude toward the world and the problem of existence, is not conducive to abstract exposition. Summoned to speak, as now, I seem to myself a little like Faust, when Gretchen asks him how he stands about religion.

You certainly do not mean to put me through my catechism, but in practice your inquiry comes to much the same thing. For truly I find it almost easier—in my position—to say how I feel about religion than about philosophy. I do, indeed, disclaim any doctrinaire attitude in spiritual matters. The ease with which some people let the word God fall from their lips—or even more extraordinarily from their pens—is always a great astonishment to me. A certain modesty, even embarrassment, in things of religion is clearly more fitting to me and my kind than any posture of bold self-confidence. It seems that only by indirection can we approach the subject: by the parable, the ethical symbolism wherein, if I may so express myself, the concept becomes secularized, is temporarily divested of its priestly garment and contents itself with the humanly spiritual.

I read lately in a treatise by a learned friend something about the origin and history of the Latin word *religio*. The verb *relegere* or *religare* from which it is thought to derive means originally in its profane sense to take care, to pay heed, to bethink oneself. As the opposite of *neglegere* (neglect, *negligere*) it means an attentive, concerned and careful, conscientious, cautious attitude—the opposite, as I said, of all carelessness and negligence. And the word *religio* seems to have retained throughout the Latin age this sense of conscientiousness, of conscientious scruples. It is thus used, without necessary reference to religious, godly matters, in the very oldest Latin literature.

I was glad to hear all that. Well, I said to myself, if that is being religious, then every artist, simply in his character as artist, may venture to call himself a religious man. For what is more contrary to the artist's very nature than carelessness or neglect? What characterizes more strikingly his moral standards, what is more inherent in his very being than carefulness, than attentiveness, conscientiousness, caution, profound concern—than *care*, altogether and in general? The artist, the workman, is of course the careful human being par excellence; the intellectual man is that anyhow, and the artist, using his plastic gift to build a bridge between life and mind, is but a variation on the type—shall we say a peculiarly gratifying and functional freak? Yes, carefulness is the predominant trait of such a man: profound and sensitive attention to the will and the activities of the universal spirit; to change in the garment of the truth; to the just and needful thing, in other words to the will of God, whom the man of mind and spirit must serve, heedless of the hatred he arouses among stupid or frightened people, people obstinately attached by their interests to obsolete or evil phases of the age.

Well, then, the artist, the poet—by virtue of his care not only for his own product but for the Good, the True, and the will of God—he is a religious man. So be it. After all, that was what Goethe meant, when he extolled the human lot in those loving-kindly words:

*Denkt er ewig sich ins Rechte,*
*Ist er ewig schön und gross.*

Again, and in other words: for me and my kind the religious is lodged in the human. Not that my humanism springs from a deification of humanity—verily there is small occasion for that! Who could find the heart, contemplating this crackbrained species of ours, to indulge in optimistic rhetoric, when his words are daily given the lie by the harsh and bitter facts? Daily we see it commit all the crimes in the Decalogue; daily we despair of its future; all too well we understand why the angels in heaven from the day of its creation have turned up their noses at sight of the Creator's incomprehensible partiality for this so doubtful handiwork of his. And yet—today more than ever —I feel we must not, however well-founded our doubts, be betrayed into mere cynicism and contempt for the human race. We must not—despite all the evidence of its fantastic vileness—forget its great and honorable traits, revealed in the shape of art, science, the quest for truth, the creation of beauty, the conception of justice. Yes, it is true, we succumb to spiritual death when we show ourselves callous to that great mystery on which we are touching whenever we utter the words "man" and "humanity."

Spiritual death. The words sound alarmingly religious; they sound deadly serious. And truly the whole question of the human being and what we think about him is put to us today with a life-and-death seriousness unknown in times that were not so stern as ours. For everybody, but most particularly for the artist, it is a matter of spiritual life or spiritual death; it is, to use the religious terminology, a matter of salvation. I am convinced that that writer is a lost man who betrays the things of the spirit by refusing to face and decide for himself the human problem, put, as it is today, in political terms. He will inevitably be stunted. And not alone will his work suffer, his talent decline, until he is incapable of giving life to anything he produces. No, even his earlier work, created before he thus rendered himself culpable, and once good and living, will cease to be so, it will crumble to dust before men's eyes. Such is my belief; I have such cases in mind.

Have I said too much, in saying that the human being is a great mystery? Whence does he come? He springs from nature, from animal nature, and behaves unmistakably after his kind. But in him nature becomes conscious of herself. She seems to have brought him forth not alone to make him lord over his own being—that is only a phrase for something with much deeper meaning. In him she lays herself open to the spiritual; she questions, admires, and judges herself in him, as in a being who is at once herself and a creature of a higher order. To become conscious, that means to acquire a conscience, to know good and evil. And nature, below the human level, does not know them. She is "innocent." In the human being she becomes guilty —that is the "Fall." The human being is nature's fall from a state of innocency; but it is not a decline, it is rather an ascent, in that a state of conscience is higher than a state of innocence. What Christians call "original sin" is more than just a piece of priestcraft devised to keep men under the Church's thumb. It is a profound awareness in man as a spiritual being of his own natural infirmity and proneness to err, and of his rising in spirit above it. Is that disloyalty to nature? Not at all. It is a response to her own deepest desire. For it was to the end of her own spiritualization that she brought man forth.

These are ideas both Christian and humane; and there is much evidence that we shall do well today to emphasize the Christian character of the culture of our Western world. I feel the strongest antipathy for the half-educated mob that today sets itself up to "conquer Christianity." But equally strong is my belief that the humanity of the future—that new human and universal feeling now in process of birth, drawing life from efforts and experiments of all sorts and kinds and striven after by the choice and master spirits of the age—that humanity will not exhaust itself in the spirituality of the Christian faith, in the Christian dualism of soul and body, spirit and life, truth and "the world."

I am convinced that of all our strivings, only those are good and worth while which contribute to the birth of this new human feeling, under whose shelter and sway, after the passing of our present forlorn and leaderless stage, all humanity will live. I am convinced that my own strivings after analysis and synthesis have meaning and value only as they stand in groping, intuitive, tentative relation to this coming birth. In fact, I believe in the coming of a new, a third humanism, distinct, in complexion and fundamental temper, from its predecessors. It will not flatter mankind, looking at it through rose-colored glasses, for it will have had experiences of which the others knew not. It will have stouthearted knowledge of man's dark, daemonic, radically "natural" side; united with reverence for his superbiological, spiritual worth. The new humanity will be universal—and it will have the artist's attitude: that is, it will recognize that the immense value and beauty of the human being lie precisely in that he belongs to the two kingdoms, of nature and spirit. It will realize that no romantic conflict or tragic dualism is inherent in the fact; but rather a fruitful and engaging combination of destiny and free choice. Upon that it will base a love for humanity in which its pessimism and its optimism will cancel each other out.

When I was young, I was infatuated with that pessimistic and romantic conception of the universe which set off against each other life and spirit, sensuality and redemption, and from which art derived some most compelling effects—compelling, and yet, humanly speaking, not quite legitimate, not quite genuine. In short, I was a Wagnerite. But it is very likely in consequence of riper years that my love and my attention have more and more fixed upon a far happier and saner model: the figure of Goethe, that marvelous combination of the daemonic and the urbane in him, which made him the darling of mankind. It was not lightly that I chose—for the hero of that epic which is becoming my lifework—a man "blest with blessing from the heavens above and from the depths beneath."

Jacob the father pronounced this blessing upon Joseph's head. It was not a wish that he might be blest, but a statement that he was so, and a wish for his happiness. And for me, it is the most compendious possible formulation of my ideal humanity. Wherever, in the realm of mind and personality, I find that ideal manifested, as the union of darkness and light, feeling and mind, the primitive and the civilized, wisdom and the happy heart—in short as the humanized mystery we call man: there lies my profoundest allegiance, therein my heart finds its home. Let me be clear: what I mean is no subtilization of the romantic, no refinement of barbarism. It is nature clarified, it is culture; it is the human being as artist, and art as man's guide on the difficult path toward knowledge of himself.

All love of humanity is bound up with the future; and the same is true of love of art. Art is hope. . . . I do not assert that hope for the future of mankind rests upon her shoulders; rather that she is the expression of all human hope, the image and pattern of all happily balanced humanity. I like to think—yes, I feel sure—that a future is coming, wherein we shall condemn as black magic, as the brainless, irresponsible product of instinct, all art which is not controlled by the intellect. We shall condemn it in the same degree to which it is exalted in ages weak, like the one we live in, on the human side. Art, indeed, is not all sweetness and light. But neither is she altogether the dark, blind, monstrous brood of the tellurian depths. She is not just "life." The artist of the future will have a clearer, happier vision of his art as "white" magic: as a winged, hermetic, moon-sib intercessor between life and spirit. For all mediation is itself spirit.

THOMAS MANN

# JACQUES MARITAIN

*Jacques Maritain is outstanding among modern Catholic philosophers. He is distinguished by the humanity and subtlety of his thought, no less than by the range of his knowledge.*

*Born in 1882, of Protestant family, he studied philosophy at the Sorbonne, became a follower of Henri Bergson, and in 1906, under the influence of Léon Bloy, was converted to Catholicism. His researches have centered in the Angelic Doctor, Thomas Aquinas, but he has also written on themes not deriving from his scholastic studies. He has lectured at the Universities of Toronto and Chicago and is at present professor of philosophy at the Institut Catholique, Paris.*

*Among his books available in English are: 'Art and Scholasticism' (1930); 'An Introduction to Philosophy' (1930); 'Religion and Culture' (1931); 'The Angelic Doctor' (1931); 'The Degrees of Knowledge' (1937); and 'True Humanism' (1938).*

*The following essay is translated from the French by Fenton Moran.*

# *Jacques Maritain*

I WAS brought up as a child in "liberal Protestantism." Later I made the acquaintance of the different phases of lay thought. In the end the scientist and phenomenist philosophy of my teachers at the Sorbonne made me despair of reason. For a moment I believed I might find complete certitude in the sciences, and Félix Le Dantec thought that my fiancée and I would become disciples of his biological materialism. (The best thing that I owe to my studies at that time is that they brought me into touch, at the School of Sciences, with the woman who, ever since, in all my work, has always been at my side in a perfect and blessed union.) Bergson was the first to fulfill our deep desire for metaphysical truth by giving us back the sense of the absolute.

Before being attracted to St. Thomas Aquinas, the great influences I underwent were those of Charles Péguy, Bergson, and Léon Bloy. A year after meeting Bloy, my wife and I received Catholic baptism, choosing him as our godfather.

It was after my conversion to Catholicism that I made the acquaintance of St. Thomas. After my "passionate pilgrimage" among all the doctrines of modern philosophers, in whom I had discovered nothing but disenchantment and splendid uncertainties, I felt, as it were, an illumination of the reason. My vocation as philosopher became clear to me. "*Woe is me should I not thomistize,*" I wrote in one of my first books. And through thirty years of work and combat I have followed in this path, with a feeling that I could understand more completely the gropings, the discoveries, and the travail of modern thought, as I tried to throw upon them more of the light which comes to us from a wisdom which, resisting the fluctuations of time, has been worked out through the centuries.

In order to advance along this way, we are constantly obliged to bring together singularly distant extremes (for no solution of our problems can be found *ready-made* in the legacy of the ancients). We are also obliged to make the difficult separation between the pure substance of those truths, which many "moderns" reject as a mere jumble of the opinions of the past, and all the dross of prejudice, worn-out expressions, and arbitrary constructions, which many "traditionalists" confuse with that which really deserves intellectual veneration.

I have mentioned the different phases through which I passed because they gave me the opportunity of experiencing personally the state of mind of the idealistic freethinker, of the inexperienced convert, and of the Christian who becomes aware, as his faith takes root, of the purifications to which it must be subjected. I was likewise enabled to acquire some experimental idea of what the antireligious camp and the so-called *orthodox* (*bien pensant*) camp are worth. Neither of them is worth much. To my way of thinking, God trains us, through our disillusionments and mistakes, to understand at last that we must believe only in Him and not in men, which places us in the proper position to marvel at all the good which is in men in spite of everything and all the good which they do in spite of themselves.

This is not the proper place to expound propositions of speculative philosophy. I shall say only that I consider Thomistic philosophy as a living and up-to-date philosophy, having all the greater power for the conquest of new fields of discovery as its principles are firmer and more organically cemented. When they behold the succession of scientific hypotheses, certain minds are surprised that it should, today, be possible to draw inspiration from metaphysical principles recognized by Aristotle and Thomas Aquinas and rooted in the most ancient intellectual heritage of our kind. To this I reply that the telephone and the radio do not prevent men from still having two arms, two legs, and two lungs, from falling in love and searching for happiness like their faraway ancestors. Moreover, truth recognizes no chronological criteria and the art of the philosopher cannot be confused with that of fashion.

Going still further, it must be explained that progress takes place in the sciences of phenomena, in which the "problem" aspect is very marked, principally by the *substitution* of one theory for another theory which took account of a lesser number of known facts and phenomena; whereas with metaphysics and philosophy, where the "mystery" aspect predominates, progress takes place principally by *deeper penetration.* In addition, the different philosophical systems, however ill-founded they may be, constitute, when taken together, a kind of virtual and fluent philosophy, overlapping contrary formulations and hostile doctrines and supported by the elements of truth they all contain. If, therefore, a body of doctrine exists among men, entirely supported by true principles, it will progressively (and more or less tardily, due to the laziness of its advocates) incorporate in itself and *realize* this virtual philosophy, thereby giving it form and organization. Such is my idea of "progress" in philosophy. The works of Prof. Mortimer J. Adler, especially his book *Art and Prudence,* are happy proof that a similar conception is appearing in contemporary American philosophy.

If after that I say that the metaphysics which I hold to be well founded in truth can be described as critical realism and as a philosophy of intelligence and of being, or still more precisely of *existing* considered as the act and perfection of all perfections, these formulas will doubtless be of interest only to specialists. A few reflections on the historical significance of modern philosophy will no doubt be more appropriate.

In the Middle Ages, philosophy was, in fact, usually treated as an instrument in the service of theology. Culturally, it was not in the state required by its nature. The coming of a philosophical or profane wisdom which had completed its own formation for itself and according to its own finalities, responded, therefore, to a historical necessity. But unfortunately this work was brought about under the emblem of separatism and a sectarian rationalism; Descartes *separated* philosophy from all higher wisdom, from everything in man which comes from above man. I am certain that what the world and civilization have lacked for three centuries has been a philosophy which would have developed its autonomous exigencies in a Christian climate, a wisdom of reason not closed but open to the wisdom of grace. Reason must battle today with an irrationalist deification of elemental and instinctive forces, which threatens to ruin the whole of civilization. In this struggle, reason's task is one of integration; understanding that the intelligence is not the enemy of mystery but rather lives by it, it must *re-enter into intelligence* with the irrational world of affectivity and instinct, as with the world of the will, of liberty and of love, as with the suprarational world of grace and the Divine Life.

The dynamic harmony of the degrees of knowledge will be made manifest at the same time. From this standpoint, the problem peculiar to the age we are entering will be, so it seems, to reconcile *science* and *wisdom.* The sciences themselves seem to invite the intelligence to this task. We see them being stripped of the traces of materialistic and mechanistic metaphysics which hid their true features. They call for a philosophy of nature, and from the marvelous progress of contemporary physics, the savant can regain a sense of the mystery announced by the atom, as by the universe. A critique of knowledge formed in a truly realist and metaphysical spirit thenceforth has a chance to be heard when it predicates the existence of structures of knowledge specifically and hierarchically distinct (distinct, but not separate) and shows that they correspond to original types of explanation which could not be substituted one for the other.

The Greeks recognized the great truth that contemplation is in itself superior to action. But they at once transformed it into a great error: they believed that humankind exists for the benefit of a few intellectuals. According to their way of thinking, philosophers were a category of specialists living a suprahuman life, and ordinary human life, which is civic or political life, existed for their service. For the service of the latter, in turn, there was the subhuman life of labor, that is to say, ultimately, the life of the slave. The lofty truth of the superiority of the contemplative life was thus tied to a contempt for labor and to the evil of slavery.

All this was transfigured by Christianity. Christianity taught men that love is worth more than intelligence. It transformed the notion of contemplation which henceforth did not stop with the intellect but with the love of God, its object. It restored to action its human significance of service to one's neighbor and rehabilitated labor by showing forth in it, as it were, an import of natural redemption and a natural prefiguration of the communication of charity. It summoned to the contemplation of saints and to perfection, not a few specialists or privileged persons, but all men, who, symmetrically, are all bound by the law of labor. Man is *at once* Homo faber and Homo sapiens, but he is Homo faber before becoming truly in act, and in order to become, Homo sapiens. Thus the Greek idea of the superiority of the contemplative life was preserved by Christianity, but through a transformation and by freeing it from the error by which it had been tainted.

The contemplation of saints completes and consummates a natural aspiration to contemplation which is consubstantial in man and of which the wise men of India and Greece in particular give testimony. In supernatural contemplation, it is through love that the knowledge of divine things becomes experimental and fruitful. For the very reason that it is the work of love in act, it passes also into action by virtue of the very generosity and abundance of love, which is the gift of self. It is then that action issues forth from the superabundance of contemplation, and this is why, far from suppressing action or obstructing it, contemplation gives it life. It is in this sense, which goes back to the essential generosity of the contemplation of love, that with Bergson we must recognize in the superabundance and excess of the gift of self shown by the Christian mystics, a sign of their success in reaching the heroic peaks of human life.

The pursuit of supreme contemplation and the pursuit of supreme liberty are two aspects of the same pursuit. In the order of the spiritual life, man aspires to perfect and absolute freedom, and therefore to a superhuman state. The men of wisdom of all times have given evidence of this. The function of the law is a function of protection and education of liberty, the function of a pedagogue. At the conclusion of this tutelage, the perfect man is freed from every servitude, even, St. Paul says, from the servitude of the law, because he does spontaneously what the law demands and is one spirit with the Creator.

The pursuit of liberty is still, to my way of thinking, at the bottom of the social and political problem. But here, in the order of temporal life, it is not a divine liberty which is the object of our desires, but rather a liberty proportionate to the state of man and to the natural possibilities of our earthly existence. We must make no mistake about the nature of the object thus pursued. It is not simply the protection of *free will* in each of us, nor is it the *liberty of power* of the social community. It is the *liberty of expansion* of the human persons which make up a people and participate in its virtues. Organized society is intended to develop conditions of life in common which, while insuring first of all advantages and peace to the whole, help each person in a positive manner progressively to conquer this freedom of expansion which consists above all in the flowering of moral and rational life.

So justice and love are the very foundations of the life of society, which must subject to truly human advantages all manner of material advantages, technical progress, and the implements of power, which also form part of society's common good.

I believe that historical conditions and the yet inferior state of development of humanity make it difficult for organized society fully to reach its objective, and that in respect to the possibilities which the Gospel brings us and the demands it makes on us in the social-temporal domain, we are still in a prehistoric age. As we can see today in the psychoses of the masses which adore Stalin or Hitler, or dream of exterminating certain classes which they consider diabolical, such as "the Reds" or "the Fascists" or "the Jews," human collectivities bear such a burden of animality, easily inclined to morbidity, that it will take centuries still for the human personality to be able really to take on among the masses the breadth of life to which it aspires. We can see, then, that the objective toward which organized society tends by its very nature is to procure the common advantage of the multitude in such a manner that the individual person, not only the one belonging to a privileged class but the members of the whole mass, may truly reach that measure of independence which is proper to civilized life and which is insured alike by the economic guarantees of work and property, political rights, civic virtues, and the cultivation of the mind.

These conceptions belong to wider general views which seem to me most fittingly designated under the term *integral humanism,* and which involve a whole philosophy of modern history. Such a humanism, considering man in the integrality of his natural and his supernatural being and setting no limits *a priori* on the descent of divinity into man, can also be called Humanism of the Incarnation.

In the social-temporal order, it does not call on man to sacrifice himself for any imperialism, be it of the race, of the class, or of the nation. It calls upon him to sacrifice himself to a better life for his brothers and to the concrete good of the community of human persons. Thus it can only be a heroic humanism.

It has often been remarked that middle-class liberalism, which tries to base everything on the individual considered as a little god and on his gracious pleasure, on absolute freedom of property, commerce, and the pleasures of life, must inevitably lead to a despotic paternalism of the state. The reign of the Greater Number produces an omnipotent state of the ruminant or plutocratic type. Communism may be regarded as a reaction against this individualism. It claims to lead to the absolute release of man who is supposed to become the god of history, but in reality this release, presuming that it were accomplished, would then be that of man taken collectively, not of the human person. Society as an economic community would enslave the whole life of the person, because economic functions would become the essential work of civil society instead of serving the liberty of expansion of the person. We already see in Russia that what is represented as the release of man taken collectively would be the enslavement of all individuals.

As for the anticommunist and anti-individualist reactions of the totalitarian or dictatorial type, it is not in the name of the social community and of the liberty of man considered collectively, but in the name of the sovereign dignity of the state, which is a state of the carnivorous type, or in the name of the spirit of a people, or in the name of a race and blood, that they would turn man over bodily to a social entity in which the person of the chief is the only one to enjoy, properly speaking, the privileges of a human personality. This is why totalitarian states, having need for themselves of the entire devotion of the human person for which they have neither feeling nor respect, inevitably seek to find a principle of human exaltation in myths of external grandeur and in the never-ending struggle for power and prestige. By its very nature this leads to war and the auto-destruction of the civilized community. If there are churchmen who count on dictatorships of this kind to promote the religion of Christ and Christian civilization, they forget that the totalitarian phenomenon is an aberrant religious phenomenon in which a kind of earthly mysticism devours every other sort of mysticism and will tolerate no other one beside itself.

Confronted with bourgeois liberalism, communism and totalitarianism, what we need is a new solution, at once personalistic and communal, which views human society as the organization of liberties. We are thus led to a conception of democracy differing fundamentally from that of Jean-Jacques Rousseau and which we might call *pluralist*, because it requires that the state insure the organic liberties of the different spiritual families and the different social bodies assembled within it, beginning with the natural basic community, the society of the family. The tragedy of modern democracies is that, under the appearances of an error—the deification of a fictitious individual closed to all realities from above—they have sought something good, the expansion of the personality open to realities from above and to the common service of justice and friendship. Our personalist democracy is really inconceivable without those superelevations which nature and temporal civilizations receive, in their own order, from the energies of the Christian leaven.

I am certain that the coming of such a democracy, which presupposes class antagonism overcome, requires that we go beyond capitalism and beyond socialism, which are both tainted by a materialistic conception of life.

I would remark that Christians today find themselves confronted, in the social-temporal order, with problems similar to those which their forefathers encountered, in the sphere of the philosophy of nature, in the sixteenth and seventeenth centuries. At that time modern physics and astronomy, which were beginning, were bound up with the philosophical systems set up against tradition. The champions of tradition did not know how to make the necessary distinctions. They took sides against what was going to become modern science at the same time as against the philosophical errors which, in the beginning, parasitized it. Three centuries have been necessary to clear up this misunderstanding, if it can be said that the world is indeed clear of it. It would be disastrous today to revive the same errors in the sphere of practical and social philosophy.

As Pope Pius XI has put it, the great scandal of the nineteenth century is the divorce between the working classes and the Church. In the temporal order, the moral secession of the working masses with regard to the political community is a tragedy of a like nature. The awakening of what the socialist vocabulary calls class consciousness in the working multitudes appears to us as an important step forward if we regard it as the arousing of a consciousness of human dignity, rebuffed and humiliated, and of a consciousness of a vocation. But it has been tied up to an historic calamity in that this awakening of consciousness has been poisoned by the evangel of despair and social warfare which is at the bottom of the Marxian idea of class strife and the dictatorship of the proletariat. In the nineteenth century, the blindness of the owning classes thrust the working masses into just this *secessionist* concept which Marx advocated and which calls upon the proletarians of all countries to consider no other common good than that of their own class.

Whoever has pondered these fundamental facts and the history of the labor movement has understood that the temporal and spiritual problem of the *reintegration of the masses* is the central problem of our times. In my opinion, it is only an artificial and illusory solution of this problem to endeavor, as in National-Socialist Germany, to manufacture a race of happy slaves through violence, accompanied by certain material improvements which are good in themselves but which are brought about in a spirit of domination, and by a psychotechnic solicitude which is bound to satisfy appetites by putting them to sleep. However difficult, slow, and painful it may be, the reintegration of the proletariat in the national community, to collaborate heart and soul in the work of the community and not to exercise a class dictatorship over it, can take place *really*, that is to say *humanly*, only by a remolding of the social structures accomplished in a spirit of justice. I am not sufficiently naïf to believe that this reintegration can be brought about without collisions and without sacrifices, on the one hand for the well-being of favored sons of fortune and on the other for the theories and the destructive instincts of revolutionary fanatics. But I am certain that it requires, above all, a free co-operation on the part of the elite of the working classes and the masses who follow their lead, in a better general understanding of historical realities, and a consciousness of the dignity of the human being as worker and citizen, which is not effaced but rather heightened. In the same way, the return of the masses to Christianity will be brought about only through love—and I mean that love which is stronger than death, the fire of the Gospel.

We shall never give up the hope of a new Christendom, of a new temporal order inspired by Christianity. Now, if it is true that the means must correspond to the end and are themselves the end, as it were in the state of formation and preparation, it is then clear that in order to prepare a Christian social order, Christian means are needed, that is to say, true means, just means, means which are animated, even when they are perforce harsh, by a true spirit of love. In two books published in 1930 and 1933,[1] I have already dwelt at length on these axiomatic truths. Nothing can be graver or more scandalous than to see, as we have seen for some years past in certain countries, the iniquitous and barbarous means employed by men who invoke a Christian order and a Christian civilization. Aldous Huxley, among others, has denounced the madness of wishing to produce good ends by bad means. Henri de Man has explained that in the means the end is already preformed. Will Christians ever understand? It is a truth laid down in the very nature of things that Christendom will be made over by Christian means or will be completely unmade.

The present state of the nations obliges us to record that never have the mind and the spirit been so thoroughly rebuffed in the world. In the end, however, pessimism is always the victim of its own deceit. It disregards the great law which might be called the law of the double energy movement of history. While the wear and tear of time naturally dissipates, and degrades, the things of this world and the energy of history, the creative forces which are charac-

[1] *Religion and Culture; Freedom in the Modern World;* since translated into English and published by Sheed and Ward.

teristic of the spirit and of liberty, and are also their witness, and which normally find their point of application in the effort of the few—destined thereby to sacrifice—constantly revitalize the quality of this energy. Such is the work accomplished in history by the sons of God; such is the work of Christians if they do not give the lie to their name.

This work is not understood at all if it is imagined that it claims to be able to set up a state in the world from which all evil and all injustice would be banished. Naturally, on this ground it would be too easy, in view of the results obtained, stupidly to dismiss Christians as Utopians. What the Christian has to do is to maintain and increase in the world an internal tension and that movement of slow and painful delivery, which comes from the invisible powers of truth and justice, goodness and love, acting upon the mass in opposition to them. This work cannot be in vain and it cannot but bear fruit.

Woe to the world should the Christians turn their back on it, should they fail to do *their job,* which is to heighten here on earth the charge and tension of spirituality; should they listen to those blind leaders of the blind who seek the means to order and to good in things which are in their very nature dissolution and death. We have no illusions about the misery of human nature and the wickedness of the world. But we have no illusions either about the blindness and the harm worked by those pseudo-realists who cultivate and exalt evil to fight against evil and who look upon the Gospel as a decorative myth which could not be taken seriously without wrecking the machinery of the world. They themselves do their part in ruining this unhappy world and driving it to folly and despair.

One of the gravest lessons we receive from the experience of life is that, in the practical behavior of most of us, all those things which are in themselves good—science, technical progress, culture, etc., the knowledge of moral laws too, and even religious faith itself, faith in the living God (during the civil war in Spain, the inhuman feelings which have swept over both "crusaders" and "reds" have demonstrated what we are saying)—all these things, *without love and good will,* only serve, in fact, to make men more wicked and more unhappy. This is because, without love and charity, man turns into evil the best that is in him.

Once we have understood this, we no longer put our hope here on earth save in that good will of which the Gospel speaks, in that obscure strength of a bit of real goodness which brings forth life and brings it forth without cease in the most hidden recesses of things. Nothing is more destitute, nothing is more secret, nothing is nearer to the weakness of childhood. And there is no more fundamental, no more effective wisdom than that simple and tenacious confidence—not in the weapons of force and cleverness and malice, which though they always triumph at the outset, a grain of sand suffices to ruin, but in the resources of personal courage and good will. Through this kind of lightness of heart flows the force of nature and of the Author of nature.

*Yous, Toronto, Canada*

JACQUES MARITAIN

# JULES ROMAINS

*Jules Romains is one of the world's leading literary figures. He has won distinction as poet, dramatist, essayist, medical researcher. Creator of the masterly series 'Men of Good Will,' he stands with Balzac and Zola as a portraitist of French life. His temperament is marked by tireless energy and curiosity, controlled power of thought, and, at the same time, by a vivid interest in certain superficially non-rational phenomena. He is best known to the English-speaking world by his 'Men of Good Will,' which will run to twenty-seven volumes in French and of which fourteen have so far appeared in translation. Also notable are his trilogy 'Psyche,' his successful plays 'Knock' and 'The Dictator,' and his researches into extraretinal vision.*

*Jules Romains was born in 1885 in the village of Saint-Julien Chapteuil (Haute-Loire) but passed his childhood and youth in Paris. He received a thorough education, both humanistic and scientific, and, after being graduated from the University of Paris, taught philosophy for ten years. His reputation was already secure before the War. His unanimist theories of art and life were debated by intellectuals everywhere.*

*Romains has interested himself in European politics, in science, in travel (he seems to have been everywhere), and in what may be called the field of intellectual co-operation. He is international president of the Federated P.E.N. Clubs.*

*The following essay is translated from the French by Christopher Lazare.*

# *Jules Romains*

To ask someone to tell you what he thinks of the principal problems facing man and, so far as possible, of the general nature of things, is to throw him into considerable, even painful, difficulty, should he be a person with a really active and living conception of the mind's function.

The only persons such a question would not embarrass are either those who have once for all yielded their allegiance to a creed provided for them (and it is not often that such a creed—whether it be a religion or a doctrine—offers a solution for all the problems in their current form), or else those who, after a period of research, have arrested the activity of their minds by freezing it into a system.

As far as I am concerned, I have always tried to avoid either of these easy attitudes, not because of any natural restlessness or taste for change, but because of the significance I attribute to the mind. For me the function of the mind consists in evolving an always more satisfactory and feasible awareness of reality. There is always some aspect of reality for the mind to uncover, some aspect it has not discerned before, or which it has sized up badly. On the other hand, reality itself is changing more or less quickly. When the mind, therefore, is impeded by a system or credo, it is really reduced to losing contact with reality. It becomes resigned to an increasing gap between reality and itself. It might be noted that this process is not without an analogy to madness. In a sense, any system necessarily evinces some of the features of delirium. I might add, in all fairness, that in the human order, systematic doctrines, through the influence they exercise, have the power to *modify* reality. It is, consequently, not absurd for a thinker, though he does not even *in petto* attribute a definite value to his system, to attempt to enforce it to the extent to which he expects it to alter reality. This belief, it is true, is only justifiable in the case of the thinker who deals in human values. The pure metaphysician who expects his system to alter the cosmos and thus post-justify itself might be accused of simple lunacy.

What I have just observed concerning the function of the mind is not fundamentally denied by anyone. Who indeed would contest that man's discoveries in all their forms, his awareness of himself and the world, are the result of an endless series of approximations and revisions? Who would suggest that this series might be terminated at any given point?

Of course, we readily grant to the *individual* the right to put a stop to his own intellectual functioning, even before death forcibly intervenes to do it for him. But I have always refused to take advantage of this privilege. I hope to continue to live intellectually as long as I do physically. Consequently, I hope to continue to resolve my ideas on all subjects, constantly bringing them closer to reality, thanks to new reflections and experiences—my own as well as those of others.

Therefore, what I say below represents only conclusions with which I would identify myself if I were obliged to stop thinking today. Still, should I, in attempting to formulate them in so few words, deprive them of all subtlety and discrimination? Should I not carefully weigh everything I say? Nothing is more difficult for a human being, even an experienced one, than to take account at a given moment of *everything* he thinks.

It might readily be gathered from what has gone before that I am neither a skeptic nor a pessimist.

I am no skeptic. True, I do not believe the mind capable

of reading the absolute and definitive truth on any point; in fact, I believe that, after having neared the truth, it may even swerve from it for a time. But I believe that in the course of history—but only on condition that civilization is not interrupted by catastrophe—truth will be approached more and more closely. This in itself is a kind of optimism. I believe also that the mind's main difficulty does not lie so much in arriving at conclusions true for one particular order of experience. The difficulty lies in discovering a means of co-ordinating conclusions reached while working on different kinds of reality or while reaching out in various directions whose nature changes with each particular epoch.

For example, it is very difficult to reconcile the admittedly precise ideas of modern science in the realm of physical phenomena with the perhaps equally valuable ideas reached in those epochs when man was concerned with spiritual or psychic phenomena, ideas which may have just as much validity today for those who live apart from physical methods and devote themselves to research on the spiritual or psychic plane. I certainly do not think that modern science, so often denounced as materialistic, is threatened by a revolution that would destroy its tested results. The only results which may be threatened are those based on overgeneralized, premature, or uncertain hypotheses. However, science may one day find itself confronted by results so coherent and conclusive, achieved through methods still roughly described as "psychic," that it will be impossible for it to regard these results, as it now does, as null and void. Many people believe that, from that moment on, things will arrange themselves without difficulty, what is called "positive" science having nothing to do except peaceably to conserve its actual domain, and, beyond its own frontiers, permitting the development of entirely different knowledge, which today it treats as pure superstition or relegates to the "unknowable," abandoning it disdainfully to metaphysics. But things will not be so accommodating. Once the most important results of psychic experimentation are proved—if they need be—and officially recognized as "truths," positive science will be challenged *within its own province*. It will then become necessary for human consciousness, which up to this point has chosen to be unaware of the approaching conflict through fear of the responsibilities involved, to resort to arbitration. That would be a grave crisis, as grave as the crisis caused by the application of scientific discoveries to the industrial technique. It might change the life of humanity itself.

I believe this crisis to be possible, probable, even imminent. That is because I am on the one hand a *rationalist* in the sense that I have entire confidence in the results of reasoning that is correct and free of the *a priori* method, also in the sense that I attribute to reason the right to investigate critically all types of experience. But, on the other hand, I believe that experience always has the last word. (This principle—call it Baconian, if you will—is the one that guided me some years ago in my work on extraretinal vision and my consequent struggle with official scientific authority.) I shall never admit that reason should refuse to consider a fact of experience merely because it is improbable and contrary to the postulates of science to date. All the worse for science to date. Taking into account the new fact, it must simply begin anew its exposition of the nature of things. For example: perhaps some day two or three experiments only, but conducted under absolutely rigorous critical control, will demonstrate that certain persons in a particular psychic state are able to foresee and describe a future event in a way that excludes all possibility of explanation through coincidence, logical foresight, the realization of some unconscious desire, or suggestion. When this happens I hold that human reason will have to discard very nearly all its current ideas about time, space, causality, the determinism or indeterminism of phenomena, human free will, the nature of the soul and the cosmos, etc. . . .

Briefly, this would be the greatest revolution conceivable. I find it astounding that our present representatives of science and philosophy are satisfied to give but half an ear to those who speak to them of the facts of prevision, or to chat idly about these facts with their friends after dinner. Should they not instead admit that there is not at the present time a single scientific or philosophic question nearly so important, and that, with responsible people affirming the existence of such facts of experiences, their first duty is to proceed to an exceedingly attentive, patient, and impartial study of them? A lesser revolution but none the less a serious one would occur in our ideas and sentiments if life after death, of whatever form and duration, could be proved a fact by scientific investigation instead of being relegated, as it is today, to arbitrary faith.

In some respects, I am even a *sur-rationalist,* in the sense that I readily attribute to the soul, in certain individual and privileged cases, the power of discovering reality by direct inspiration. I believe that such inspirations have occurred often enough in the history of the human soul. But—and I emphasize this because it is the source of much confusion—to me the rule seems to be that these profoundly credible illuminations occur time and again amidst a multitude of states of consciousness which may resemble them but which are merely dreams or illusions. The role of reason, in this case, is not to influence the soul to reject all these states without distinction, but to help it, by confronting them with reality, to recognize those illuminations that are genuine.

I have used the word soul several times. In truth I accord the spiritual and psychic an eminent place in the universe. I am not at all inclined to believe that consciousness and the intellect are superimposed and episodic phenomena in their relationship to the forces and mechanisms of the material world. I do not conceive as yet, and perhaps I never shall, what type of relationship unites matter and spirit in the cosmos. Nor do I know whether the spiritual is coextensive with the realm of material phenomena, or whether, on the other hand, it occupies a privileged zone. Traditional metaphysics would say that the question lacks meaning, that the spiritual principle has no connection with space. I am not quite so sure. I do not believe that space is by nature any more foreign to the structure of spiritual reality than is time. That is what permits me to attach special importance to the notion of the "psychic continuum." Let me explain what I mean. I do not deny the existence of those concrete, well-defined forms that we may call individual souls. But I am inclined to think they are linked and supported by a vast, diffused spirituality whose limits perhaps coincide with those of the cosmos itself, and to which space, with certain of its restrictions and privileges, is probably not indifferent.

I believe particularly that the facts of *proximity* may hold as much significance for individual "souls" or "psychic entities" as they do for physical bodies. Or even perhaps that proximity between one and another element of the cosmos might precipitate a relationship, psychic in nature, or enhance such a relationship if it already exists. "Proximity augments," as I once wrote; "it feeds on reality." The words were meant to convey some idea of the fundamental rapport between what appears to us as matter and what appears to us as spirit.

From such a viewpoint, *groups* take on a notable significance. In my opinion, the general nature of reality might very profitably be examined in the light of this idea of the *group*. We might seek to discover, for example, what there is about elementary things of all sorts that causes us to believe they are possessed of a certain unity when interrelated, and form something greater than themselves. We

*Lazarnick, New York*

Jules Romains

would realize that the question is very complex and obscure. We might, for example, establish an infinity of intermediary cases between two extremes. One of these extremes might be an arbitrary collection of objects which we group together only by some convention, objects that may not even at all times share a physical proximity or some common relationship. The other extreme might be some such organism as the human body. We would be extremely confused by those intermediary cases where we could not tell whether we were still dealing with a disparate collection of objects or beings, or whether we were being confronted by the beginnings of an organic unity. We would also find that it is not as simple as it seems, to determine which is, and which is not, an *organic bond*; and that in the case of those organisms whose unity is unquestionable, the bond cannot be perceived and manifests itself only in its effects. Then, after careful examination, it will become even more of a problem to decide which of these effects are sufficiently pronounced to warrant on their evidence alone a belief in the existence of such a bond.

Naturally, it is with respect to living creatures that the question becomes most acute. One of my first scientific tasks consisted precisely in seeking to find out how, in the microorganic world, these ambiguously grouped forms present themselves, forms which it is difficult to consider simple collections of unrelated entities, but which cannot be classified as unified and self-sufficient organisms.

But it is in the human sphere that the problem takes on breadth and vital interest. The reader may know that I have devoted a great deal of attention to human groups. When *unanimism* is discussed it ordinarily designates a specialized study, largely a literary one, of the life of human groups, and the relationship between the individual and these groups.

I believe, in fact, that the adventure of humanity is essentially an adventure of groups. It is also an adventure of individuals in conflict with groups or with each other. This conflict is maintained under conditions which bring into constant play the aptitude for forming multiple ties, truly biological associations, as well as the aptitude for warding off the forces of "dispossession," both spiritual and physical, which groups or collectivities of various kinds may exercise over the individual.

Reduced to its simplest form this statement contains very little originality. The life of society, at whatever level, has always been considered important as a key to the explanation of human action.

Experience, however, has proved that this bare statement takes on a special power of illumination when one endows the idea of the group with its full richness of content, its efficacy, one might almost say its virulence. Especially when one need not be afraid to look for the organic bond elsewhere than in mere metaphors and abstractions.

This patient and painstaking quest for the organic bond down to its weakest manifestation is in brief the essence of unanimism: a quest rather than a doctrine.

It will be noted that this quest profits by one very remarkable circumstance. Man forms part of the groups, the organizations, the associations which he seeks to understand. The situation is analogous to that in which he finds himself when he attempts to probe human consciousness. As he himself is "human consciousness," the facts he investigates occur within him, form a part of himself. He manages to grasp many of them, and to grasp them (without detriment to other methods) in a firm and essential way by the direct means of introspection, that is to say by consciousness carried to a high degree of acuteness and subtlety. There is a direct connection of the same kind between man and the groups or communities of which he is part. This connection cannot be questioned even by the most positivist, the most critical minds. They, for instance, admit that as part of society we can, more readily than if we were not part of it, take account of the internal mechanisms of that society and understand the *raison d'être* of the varied behavior of social man, his customs and manners, the influence exerted on him by group emotions, public institutions, etc.—even if this internal awareness does not reveal everything. But I for one go further. I hold, on the basis of an experience of a special nature, that we are able, with the aid of certain refinements of attention, to grasp the interhuman organic bond, even in its most essential and invisible form, its most fugitive nascent stages. This is, if you will, the counterpart of introspection when it functions most profoundly and permits us to grasp the psychic reality within us.

Now it becomes a question of reaching a psychic reality which is not external to us but which envelopes us. I am far from believing—even if I have appeared to say so at certain times—that this enveloping psychic reality does not exceed the bounds of human groups. But human groups elaborate and condense it in a fashion, raise it one degree higher, just as the human consciousness condenses and raises to a higher plane some psychic reality which exceeds the limitations of personal identity.

It is not astonishing—and I emphasize this—that I have attributed a prominent part in this investigation to literature in all its forms. Literature has, for the same reasons, played an important part in the investigation of the spirit.

I have been reproached for having "deified" the group. And it is true I have pronounced words on the subject dangerous to the extent that they might provoke a confusion between the order of fact and the order of right, between the real and the desirable. That groups, having achieved a certain degree of organic reality, should be termed by the poet "gods" or, better, "divine animals"—this is merely to express on the lyric or mystic plane a real fact. That fact arises from the disproportion in dimension and power (physical and psychic) between groups and individuals. It implies the change of magnitude occurring when one rises from one plane to the other. But it would obviously be hazardous to draw from this the unqualified conclusion that the group as opposed to the individual is always right, and that the individual's only attitude should be submission and worship.

In any case, formerly no less than now, I have always insisted that the power of the group over the individual is justified only to the extent to which it finds expression in and by the spontaneity of the individual. I condemned the restrictions imposed upon the individual from without by society and its institutions. As forcibly as I could, I emphasized the contrast between "society," conceived as a system of restraints and conventions, and "the unanimous life," conceived as the "free respiration" of human groups and implying the voluntary surrender of the individual to their influence and attractions. I indicated the danger lying in the very idea of the state, with all its germs of juridical formalism and of oppression. I even declared that a certain infusion of "anarchy" is indispensable to avert the demoniacal mechanization of society and salvage "the unanimous life." On the other hand, I have always maintained the extreme importance—for good or evil—of the leader.

The political and social events of the last twenty years have but confirmed these opinions. It has been said, ironically—and hardly to make me feel happy—that the founders of totalitarian governments are to some extent my disciples. My reply was that these governments are merely a burlesque of unanimism, and that they err and err gravely in two important respects. First, they proceed by coercion and are as far as possible from fostering the "free respiration" of the masses. Second, they have a shockingly oversimplified idea of unanimity. They interpret it as an inexorable uniformity of thought, an inflexible and sterile "union." Unanimism postulates the richest possible variety of individual states of consciousness, in a "harmony" made valuable by its richness and density. This harmony is necessary before any glimpse can be given of the birth of those states of consciousness that transcend the individual spirit.

My chief objections to the Soviet commune are based on the same reasons. I regret that constraint, juridical abstractions, the oppressive mechanism of institutions, the state, should so greatly dominate social spontaneity, collective pleasure, diversity of life experience.

I am not blind to the fact that a totalitarian government, such as a dictatorship, may obtain concrete results more quickly and radically than another. I realize that it is a question of abolishing ancient abuses, of wiping out recalcitrance, of founding a new order. But this short cut is made possible only by violence and destruction; by sacrificing worthy individuals and entire classes; by the imposition upon an entire generation of a restrained and constricted life, the rewards of which are the hypothetical happiness of future generations. It is excellent for each generation to show concern and love for the future. But I am completely opposed to the idea of one generation sacrificing itself to those following it. History has always shown that to be a fool's bargain. There is no reason why such sacrifices might not be repeated indefinitely to the end of time, always for the benefit of some future generation or, in other words, for the benefit of a consuming myth. This Moloch future is a survival of the old ferocious divinities, a survival, in its pathology and inadaptability to reality, of Messianism. What is more objectionable, it authorizes all the errors of fanaticism while withholding them from the sanction of experience. The present has its rights and duties to itself. The wisest, or the least foolish, eras have been those which thought of themselves first. At the same time, they have worked better for the future than the others, not in bequeathing it systems to be revised, feuds to be settled, ruins to be reconstructed, but in leaving behind a certain apprenticeship to happiness. Let us add that the accomplishments of coercion rarely endure. That succeeding generation whose happiness, by sacrificing your own, you think you have established, is usually in the greatest haste to undo your work.

The fault I now find in ideas I formerly held, a fault I have corrected, is in not having sufficiently emphasized the role of reason in individual or collective life. Without a vigilant and unimpeded exercise of the reason no lasting progress can be established for humanity, and all evils become possible. Now, reason functions only on the plane of individual consciousness, or among individual consciousnesses which reject all collective emotion, all coercion by the group. It follows that I believe in the permanent value of democratic principles and in fundamental democratic institutions: a government created by assemblies duly elected and self-checked, and thus, by opinions formed as liberally as possible with absolute respect for the rights of the individual. Democratic governments are certainly the only ones which offer unanimous and spiritual life its freest scope, thanks to which the unanimism of action now developing in the masses can be preserved from barbarous deviations and slowly become impregnated with reason.

I do not believe the future of humanity is hopeless, despite the great perils which beset it under our very eyes. But salvation will not come automatically. Even if time is merely an illusion, events still occur as though history were a series of crossroads, and as though at each crossroad, the forceful exertion of will of a man or of several men (or, it may be, the lack of will and abandonment to blind chance) gave events a direction which formerly was merely one possibility among many but which subsequently became irrevocable. I therefore firmly believe in men of will as factors in history, and I attach great importance to whether or not they be men of good will.

I have no fear of mechanization. It is sufficient to know how to take advantage of it, just as it is necessary to know how to use the machines themselves.

I believe, despite unfavorable present indications, that humanity is tending toward the suppression of war; toward the intellectual and economic emancipation, by democratic means, of the masses; toward the diminishing, if not the abolition, of class distinctions and political frontiers; toward the cure of the psychosis of nationalism; toward an international police and a federal government of the world.

It depends upon us to make this take place as soon as possible, and to prevent great, almost irreparable, misfortunes from occurring in the interim.

As for my ideas on personal conduct, they are either to be found in my remarks above, or are a consequence of them. I limit myself to mentioning the most salient points.

First, I must stress the fact that my views seek to rehabilitate the *art of living* as against those moral compulsions which the moderns have abused. I consider it more important to teach man how to live, than to crush him under the weight of his duties. I believe that one of the primary tasks of education lies in making the individual enjoy society, and that society should subtly affect the individual with a sympathy for it, not a fear of it. The essential chapters of my ethics would be entitled: social agreement, spontaneity, reason, happiness. I would assign an important place to the development of the instincts. I would consider it an important task, on the one hand, to reconcile sexuality with clear conscience in all men, and on the other hand, to raise the level of sexuality so that it might accord with the lyric forms of social and universal feeling.

Finally, I would insist that, with the exception of a small number of very general rules applicable to all men, the formulas and recipes for the art of living must vary in accordance with the condition, vocation, and purpose of each individual.

So far I have not mentioned God, in the usual sense of the word. That is because I find it difficult to say anything certain or even plausible on the subject. It can at most be suggested that the God of traditional metaphysics, perfect, infinite, creator, and all-powerful ruler of the universe, is highly improbable. The probability continues to decrease as our knowledge of the universe grows and becomes richer. The crude, fortuitous elements of the universe, its intolerable contradictions, the frightful, gratuitous waste inherent in it—to cite only a few shortcomings among many—scarcely make it seem possible that an intelligence has from the beginning been in perfect control of the cosmos in all its aspects. Then, if it is not an intelligence—as intuitive as you wish—it is nothing which could possibly control the universe. Even if we envision a more or less imminent upheaval in the positive sciences due to discoveries made in the "psychic" ones, whatever we know of the latter hardly suggests that their triumph would restore to his throne the God of classical metaphysics. Far from it. Certain minds find satisfaction in the not unseductive hypothesis of a God of considerable power but nevertheless limited in his attributes, means, and competency (in reality this is much closer to the God of primitive Christianity); one who perhaps rules over only one division of the cosmos and must defend himself against evil forces, or against mere chance—even perhaps against his neighbors. (We would have to come to his assistance.) Such a return to humanity's ancestral notions is not necessarily absurd. Such a God would escape those purely metaphysical concepts impossible of demonstration, and would enter, at least theoretically, the realm of an experimental metaphysic. His weakness would be an anthropomorphism even more accentuated than that of the traditional God.

When unanimism used the word "god" with reference to those collective beings who have arrived at a certain stage of unified awareness, it was no doubt being a little extreme. But here lay the nub of the matter: the idea of divinity seemed bound up with the phenomenon of a psychism which, though still rudimentary in itself, represented a state of spiritual reality radically different from and superior to our own, not simply in degree but in kind. It was to our consciousness what our consciousness may be to the vital elements of which we are composed. In short, the divine was no longer the human carried to some ultimate point of perfection. It now became another type of reality, manifesting itself in relatively rudimentary forms, vastly removed from the perfection proper to it. What is it then, in reality? On which side is there more reason and shall we be able to recognize it for ourselves some day? It is, as a matter of fact, the old question of the nature of God coming up again, with some new light thrown upon it, but whose solution we will have to approach with more caution than before.

# GEORGE SANTAYANA

*George Santayana's philosophy cannot be pigeonholed, a fact which doubtless gives him the intensest satisfaction. He irritates many of his philosophical colleagues because he writes so well, infusing into his thought a poetic feeling to match which one must go back to his master, Plato. To the student he is best known by his 'Life of Reason' and his later systematic work, 'The Realms of Being.' To the general public he is famous as the author of 'The Last Puritan,' a best-selling novel, his only one, the product of his mature years. Both his books and his teaching have had a great influence on American thought. One of his disciples, Irwin Edman, sums up Santayana in these words: "The net impression left by the total body of Santayana's work is that of a philosopher who realizes that all religions and philosophies are murmurs, at once lyric and dramatic, in which the spirit of man has been talking to itself."*

*In addition to 'The Life of Reason' (1905-6), 'The Realms of Being' (1937), and 'The Last Puritan' (1935), Santayana's other major works include 'The Genteel Tradition at Bay' (1931); 'Soliloquies in England and Later Soliloquies' (1922); 'Interpretations of Poetry and Religion' (1900); and 'Winds of Doctrine' (1913).*

*The essay which follows provides the reader with all necessary biographical details. The only contribution not written especially for this book, it originally appeared in 1930, as part of a symposium called 'Contemporary American Philosophy,' published by the Macmillan Company, through whose courteous permission it is here reprinted. It was called 'A Brief History of My Opinions.'*

# *George Santayana*

How came a child born in Spain of Spanish parents to be educated in Boston and to write in the English language? The case of my family was unusual. We were not emigrants; none of us ever changed his country, his class, or his religion. But special circumstances had given us hereditary points of attachment in opposite quarters, moral and geographical; and now that we are almost extinct—I mean those of us who had these mixed associations—I may say that we proved remarkably staunch in our complex allegiances, combining them as well as logic allowed, without at heart ever disowning anything. My philosophy in particular may be regarded as a synthesis of these various traditions, or as an attempt to view them from a level from which their several deliverances may be justly understood. I do not assert that such was actually the origin of my system: in any case its truth would be another question. I propose simply to describe as best I can the influences under which I have lived, and leave it for the reader, if he cares, to consider how far my philosophy may be an expression of them.

In the first place, we must go much farther afield than Boston or Spain, into the tropics, almost to the antipodes. Both my father and my mother's father were officials in the Spanish civil service in the Philippine Islands. This was in the 1840's and 1850's, long before my birth; for my parents were not married until later in life, in Spain, when my mother was a widow. But the tradition of the many years which each of them separately had spent in the East was always alive in our household. Those had been, for both, their more romantic and prosperous days. My father had studied the country and the natives, and had written a little book about the island of Mindanao; he had been three times round the world in the sailing ships of the period, and had incidentally visited England and the United States, and been immensely impressed by the energy and order prevalent in those nations. His respect for material greatness was profound, yet not unmixed with a secret irony or even repulsion. He had a seasoned and incredulous mind, trained to see other sorts of excellence also: in his boyhood he had worked in the studio of a professional painter of the school of Goya, and had translated the tragedies of Seneca into Spanish verse. His transmarine experiences, therefore, did not rattle, as so often happens, in an empty head. The sea itself, in those days, was still vast and blue, and the lands beyond it full of lessons and wonders. From childhood I have lived in the imaginative presence of interminable ocean spaces, coconut islands, blameless Malays, and immense continents swarming with Chinamen, polished and industrious, obscene and philosophical. It was habitual with me to think of scenes and customs pleasanter than those about me. My own travels have never carried me far from the frontiers of Christendom or of respectability, and chiefly back and forth across the North Atlantic—thirty-eight fussy voyages; but in mind I have always seen these things on an ironical background enormously empty, or breaking out in spots, like Polynesia, into nests of innocent parti-colored humanity.

My mother's figure belonged to the same broad and somewhat exotic landscape; she had spent her youth in the same places; but the moral note resounding in her was somewhat different. Her father, José Borrás, of Reus in Catalonia, had been a disciple of Rousseau, an enthusiast and a wanderer: he taught her to revere pure reason and republican virtue and to abhor the vices of a corrupt world. But her own temper was cool and stoical, rather than ardent, and her disdain of corruption had in it a touch of elegance. At Manila, during the time of her first marriage, she had been rather the grand lady, in a style half Creole, half early Victorian. Virtue, beside those tropical seas, might stoop to be indolent. She had given a silver dollar every morning to her native major-domo, with which to provide for the family and the twelve servants, and keep the change for his wages. Meantime she bathed, arranged the flowers, received visits, and did embroidery. It had been a spacious life; and in our narrower circumstances in later years the sense of it never forsook her.

Her first husband, an American merchant established in Manila, had been the ninth child of Nathaniel Russell Sturgis, of Boston (1779-1856). In Boston, accordingly, her three Sturgis children had numerous relations and a little property, and there she had promised their father to bring them up in case of his death. When this occurred, in 1857, she therefore established herself in Boston; and this fact, by a sort of prenatal or pre-established destiny, was the cause of my connection with the Sturgis family, with Boston, and with America.

It was in Madrid in 1862, where my mother had gone on a visit intended to be temporary, that my father and she were married. He had been an old friend of hers and of her first husband's, and was well aware of her settled plan to educate her children in America, and recognized the propriety of that arrangement. Various projects and combinations were mooted: but the matter eventually ended in a separation, friendly, if not altogether pleasant to either party. My mother returned with her Sturgis children to live in the United States and my father and I remained in Spain. Soon, however, this compromise proved unsatisfactory. The education and prospects which my father, in his modest retirement, could offer me in Spain were far from brilliant; and in 1872 he decided to take me to Boston, where, after remaining for one cold winter, he left me in my mother's care and went back to Spain.

I was then in my ninth year, having been born on December 16, 1863, and I did not know one word of English. Nor was I likely to learn the language at home, where the family always continued to speak a Spanish more or less pure. But by a happy thought I was sent during my first winter in Boston to a kindergarten, among much younger children, where there were no books, so that I picked up English by ear before knowing how it was written: a circumstance to which I probably owe speaking the language without a marked foreign accent. The Brimmer School, the Boston Latin School, and Harvard College then followed in order: but apart from the taste for English poetry which I first imbibed from our excellent English master, Mr. Byron Groce, the most decisive influences over my mind in boyhood continued to come from my family, where, with my grown-up brother and sisters, I was the only child. I played no games, but sat at home all the afternoon and evening reading or drawing; especially devouring anything I could find that regarded religion, architecture, or geography.

In the summer of 1883, after my freshman year, I returned for the first time to Spain to see my father. Then, and during many subsequent holidays which I spent in his company, we naturally discussed the various careers that might be open to me. We should both of us have liked the Spanish army or diplomatic service: but for the first I was already too old, and our means and our social relations hardly sufficed for the second. Moreover, by that time I felt like a foreigner in Spain, more acutely so than in America, although for more trivial reasons: my Yankee manners seemed outlandish there, and I could not do myself justice in the language. Nor was I inclined to overcome this handicap, as perhaps I might have done with a little effort: nothing in Spanish life or literature at that time particularly attracted me. English had become my only possible instrument, and I deliberately put away everything that might confuse me in that medium. English, and the whole Anglo-Saxon tradition in literature and philosophy, have always been a medium to me rather than a source. My natural affinities were elsewhere. Moreover, scholarship and learning of any sort seemed to me a means, not an end. I always hated to be a professor. Latin and Greek, French, Italian, and German, although I can read them, were languages which I never learned well. It seemed an accident to me if the matters which interested me came clothed in the rhetoric of one or another of these nations: I was not without a certain temperamental rhetoric of my own in which to recast what I adopted. Thus in renouncing everything else for the sake of English letters I might be said to have been guilty, quite unintentionally, of a little stratagem, as if I had set out to say plausibly in English as many un-English things as possible.

This brings me to religion, which is the head and front of everything. Like my parents, I have always set myself down officially as a Catholic: but this is a matter of sympathy and traditional allegiance, not of philosophy. In my adolescence, religion on its doctrinal and emotional side occupied me much more than it does now. I was more unhappy and unsettled; but I have never had any unquestioning faith in any dogma, and have never been what is called a practicing Catholic. Indeed, it would hardly have been possible. My mother, like her father before her, was a Deist: she was sure there was a God, for who else could have made the world? But God was too great to take special thought for man: sacrifices, prayers, churches, and tales of immortality were invented by rascally priests in order to dominate the foolish. My father, except for the Deism, was emphatically of the same opinion. Thus, although I learned my prayers and catechism by rote, as was then inevitable in Spain, I knew that my parents regarded all religion as a work of human imagination: and I agreed, and still agree, with them there. But this carried an implication in their minds against which every instinct in me rebelled, namely that the works of human imagination are bad. No, said I to myself even as a boy: they are good, they alone are good; and the rest—the whole real world—is ashes in the mouth. My sympathies were entirely with those other members of my family who were devout believers. I loved the Christian epic, and all those doctrines and observances which bring it down into daily life: I thought how glorious it would have been to be a Dominican friar, preaching that epic eloquently, and solving afresh all the knottiest and sublimest mysteries of theology. I was delighted with anything, like Mallock's *Is Life Worth Living?*, which seemed to rebuke the fatuity of that age. For my own part, I was quite sure that life was not worth living; for if religion was false everything was worthless, and almost everything, if religion was true. In this youthful pessimism I was hardly more foolish than so many amateur medievalists and religious esthetes of my generation. I saw the same alternative between Catholicism and complete disillusion: but I was never afraid of disillusion, and I have chosen it.

Since those early years my feelings on this subject have become less strident. Does not modern philosophy teach that our idea of the so-called real world is also a work of imagination? A religion—for there are other religions than the Christian—simply offers a system of faith different from the vulgar one, or extending beyond it. The question is which imaginative system you will trust. My matured conclusion has been that no system is to be trusted, not even that of science, in any literal or pictorial sense; but all systems may be used and, up to a certain point, trusted as symbols. Science expresses in human terms our dynamic relation to surrounding reality. Philosophies and religions, where they do not misrepresent these same dynamic relations and do not contradict science, express destiny in moral dimensions, in obviously mythical and poetical images: but how else should these moral truths be expressed at all in a traditional or popular fashion? Religions are the great fairy tales of the conscience.

When I began the formal study of philosophy as an undergraduate at Harvard, I was already alive to the fundamental questions, and even had a certain dialectical nimbleness, due to familiarity with the fine points of theology: the arguments for and against free will and the proofs of the existence of God were warm and clear in my mind. I accordingly heard James and Royce with more wonder than serious agreement: my scholastic logic would have wished to reduce James at once to a materialist and Royce to a solipsist, and it seemed strangely irrational in them to resist such simplification. I had heard many Unitarian sermons (being taken to hear them lest I should become too Catholic), and had been interested in them so far as they were rationalistic and informative, or even amusingly irreligious, as I often thought them to be: but neither in those discourses nor in Harvard philosophy was it easy for me to understand the Protestant combination of earnestness with waywardness. I was used to seeing water flowing from fountains, architectural and aboveground: it puzzled me to see it drawn painfully in bucketfuls from the subjective well, muddied, and half spilt over.

There was one lesson, however, which I was readier to learn, not only at Harvard from Professor Palmer and afterwards at Berlin from Paulsen, but from the general temper of that age well represented for me by the *Revue des Deux Mondes* (which I habitually read from cover to cover) and by the works of Taine and of Matthew Arnold—I refer to the historical spirit of the nineteenth century, and to that splendid panorama of nations and religions, literatures and arts, which it unrolled before the imagination. These picturesque vistas into the past came to fill in circumstantially that geographical and moral vastness to which my imagination was already accustomed. Professor Palmer was especially skillful in bending the mind to a suave and sympathetic participation in the views of all philosophers in turn: were they not all great men, and must not the aspects of things which seemed persuasive to them be really persuasive? Yet even this form of romanticism, amiable as it is, could not altogether put to sleep my scholastic dogmatism. The historian of philosophy may be as sympathetic and as self-effacing as he likes: the philosopher in him must still ask whether any of those successive views were true, or whether the later ones were necessarily truer than the earlier: he cannot, unless he is a shameless sophist, rest content with a truth pro tem. In reality the sympathetic reconstruction of history is a literary art, and it depends for its plausibility as well as for its materials on a conventional belief in the natural world. Without this belief no history and no science would be anything but a poetic fiction, like a classification of the angelic choirs. The necessity of naturalism as a foundation for all further serious opinions was clear to me from the beginning. Naturalism might indeed be criticized —and I was myself intellectually and emotionally predisposed to criticize it, and to oscillate between supernaturalism and solipsism—but if naturalism was condemned, supernaturalism itself could have no point of application in the world of fact; and the whole edifice of human knowledge would crumble, since no perception would then be a report and no judgment would have a transcendent object. Hence historical reconstruction seemed to me more honestly and solidly practiced by Taine, who was a professed naturalist, than by Hegel and his school, whose naturalism, though presupposed at every stage, was disguised and distorted by a dialectic imposed on it by the historian and useful at best only in simplifying his dramatic perspectives and lending them a false absoluteness and moralistic veneer.

The influence of Royce over me, though less important in the end than that of James, was at first much more active. Royce was the better dialectician, and traversed subjects in which I was naturally more interested. The point that particularly exercised me was Royce's Theodicy or justification for the existence of evil. It would be hard to exaggerate the ire which his arguments on this subject aroused in my youthful breast. Why that emotion? Romantic sentiment that could find happiness only in tears and virtue only in heroic agonies was something familiar to me and not unsympathetic: a poetic play of mine, called *Lucifer*, conceived in those days, is a clear proof of it. I knew Leopardi and Musset largely by heart; Schopenhauer was soon to become, for a brief period, one of my favorite authors. I carried Lucretius in my pocket: and although the spirit of the poet in that case was not romantic, the picture of human existence which he drew glorified the same vanity. Spinoza, too, whom I was reading under Royce himself, filled me with joy and enthusiasm: I gathered at once from him a doctrine which has remained axiomatic with me ever since, namely that good and evil are relative to the natures of animals, irreversible in that relation, but indifferent to the march of cosmic events, since the force of the universe infinitely exceeds the force of any one of its parts. Had I found, then, in Royce only a romantic view of life, or only pessimism, or only stoical courage and pantheistic piety, I should have taken no offense, but readily recognized the poetic truth or the moral legitimacy of those positions. Conformity with fate, as I afterwards came to see, belongs to post-rational morality, which is a normal though optional development of human sentiment: Spinoza's "intellectual love of God" was a shining instance of it.

But in Royce these attitudes, in themselves so honest and

noble, seemed to be somehow embroiled and rendered sophistical: nor was he alone in this, for the same moral equivocation seemed to pervade Hegel, Browning, and Nietzsche. That which repelled me in all these men was the survival of a sort of forced optimism and pulpit unction, by which a cruel and nasty world, painted by them in the most lurid colors, was nevertheless set up as the model and standard of what ought to be. The duty of an honest moralist would have been rather to distinguish, in this bad or mixed reality, the part, however small, that could be loved and chosen from the remainder, however large, which was to be rejected and renounced. Certainly the universe was in flux and dynamically single: but this fatal flux could very well take care of itself; and it was not so fluid that no islands of a relative permanence and beauty might not be formed in it. Ascetic conformity was itself one of these islands: a scarcely inhabitable peak from which almost all human passions and activities were excluded. And the Greeks, whose deliberate ethics was rational, never denied the vague early Gods and the environing chaos, which perhaps would return in the end: but meantime they built their cities bravely on the hilltops, as we all carry on pleasantly our temporal affairs, although we know that tomorrow we die. Life itself exists only by a modicum of organization, achieved and transmitted through a world of change: the momentum of such organization first creates a difference between good and evil, or gives them a meaning at all. Thus the core of life is always hereditary, steadfast, and classical; the margin of barbarism and blind adventure round it may be as wide as you will, and in some wild hearts the love of this fluid margin may be keen, as might be any other loose passion. But to *preach* barbarism as the only good, in ignorance or hatred of the possible perfection of every natural thing, was a scandal: a belated Calvinism that remained fanatical after ceasing to be Christian. And there was a further circumstance which made this attitude particularly odious to me. This romantic love of evil was not thoroughgoing: willfulness and disorder were to reign only in spiritual matters; in government and industry, even in natural science, all was to be order and mechanical progress. Thus the absence of a positive religion and of a legislation, like that of the ancients, intended to be rational and final, was very far from liberating the spirit for higher flights: on the contrary, it opened the door to the pervasive tyranny of the world over the soul. And no wonder: a soul rebellious to its moral heritage is too weak to reach any firm definition of its inner life. It will feel lost and empty unless it summons the random labors of the contemporary world to fill and to enslave it. It must let mechanical and civic achievements reconcile it to its own moral confusion and triviality.

It was in this state of mind that I went to Germany to continue the study of philosophy—interested in all religious or metaphysical systems, but skeptical about them and scornful of any romantic worship or idealization of the real world. The life of a wandering student, like those of the Middle Ages, had an immense natural attraction for me—so great, that I have never willingly led any other. When I had to choose a profession, the prospect of a quiet academic existence seemed the least of evils. I was fond of reading and observation, and I liked young men; but I have never been a diligent student either of science or art, nor at all ambitious to be learned. I have been willing to let cosmological problems and technical questions solve themselves as they would or as the authorities agreed for the moment that they should be solved. My pleasure was rather in expression, in reflection, in irony: my spirit was content to intervene, in whatever world it might seem to find itself, in order to disentangle the intimate moral and intellectual echoes audible to it in that world. My naturalism or materialism is no academic opinion: it is not a survival of the alleged materialism of the nineteenth century, when all the professors of philosophy were idealists: it is an everyday conviction which came to me, as it came to my father, from experience and observation of the world at large, and especially of my own feelings and passions. It seems to me that those who are not materialists cannot be good observers of themselves: they may hear themselves thinking, but they cannot have watched themselves acting and feeling; for feeling and action are evidently accidents of matter. If a Democritus or Lucretius or Spinoza or Darwin works within the lines of nature, and clarifies some part of that familiar object, that fact is the ground of my attachment to them: they have the savor of truth; but what the savor of truth is, I know very well without their help. Consequently there is no opposition in my mind between materialism and a Platonic or even Indian discipline of the spirit. The recognition of the material world and of the conditions of existence in it merely enlightens the spirit concerning the source of its troubles and the means to its happiness or deliverance; and it was happiness or deliverance, the supervening supreme expression of human will and imagination, that alone really concerned me. This alone was genuine philosophy; this alone was the life of reason.

Had the life of reason ever been cultivated in the world by people with a sane imagination? Yes, once, by the Greeks. Of the Greeks, however, I knew very little: the philosophical and political departments at Harvard had not yet discovered Plato and Aristotle. It was with the greater pleasure that I heard Paulsen in Berlin expounding Greek ethics with a sweet reasonableness altogether worthy of the subject: here at last was a vindication of order and beauty in the institutions of men and in their ideas. Here, through the pleasant medium of transparent myths or of summary scientific images, like the water of Thales, nature was essentially understood and honestly described; and here, for that very reason, the free mind could disentangle its true good, and

*Elliot and Fry*

George Santayana

could express it in art, in manners, and even in the most refined or the most austere spiritual discipline. Yet, although I knew henceforth that in the Greeks I should find the natural support and point of attachment for my own philosophy, I was not then collected or mature enough to pursue the matter; not until ten years later, in 1896-97, did I take the opportunity of a year's leave of absence to go to England and begin a systematic reading of Plato and Aristotle under Dr. Henry Jackson of Trinity College, Cambridge. I am not conscious of any change of opinion supervening, nor of any having occurred earlier; but by that study and change of scene my mind was greatly enriched; and the composition of *The Life of Reason* was the consequence.

This book was intended to be a summary history of the human imagination, expressly distinguishing those phases of it which showed what Herbert Spencer called an adjustment of inner to outer relations; in other words, an adaptation of fancy and habit to material facts and opportunities. On the one hand, then, my subject being the imagination, I was never called on to step beyond the subjective sphere. I set out to describe, not nature or God, but the ideas of God or nature bred in the human mind. On the other hand, I was not concerned with these ideas for their own sake, as in a work of pure poetry or erudition, but I meant to consider them in their natural genesis and significance; for I assumed throughout that the whole life of reason was generated and controlled by the animal life of man in the bosom of nature. Human ideas had, accordingly, a symptomatic, expressive, and symbolic value: they were the inner notes sounded by man's passions and by his arts: and they became rational partly by their vital and inward harmony—for reason is a harmony of the passions—and partly by their adjustment to external facts and possibilities—for reason is a harmony of the inner life with truth and with fate. I was accordingly concerned to discover what wisdom is possible to an animal whose mind, from beginning to end, is poetical: and I found that this could not lie in discarding poetry in favor of a science supposed to be clairvoyant and literally true. Wisdom lay rather in taking everything good-humoredly, with a grain of salt. In science there was an element of poetry, pervasive, inevitable, and variable: it was strictly scientific and true only insofar as it involved a close and prosperous adjustment to the surrounding world, at first by its origin in observation and at last by its application in action. Science was the mental accompaniment of art.

Here was a sort of pragmatism: the same which I have again expressed, I hope more clearly, in one of the *Dialogues in Limbo* entitled "Normal Madness." The human mind is a faculty of dreaming awake, and its dreams are kept relevant to its environment and to its fate only by the external control exercised over them by Punishment, when the accompanying conduct brings ruin, or by Agreement, when it brings prosperity. In the latter case it is possible to establish correspondences between one part of a dream and another, or between the dreams of separate minds, and so create the world of literature, or the life of reason. I am not sure whether this notion, that thought is a controlled and consistent madness, appears among the thirteen pragmatisms which have been distinguished, but I have reason to think that I came to it under the influence of William James; nevertheless, when his book on *Pragmatism* appeared about the same time as my *Life of Reason*, it gave me a rude shock. I could not stomach that way of speaking about truth; and the continual substitution of human psychology—normal madness, in my view—for the universe, in which man is but one distracted and befuddled animal, seemed to me a confused remnant of idealism, and not serious.

The William James who had been my master was not this William James of the later years, whose pragmatism and pure empiricism and romantic metaphysics have made such a stir in the world. It was rather the puzzled but brilliant doctor, impatient of metaphysics, whom I had known in my undergraduate days, one of whose maxims was that to study the abnormal was the best way of understanding the normal; or it was the genial author of *The Principles of Psychology,* chapters of which he read from the manuscript and discussed with a small class of us in 1889. Even then what I learned from him was perhaps chiefly things which explicitly he never taught, but which I imbibed from the spirit and background of his teaching. Chief of these, I should say, was a sense for the immediate: for the unadulterated, unexplained, instant fact of experience. Actual experience, for William James, however varied or rich its assault might be, was always and altogether of the nature of a sensation: it possessed a vital, leaping, globular unity which made the only fact, the flying fact, of our being. Whatever continuities of quality might be traced in it, its existence was always momentary and self-warranted. A man's life or soul borrowed its reality and imputed wholeness from the intrinsic actuality of its successive parts; existence was a perpetual rebirth, a traveling light to which the past was lost and the future uncertain. The element of indetermination which James felt so strongly in this flood of existence was precisely the pulse of fresh unpredictable sensation, summoning attention hither and thither to unexpected facts. Apprehension in him being impressionistic—that was the age of impressionism in painting too—and marvelously free from intellectual assumptions or presumptions, he felt intensely the fact of contingency, or the contingency of fact. This seemed to me not merely a peculiarity of temperament in him, but a profound insight into existence, in its inmost irrational essence. Existence, I learned to see, is intrinsically dispersed, seated in its distributed moments, and arbitrary not only as a whole, but in the character and place of each of its parts. Change the bits, and you change the mosaic: nor can we count or limit the elements, as in a little closed kaleidoscope, which may be shaken together into the next picture. Many of them, such as pleasure and pain, or the total picture itself, cannot possibly have pre-existed.

But, said I to myself, were these novelties for that reason unconditioned? Was not sensation, by continually surprising us, a continual warning to us of fatal conjunctions occurring outside? And would not the same conjunctions, but for memory and habit, always produce the same surprises? Experience of indetermination was no proof of indeterminism; and when James proceeded to turn immediate experience into ultimate physics, his thought seemed to me to lose itself in words or in confused superstitions. Free will, a deep moral power contrary to a romantic indetermination in being, he endeavored to pack into the bias of attention—the most temperamental of accidents. He insisted passionately on the efficacy of consciousness, and invoked Darwinian arguments for its utility—arguments which assumed that consciousness was a material engine absorbing and transmitting energy; so that it was no wonder that presently he doubted whether consciousness existed at all. He suggested a new physics or metaphysics in which the essences given in immediate experience should be deployed and hypostatized into the constituents of nature: but this pictorial cosmology had the disadvantage of abolishing the human imagination, with all the pathos and poetry of its animal status. James thus renounced that gift for literary psychology, that romantic insight, in which alone he excelled; and indeed his followers are without it. I pride myself on remaining a disciple of his earlier unsophisticated self, when he was an agnostic about the universe, but in his diagnosis of the heart an impulsive poet: a master in the art of recording or divining the lyric quality of experience as it actually came to him or to me.

Lyric experience and literary psychology, as I have learned to conceive them, are chapters in the life of one race of animals, in one corner of the natural world. But before relegating them to that modest station (which takes nothing away from their spiritual prerogatives) I was compelled to face the terrible problem which arises when, as in modern philosophy, literary psychology and lyric experience are made the fulcrum or the stuff of the universe. Has this experience any external conditions? If it has, are they knowable? And if it has not, on what principle are its qualities generated or its episodes distributed? Nay, how can literary psychology or universal experience have any seat save the present fancy of the psychologist or the historian? Although James had been bothered and confused by these questions, and Royce had enthroned his philosophy upon them, neither of these my principal teachers seemed to have come to clearness on the subject; it was only afterwards, when I read Fichte and Schopenhauer, that I began to see my way to a solution. We must oscillate between a radical transcendentalism, frankly reduced to a solipsism of the living moment, and a materialism posited as a presupposition of conventional sanity. There was no contradiction in joining together a skepticism which was not a dogmatic negation of anything and an animal faith which avowedly was a mere assumption in action and description. Yet such oscillation, if it was to be justified and rendered coherent, still demanded some understanding of two further points: what, starting from immediate experience, was the *causa cognoscendi* of the natural world; and what, starting from the natural world, was the *causa fiendi* of immediate experience?

On this second point (in spite of the speculations of my friend Strong) I have not seen much new light. I am constrained merely to register as a brute fact the emergence of consciousness in animal bodies. A psyche, or nucleus of hereditary organization, gathers and governs these bodies, and at the same time breeds within them a dreaming, suffering, and watching mind. Such investigations as those of

Fraser and of Freud have shown how rich and how mad a thing the mind is fundamentally, how pervasively it plays about animal life, and how remote its first and deepest intuitions are from any understanding of their true occasions. An interesting and consistent complement to these discoveries is furnished by behaviorism, which I heartily accept on its positive biological side: the hereditary life of the body, modified by accident or training, forms a closed cycle of habits and actions. Of this the mind is a concomitant spiritual expression, invisible, imponderable, and epiphenomenal, or, as I prefer to say, hypostatic: for in it the moving unities and tensions of animal life are synthesized on quite another plane of being, into actual intuitions and feelings. This spiritual fertility in living bodies is the most natural of things. It is unintelligible only as all existence, change, or genesis is unintelligible; but it might be better understood, that is, better assimilated to other natural miracles, if we understood better the life of matter everywhere, and that of its different aggregates.

On the other point raised by my naturalism, namely on the grounds of faith in the natural world, I have reached more positive conclusions. Criticism, I think, must first be invited to do its worst; nothing is more dangerous here than timidity or convention. A pure and radical transcendentalism will disclaim all knowledge of fact. Nature, history, the self become ghostly presences, mere notions of such things; and the being of these images becomes purely internal to them; they exist in no environing space or time; they possess no substance or hidden parts, but are all surface, all appearance. Such a being, or quality of being, I call an essence; and to the consideration of essences, composing of themselves an eternal and infinite realm, I have lately devoted much attention. To that sphere I transpose the familiar pictures painted by the senses, or by traditional science and religion. Taken as essences, all ideas are compatible and supplementary to one another, like the various arts of expression; it is possible to perceive, up to a certain point, the symbolic burden of each of them, and to profit by the spiritual criticism of experience which it may embody. In particular, I recognize this spiritual truth in the Neoplatonic and Indian systems, without admitting their fabulous side: after all, it is an old maxim with me that many ideas may be convergent as poetry which would be divergent as dogmas. This applies, in quite another quarter, to that revolution in physics which is now loudly announced, sometimes as the bankruptcy of science, sometimes as the breakdown of materialism. This revolution becomes, in my view, simply a change in notation. Matter may be called gravity or an electric charge or a tension in an ether; mathematics may readjust its equations to more accurate observations; any fresh description of nature which may result will still be a product of human wit, like the Ptolemaic and the Newtonian systems, and nothing but an intellectual symbol for man's contacts with matter, insofar as they have gone or as he has become distinctly sensitive to them. The real matter, within him and without, will meantime continue to rejoice in its ancient ways, or to adopt new ones, and incidentally to create these successive notions of it in his head.

When all the data of immediate experience and all the constructions of thought have thus been purified and reduced to what they are intrinsically, that is, to eternal essences, by a sort of counterblast the sense of existence, of action, of ambushed reality everywhere about us, becomes all the clearer and more imperious. This assurance of the not-given is involved in action, in expectation, in fear, hope, or want: I call it animal faith. The object of this faith is the substantial energetic thing encountered in action, whatever this thing may be in itself; by moving, devouring, or transforming this thing I assure myself of its existence; and at the same time my respect for it becomes enlightened and proportionate to its definite powers. But throughout, for the description of it in fancy, I have only the essences which my senses or thought may evoke in its presence; these are my inevitable signs and names for that object. Thus the whole sensuous and intellectual furniture of the mind becomes a store whence I may fetch terms for the description of nature, and may compose the silly home poetry in which I talk to myself about everything. All is a tale told, if not by an idiot, at least by a dreamer; but it is far from signifying nothing. Sensations are rapid dreams: perceptions are dreams sustained and developed at will; sciences are dreams abstracted, controlled, measured, and rendered scrupulously proportional to their occasions. Knowledge accordingly always remains a part of imagination in its terms and in its seat; yet by virtue of its origin and intent it becomes a memorial and a guide to the fortunes of man in nature.

In the foregoing I have said nothing about my sentiments concerning esthetics or the fine arts; yet I have devoted two volumes to those subjects, and I believe that to some people my whole philosophy seems to be little but rhetoric or prose poetry. I must frankly confess that I have written some verses; and at one time I had thoughts of becoming an architect or even a painter. The decorative and poetic aspects of art and nature have always fascinated me and held my attention above everything else. But in philosophy I recognize no separable thing called esthetics; and what has gone by the name of the philosophy of art, like the so-called philosophy of history, seems to me sheer verbiage. There is in art nothing but manual knack and professional tradition on the practical side, and on the contemplative side pure intuition of essence, with the inevitable intellectual or luxurious pleasure which pure intuition involves. I can draw no distinction—save for academic programs—between moral and esthetic values: beauty, being a good, is a moral good; and the practice and enjoyment of art, like all practice and all enjoyment, fall within the sphere of morals—at least if by morals we understand moral economy and not moral superstition. On the other hand, the good, when actually realized and not merely pursued from afar, is a joy in the immediate; it is possessed with wonder and is in that sense esthetic. Such pure joy when blind is called pleasure, when centered in some sensible image is called beauty, and when diffused over the thought of ulterior propitious things is called happiness, love, or religious rapture. But where all is manifest, as it is in intuition, classifications are pedantic. Harmony, which might be called an esthetic principle, is also the principle of health, of justice, and of happiness. Every impulse, not the esthetic mood alone, is innocent and irresponsible in its origin and precious in its own eyes; but every impulse or indulgence, including the esthetic, is evil in its effect, when it renders harmony impossible in the general tenor of life, or produces in the soul division and ruin. There is no lack of folly in the arts; they are full of inertia and affectation and of what must seem ugliness to a cultivated taste; yet there is no need of bringing the catapult of criticism against it: indifference is enough. A society will breed the art which it is capable of, and which it deserves; but even in its own eyes this art will hardly be important or beautiful unless it engages deeply the resources of the soul. The arts may die of triviality, as they were born of enthusiasm. On the other hand, there will always be beauty, or a transport akin to the sense of beauty, in any high contemplative moment. And it is only in contemplative moments that life is truly vital, when routine gives place to intuition, and experience is synthesized and brought before the spirit in its sweep and truth. The intention of my philosophy has certainly been to attain, if possible, such wide intuitions, and to celebrate the emotions with which they fill the mind. If this object be esthetic and merely poetical, well and good; but it is a poetry or estheticism which shines by disillusion and is simply intent on the unvarnished truth.

# VILHJALMUR STEFANSSON

*Vilhjalmur Stefansson contributes to this book the viewpoint of a man of thought who is also a man of action, one whose life experience makes him reflect upon mankind in broad anthropological terms. One of the world's foremost explorers, he is no less noted as scientist, geographer, writer, and lecturer. He is probably the greatest living authority on all matters connected with polar and subpolar regions.*

*Born of Icelandic parentage in Manitoba in 1879, he spent his childhood and youth in the United States. After graduating from the University of Iowa, he studied at Harvard, switching from divinity to anthropology. In 1904 he made his first expedition, visiting Iceland. This was followed by a number of Arctic expeditions, in the course of which he demonstrated the feasibility of his revolutionary theory of "living off the country" both on uninhabited Arctic lands and on the drifting ice of the Polar Sea, at times hundreds of miles from shore. He has contributed steadily to popular, scientific, and technical magazines, has been since 1932 Adviser on Northern Operations to Pan American Airways, and his services to mankind have been recognized by the leading universities and learned societies of the world.*

*His publications include: 'My Life with the Eskimo' (1913); 'The Friendly Arctic' (1921); 'The Northward Course of Empire' (1922); 'Hunters of the Great North' (1922); 'Adventures in Error' (1936); 'Unsolved Mysteries of the Arctic' (1939).*

# *Vilhjalmur Stefansson*

SLIGHTLY less embarrassing than owning to a philosophy of life is confessing that you have some idea, though vague and changing, as to what constitutes the good life. My ideas of the good life come chiefly from a comparison between "civilization" and "primitive culture."

I feel that when Shaw intentionally speculates in his *Back to Methuselah* on the good life in coming millenniums, he describes unintentionally the lives of some groups of our ancestors during millenniums of the remote past. For Shaw pictures the nearly ideal condition of the future in a way that reminds us little of civilization as we have it around us today but which reminds us a great deal of what we call the lowest savagery.

So far as my picture of the good life is derived from experience, I get it mainly from people of the Stone Age with whom I lived in the Coronation Gulf district of northern Canada. Or, rather, I get from comparing ten years among savages with forty years in civilization the feeling that a better life need not be a chimera—that we have had it in the past and may attain it in the future.

With few exceptions, it is only those who know the savage at first hand that really believe his way better than ours. Nor does the savage convert everyone who sees him. He has a chance to make converts only when there are many of him and few of us, so that we are compelled to adopt his life and to live it through many years, not as visitors and patrons but as self-supporting members of the community.

Occasionally, however, it is given to comparative outsiders to see the light. Few can be more complete outsiders, as a group, than missionaries; for they go to teach and not to learn. But even among them you find understanding now and then. David Livingstone for Tropical Africa and Hudson Stuck for Arctic Alaska were great admirers of the unspoiled savage. These and a few other missionaries join the majority of scientific travelers in proclaiming that the less influenced savages are, the finer people they are.

My party of one white and three civilized western Eskimos reached the Stone Age Eskimos of Coronation Gulf in late winter, traveling by sledge in a manner to which the local people were accustomed. We four used fur garments similar to their own, and gave the impression of being not foreign though strangers. We were able to converse from the first day, for Eskimo is one language the whole way from Greenland to Bering Sea across the northern frontier of the New World.

In culture the Gulf Eskimos went back not thousands but tens of thousands of years, for they were just emerging from the age of wood and horn into the earliest period of stone. They had no elaborate technique for chipping flintlike stones in the ways characteristic of the early and middle Stone Ages of the Old World. They used copper, but without the arts which we associate with metals—they just picked up lumps of the native metal where they found them, hammered them with stone hammers, and ground them upon other stones until they were of the required size and shape. They used so much copper and used it for so many things that we named them Copper Eskimos.

Though these Stone Age people knew that certain berries and roots could be eaten, they considered them no real food but only a substitute for food in an emergency. Their proper diet was wholly from animals. Through two thirds of the year it was chiefly seal, with an occasional polar bear. During the summer third they lived mainly on caribou, with some fish. There were no large nesting or molting grounds in these districts and birds were, therefore, of little importance. There was no clothing except from the skins of animals. The tents were of skin, and so were the boats. These were kayaks, the small boats used for hunting; there were none of the large skin boats in which other groups of Eskimos travel. The only domestic beast was the dog, and he was mainly a hunting animal. There was usually not more than one dog for each hunter; so that, although the dogs were hitched to sledges in traveling, there were so few dogs in comparison with the people that essentially the people themselves were the draft animals.

The Coronation Eskimos knew of the Bear Lake forest but did not like it as a country to live in and made journeys to it only to secure timber for sledges, tent poles, and for a few other uses. They considered the treeless prairie north of the forest the best possible land in summer, and they considered the ice of the gulf and strait a proper and desirable home in winter. They were satisfied, then, with both their country and their climate, believing that any change would be for the worse.

These Stone Age people considered not only that the one proper food is meat but also that the most delicious things in the world are the preferred parts of animals. They had the highest average of good health which I have ever found in any community of like size, and most deaths among them were from accidents or old age. They had a religion by which they believed themselves able to control their environment, but it was neither a religion of hope nor of fear. There was no permanent future life; there was nothing resembling heaven or hell. The spirits were powerful but they were not in themselves good or evil, though they might do the good or evil bidding of people who controlled them—their attitude toward the spirits was something like ours toward explosives or steam power, things neutral in themselves but capable of being used for good or ill. They had as much desire to live as any of us but less fear of dying than most of us.

We met in or near Coronation Gulf several hundred Copper Eskimos who knew so little about Europeans that they saw no difference of race or nationality between me and my three Western Eskimo companions. Certain branches of the Copper people had seen white men at the time of the Franklin expeditions; two men were still living, one in Coronation Gulf and the other north in Victoria Island, who remembered these Europeans of sixty and seventy years before.

Of the seven hundred or so Stone Age people, about two hundred had been in contact with whaling ships for a few days each of two years, 1906-7 and 1907-8. Our visit to them was in 1910. There were a dozen or less who had seen David Hanbury when he passed by along the southern edge of their district in 1902. Another dozen had seen at close range some Slavey Indians, a few years before our visit, and, of course, they had seen groups of them frequently at a distance. But at least four hundred had never heard the noise which gunpowder makes when it explodes or seen the lighting of a match. They had seen pieces of cloth and believed them to be skins of animals. They had received many guns by tribe-to-tribe trade, but had secured them only when the neighbor groups had run out of ammunition. They cut the guns up to make things which they wanted, such as knives, spear points, and especially needles.

When we first lived with these people they envied us greatly just one thing we had with us, our sewing needles. Among themselves the most valuable single thing was a dog. I purchased a dog for a large knife, worth about three dollars at American wholesale prices. Later that day the man returned with the knife and with a second dog—if I would take the knife back he would give me two dogs for one needle. They explained that, although they had seen the Eskimo woman member of our party sewing before we made

*Photo by Dr. Orrin S. Wightman*

VILHJALMUR STEFANSSON

the first trade of the knife for the dog, they had not then realized that she possessed two needles. Now they understood that she had not only two but several, and she had told them that, with my consent, she was willing to give up one.

We inquired and found that, by local standards, a No. 1 size sewing needle was worth much more than any knife could be and was well worth, in the common estimation, at least two good dogs. So we made the trade.

The point of the trading story is that these Stone Age Eskimos were as yet not discontented with their copper knives, although they had been familiar for decades with the better iron knives which they themselves had made through Stone Age technique from rifle barrels and other pieces of iron. But they were far from content with their copper needles, for the shafts were necessarily stout in comparison with the size of the eye, which made it difficult to sew a waterproof seam.

Waterproof sewing is apparently one of the early discoveries of man, and there may not be any people on earth today except the Eskimos who still remember how to make, and do make, a really waterproof seam. For most or all other sewers rub grease into a seam to waterproof it, or use some trick of that sort; but the women of the Stone Age Eskimos considered it an insult if they saw anybody rubbing grease on the seam of a water boot which they had made. However, in spite of their skill, waterproof sewing was difficult with the use of a copper needle; it was to them easy with one of our steel needles.

Perhaps we have gone too far already before saying that we have no thought of deriving the health, happiness, and other details of the good life of the Copper Eskimos from their backward state—from their being still thousands of years behind us in technological development. We are merely trying to sketch briefly, without any necessary causal relation, how these people lived who were to all appearances so much happier than any other group I have ever known.

We were the first of European civilization to live with these Eskimos, and saw during the first year the gradual, and later rapid, increase of discontent—which was a decrease of happiness. Discontent grew not always along lines that would have been expected. For instance, you would think that our matches would have been coveted, but this was not the case. Their method of lighting fires by knocking together two pieces of iron pyrite had advantages which, to their minds (and even to mine later on), compensated for the disadvantages. Certainly a match is handier for things like smoking a cigarette; also for lighting a fire in good weather our matches were better. The advantage of the pyrite came out when we had to kindle a fire in a gale or in a rainstorm. It grew to be our practice, when we traveled with the Stone Age people, to light fires with matches in good weather and to borrow their technique when the weather was bad. Then there was, of course, the advantage of pyrite that two pieces of it, each the size of a lemon, would last you for years, if not for a lifetime. Nor did you have to worry about these lumps of rock to keep them dry.

As said, the Stone Age people were discontented with their needles before we came. The first discontent after that was connected with the insect pests. They had never conceived of a mosquito net that would protect your face during the day and that might be used to cover your bed at night. At first they considered our face nets and bed nets frivolous. But after a few weeks of association they began to say what a fine thing it would be if a white trader came in with enough mosquito nets so that everybody could buy one.

There were also the black flies. Eskimo garments are loose, somewhat as if the coat were a Russian blouse and the trousers in the style of our pyjamas. Besides, in the heat of the summer, with temperatures sometimes running above ninety degrees in the shade, they practically had to have rents and holes in their skin clothing. Through these holes, up their sleeves and down their necks, would crawl the black flies as if they were fleas, stinging so that the hurt was greater than the itch—or at least preceded the itch. Against these pests we wore knitted cotton shirts and drawers, with long arms and long legs, the elasticity making them tight and fly-proof around the wrist and ankle. A longing for this kind of underwear to use in summer was perhaps the basis of the second of the new discontents.

There grew slowly through the first summer an appreciation that a cloth tent was better than one of skins—lighter, less bulky, and less difficult to preserve from decay. It was not until perhaps the second or third year that there was any real discontent with the bow and arrow for caribou hunting and a desire for rifles. The appreciation of the value of fish nets, as compared with spears and hooks, developed somewhat more rapidly than the longing for guns.

During the first few years of Copper Eskimo association with Europeans there was no discontent on the score of diet. The local conception was, as said, that meat is real food and that things like cereals and vegetables are makeshifts.

The things which the Stone Age people most readily learned to eat were ones which we think of as nearly tasteless, like pilot bread; or of a "clean" taste, like weak or medium strong tea that has neither milk nor sugar. There was difficulty in learning to eat corned beef and canned salmon because of the intense dislike for salt—there is scarcely one of us with so strong a bias against garlic as every Copper Eskimo had, in 1910, against salt. For instance, if we boiled caribou meat in several pints of water and added one teaspoonful of salt, the local people would politely but firmly refuse to eat it.

The picture of Stone Age life which we have begun to sketch might not seem attractive to the reader even if we could spread it over a large canvas with the details competently and lucidly presented. We endeavor to bring out a segment of our meaning by writing a contrast between the Copper Eskimos of 1910 and those of 1939.

Perhaps the only thing with which the Coronation people are still content, as they were in 1910, is their climate. You cannot even now explain to them the weather of Hawaii or of California in such terms as to get a more favorable reply than that no doubt Europeans do like that sort of thing but they themselves would never like it. They still prefer boiled meat to any imported food; but they now feel ashamed if they do not have, especially for visitors, a few of the costly imports to offer, among them tea, coffee, sugar, salt, bread, and syrup. They are as discontented now with the sewing machines which they own as they formerly were with the copper needles. They are less content with the best rifles they can get than they were with their bows and arrows. They still enjoy their own songs most, but they feel a social need of phonographs, and there is a developing need for the radio. They know that their skin clothes are best for the climate, but fashion has laid such hold upon them that they must have clothes of silk, and of various other materials.

In 1910 they already believed in keeping up with the Joneses. In this they used to be approximately successful; for under their communistic anarchy everyone shared in the best of the foods and in the best of all materials. There was scarcely any difference between garments except that one woman could make a more attractive dress than another out of given material, or a man correspondingly could make a slightly superior bow or spear. Today keeping up with the Joneses wears a different aspect. Formerly they had in that contest no problems which we classify as economic; now they compete, or want to compete, in things which are beyond their economic reach, some of them known through hearsay but not obtainable in their country.

The breakdown in native economy, and thereby in self-respect, is more easily described, at least so far as my own experience goes, from the Mackenzie River district, several hundred miles to the west of the Copper Eskimos.

Mackenzie habits of life began to change notably with the entrance of the New England whaling fleet in 1889. I arrived there in 1906. Between that year and 1918 I saw much change; the rest to date is known to me from dependable hearsay.

Comparing the reports of Sir John Franklin with what I saw a hundred years later, I would conclude that two thousand people had decreased in a century to less than two hundred. The chief cause was measles, one epidemic of which, in the memory of those still living, had killed something like two out of three within a few weeks. Tuberculosis had been rare or absent; now it was prevalent. Digestive troubles had been few, but now they were common. Tooth decay had been unknown, but now their teeth were as bad as ours. There is no reasonable doubt that in 1820 the Mackenzie people, then in the Stone Age, were on the average as healthy as my Copper Eskimos were in 1910; but when I reached the Mackenzie district in 1906 the average Mackenzie health was probably not better than that of our worst slum districts.

The Mackenzie people, however, were not living on a slum level of poverty in 1906. They still had their economic independence and the self-respect which goes with it. How this later broke down can be shown by the story of Ovayuak.

The Hudson's Bay Company trader at Macpherson, a hundred miles to the south, had talked to me of Ovayuak as a chief. Ovayuak knew this, and when I had been living at his house as his guest for a month or two he explained to me one day why the trader called him a chief. Ovayuak knew what a chief was, both from dealings with whites and with the Loucheux Indians, and was aware that among whites and Athapascans there are people who have authority over others. Ovayuak said that no one had ever had any authority over anyone else among the Mackenzie Eskimos, so far as he knew, and that certainly he himself possessed no authority. That the trader called him a chief was, in his opinion, the result of two things: that he still held to the old ways of life, and that he was still a heathen.

Steamers come down the Mackenzie River in midsummer, usually arriving at Macpherson during early July. The first steamer brought the bishop. It was known among the converts in the Mackenzie district that the bishop wanted to see them on his annual pastoral visits. The people liked the bishop, they wanted to purchase goods that had been brought by the steamer, and they enjoyed the outing of the trip up to the Hudson's Bay post. So they streamed to Macpherson in late June.

But, said Ovayuak, the bishop's visit came in a fishing season. Not being a convert, he stayed behind and fished all summer with his family and a few who still took their lead from him. Most of the others went to meet the bishop and the traders. By the time the religious ceremonies, the feasting, and the trading were completed and the return journey made to the coast, the fishing was nearly over.

But that was only part of the difficulty. The trader had said to the Eskimo husbands that they ought to dress their wives in the best possible garments. When the reply was that the Eskimos had nothing with which to pay, the trader said that he knew them well, that they were reliable, that he would be glad to trust them, and that they could take as much cloth as they wanted, paying next year.

However, when the cloth had been sold the trader would give these men a talking-to of another sort. He would remind them that now they were in honor bound to pay for the goods a year later. They must not, therefore, spend all their time down on the coast fishing and gorging themselves;

they would now have to go up into the forest, or to certain promontories on the coast, so as to catch the mink of the woodland or the white foxes that frequent the shore floe. These would now have to be their chief concern, for they were in honor bound to see that the dealer would not suffer through having trusted them.

Accordingly, said Ovayuak, when the people returned from their summer visit to Macpherson they would explain to him that they had made promises not to stay very long at the fishing but to go to the promontories or the forest in time to be ready for the trapping season. And, said Ovayuak, naturally he could not argue against this; for, like them, he believed that a promise ought to be kept. So most of the families would scatter for the trapping districts, leaving him and his few adherents still at the fishing.

Ovayuak told me this just after the New Year. He forecast that when the midwinter days began to lengthen, visitors would begin to arrive. The trappers would now be running short of food and they would say to each other, "Let us go to Ovayuak; he has plenty of fish."

Sure enough, they began to gather. At first we took them into our house where twenty-three of us had been living in one room, but that accommodation could not be stretched for more than ten extras. So the others had to pitch tents or to build snowhouses in the neighborhood of our cabin. The stores of fish that seemed inexhaustible began to melt rapidly. There was not merely a steady increase of people, but they all had their dog teams to feed.

Everybody went out fishing every day, we locals and the visitors, but we caught perhaps only one-tenth as much as was being consumed. This went on till the fish were nearly gone. Thereupon everybody who had a sledge loaded it heavy with the last of the fish and then we scattered in all directions, to fishing and hunting districts. We went in small detachments, for it is a first principle of the hunting life that you must not travel in large groups. Two or three families would be right.

The system which I watched breaking down under the combined influence of Christianity and the fur trade, was, on its economic side, communism. Natural resources and raw materials were owned in common, but made articles were privately owned. The blubber of a seal that was needed for light and heat, or lean and fat that were needed for meals, belonged no more to the man who secured them than to anyone else. A pair of boots belonged to the woman who made them until she presented or sold them to somebody else. A meal that had been cooked was in a sense private property, but it was open to everyone under the laws of hospitality—it was very bad form to start a meal in any village without at the least sending a youngster outdoors to shout at the top of his voice that the family were about to dine or breakfast. If the houses were scattered and the people indoors, then messengers, usually children, would be sent to every household. People would come and join the family at their meal, either because they wanted the food or else for sociability. If the house was too small to accommodate everybody, then portions of cooked food were sent out to the other houses.

It is a usual belief with us that this type of communism leads to shiftlessness. But that was certainly not the case in any Eskimo community known to me, so long as they still followed the native economy.

Among the Eskimos of northern Canada there was no law except public opinion. Although no one had authority, each person had influence according to the respect won from a community which had intimate knowledge of everybody. Nobody was supposed to work if he was sick; and still the permanently handicapped were expected to work, each according to his ability. Among the Copper Eskimos, for instance, I saw a man of about forty who had been blind since he was six. He was one of the most cheerful and constant workers, but naturally could do only a few special things.

It has been a part of European ethics that a debt of honor should be paid before other debts. Thus a debt which could not be collected through legal machinery was a heavier obligation than one which had behind it the machinery and penalties of the state. With the primitive Eskimos every debt was a debt of honor; for there were no police, judges, prisons, or punishment. The force of public opinion was at least as strong in every Eskimo village for all debts as the same force was in the eighteenth and nineteenth centuries among the nobility and gentry of England with regard to a special class of debts, those of honor.

The same force which compelled the Eskimo to pay his debts compelled him to do his share of the work according to his recognized abilities. I never knew even one who didn't try his best, although there were, of course, the same differences of energy and aptitude which we find among ourselves. If there had been a shirker, he would have received the same food; but, even in a circle of punctilious courtesy he would have felt that he was not being fed gladly. It is the nearest thing to impossible, when you know how primitive society works under communistic anarchy, to conceive of anyone with that combination of indolence and strength of character which would make it possible for a well man to remain long a burden on the community.

In the few cases where strength of character is enough for running against public opinion, the issue is seldom or never on any such low plane as that of indolence. I have known one situation where a man was condemned to death. For there was no punishment among the Stone Age Eskimos except the disapproval of the community, and death—nothing in between.

The worst crime, in the view of these anarchistic communists of the Stone Age, was troublemaking—indeed, there cannot be a more antisocial quality in a society that has no legal or punitive machinery. If I am a liar, and if you go around saying I am a liar, then you are the worse of us two, for you stir up more trouble.

There is, of course, among Eskimos (as in English common law) the principle that a disagreeable truth may be told *if telling it is in the public interest.* In Eskimo practice, then, if you want to explain that I am a liar you will have to do it in some way which makes it clear that you are not merely being malicious or a gossip, but that the community needs to know, for its own good *must* know.

When the impression spreads, and is confirmed, that a certain person is a troublemaker, there begin informal discussions as to what should be done. Theoretically the troublemaker will never learn of these discussions; not even his wife or mother will tell him. In practice, however, he may be warned by a relative or friend, the informer then expecting that the troublemaker will flee to a remote community. There have been cases, however, where he does not flee but begins to swagger, carrying weapons or having them handy day and night, defying everybody.

Theoretically the execution takes place only when the community is unanimous, and then it becomes the duty of the next of kin to be executioners. This prevents blood feuds, for the avengers and those upon whom vengeance should fall are then the same persons.

When the execution is by someone who ought not to have been executioner, or when there has been a crime of anger, a feud starts and runs a course in all essentials similar to our Kentucky feuds. They may last for decades and may result in the extermination of a family. A feud ceases when one of the families is a killing ahead and picks up and moves to a great distance, settling among some other people—as if a family of

Kentucky mountaineers were to move to France or to Oregon.

We now try to summarize those things in the Stone Age life which we judge made for happiness more than do the corresponding elements of our own civilization.

The successful man stood above his fellows in nothing but their good opinion. The skillful hunter did not have better clothes than the poor hunter or the man who never could hunt—if clothes differed it was chiefly through the skill of a wife or mother as a seamstress. When the good provider brought home the only seal of the day to a village of six families there was no more food in his house than in the one next door. But he was the central figure of the community life for that day. The man who was usually the most successful hunter was usually at the center of community esteem.

Rank was determined by the things you secured and turned over to the common use. Your importance in the community depended on your judgment, your ability, and your character, but notably upon your unselfishness and kindness. Those who were useful to the community, who fitted well into the community pattern, were leaders. It was these men who were so often wrongly identified by the careless early civilized traveler and the usual trader as chiefs. They were not chiefs, for they had no authority; they had nothing but influence. People followed their advice because they believed it to be sound. They traveled with them because they liked to travel with them.

There was, of course, the negative side. If you were selfish, you were disliked. If you tried to keep more than your share, you became unpopular. If you were persistently selfish, acquisitive, and careless of the general good, you gradually became too unpopular. Realizing this, very likely you would try moving to another community and starting life there over again. If you persisted in your ways and stayed where you were, there would come a time of unanimous disapproval. You might survive for a year or even a few years as an unwanted hanger-on; but the patience of the community might any time find its limit, and there would be one more execution of a troublemaker.

Because few understand the workings of a communistic anarchy it is necessary to insist that most of the chief objections which fill our theoretical discussions of communism and of anarchy do not arise in practice.

Under the communism we are describing you don't have to accumulate food, apart from the community's store, for you are welcome to all you reasonably need of the best there is. You do not have to buy clothes, for they will be made for you either by some woman member of your family or by some woman friend who will feel about your wearing a coat of hers just the way any number of our women feel when they see their men friends wearing a garment they have knitted or a tie they have sent as a Christmas gift. You do not have to own land where no one owns land; you do not own a house because no one owns houses, or wants to. You do not have to accumulate wealth against your old age, for the community will support you as gladly when you are too old to work as it would if you had never been able to work at all—say because you had been blind from childhood.

One common arrangement of ours, however, is useful under communism, though not quite as necessary there as under rugged individualism. It is a good thing to have a family, for your children and grandchildren will look after you even more thoughtfully than mere friends. The nearest thing to an investment among the Stone Age Eskimos, the one means of providing against old age, is children. For that reason a widow without a child would have to be loved for herself alone. A widow with one child would be a desirable match. To marry a widow with three or four children was, among the Stone Age people of Coronation Gulf, the New York equivalent of marrying the widow of a millionaire.

Fortunately we do not have to debate whether little-civilized and uncivilized Eskimos are the happiest people in the world, for most travelers have agreed on their being the happiest, or at least seeming to be. What we must discuss is why they are or seem the happiest. We have space only for brief characterization of some of the chief theories.

Frequently repeated, although perhaps not often seriously maintained, is the view that uncivilized Eskimos were happy because "they don't know any better." Under this theory they are assumed to be completely without a notion of what it is that "makes life really worth living."

A frequent and popular view is that the Eskimos were happy because they "lived a natural life." Most of those who put the case that way seem to feel a natural life is the life of an animal, in the sense that the Stone Age people were free from inhibitions—that they did not have a clear differentiation between right and wrong and were consequently not under the stress of conscience and of social restraint. Few anthropologists take much stock in this explanation, for it is almost or quite a principle with them that the lower you are in the grade of civilization (i.e., the farther you are from our present civilization) the more rigid is likely to be at least that classification of right and wrong which we call taboo—like eating fish on Friday and not catching them on Sunday.

Certainly the Eskimos had plenty of taboos in many spheres, among them in dealing with food. We all know the food troubles of the Roman Catholics with Lent and with Friday. As this is being written (January, 1939) we are learning through the newspapers what a lot of trouble the Union of Soviet Socialist Republics is having with the American chess champion, Reshevsky, an orthodox New York Jew. He is the guest of the Soviets and they are looking after him the best they can. But, according to the press, they are having no end of bother in securing kosher food. One report has it that for several days the American chess prodigy was so undernourished that he could not compete in the games.

But the difficulties of Roman Catholic and of Jew with the dietary sections of their beliefs are elementary when compared with the ritual that has to be observed by at least some groups of Eskimos. I have said in print, and I might as well stick to it, that the dietary commands and prohibitions of certain Alaska groups with regard to mountain sheep alone are as difficult and extensive as the entire food section of Deuteronomy.

Eskimo conceptions of right and wrong are not the same as ours, and perhaps not even similar to ours, but they are numerous; and the inhibitions connected with them are strong. If they are the happiest people in the world, it is hard to see that freedom from a consciousness of right and wrong, and of associated guilt, can be one of the explanations.

Remember, too, that we are not trying to say in this paper that the Stone Age Eskimos had a way of life that could not be greatly improved. In our opinion, throwing out the entire dietetic section of Eskimo beliefs would simplify their problems, leading to an increase of happiness—perhaps to some improvement in even their excellent health.

An explanation with many supporters is that the Eskimos are happy because they live a natural life in the sense of doing mainly outdoor work of a sort that resembles the play of children—which, of course, is begging the question of whether the play of children is in large part an imitation of the daily work of their elders.

What Eskimos have to do is to hunt, fish, travel, and keep house. Many of our own people consider hunting, fishing, and travel such likeable occupations as to be play rather than work. Eskimos hunt across open fields instead of digging coal in a shaft; they fish in river or lake instead of tightening nuts or pounding rivets in a factory. They travel when they want to travel and stay when they want to stay. They can build in a few hours, particularly in midwinter, dwellings that are as comfortable for people living in them by Eskimo methods as our apartments are for us when we live in them by our methods. They are better protected in light and velvety suits of fur at their coldest winter weather than we are at half their frost in our stiff and twice as heavy suits and overcoats. And thus we could recite indefinitely. It is not possible to spend several years as an Eskimo among Eskimos without coming to feel that the "natural" life, as meant in this paragraph, does contribute toward average happiness.

It is said by another group of theorizers that the Eskimos were happy because they lived in a stimulating climate—that, within limits, stimulation leads to happiness. There may be something in this, for it is the experience of most of us that we feel better, and to that extent happier, on a brisk autumn morning after a frosty night than we do on a morning after one of the hot nights of July or August. Again, there is little dispute that on the Asiatic continent, for instance, you discover the highest percentage of jollity along the Arctic shore, the highest percentage of gloom, misanthropy, and melancholy along the frontiers of the Indian Ocean. Doubtless the reasons for the pessimism both of systems of thought and of individual persons in India are complicated; but it does seem likely that, unraveling this complexity, you will find among the elements those of climate—and of food.

Food brings us to the last-but-one of the common explanations of why the Eskimos are happy—it is said they are happy because they are healthy, and that they are healthy because they live a natural life (as described above) on the natural diet of man. By this view, it was only to man of three or four million years ago, when he was emerging from the anthropoid state, that vegetarianism was natural. The argument runs that the ape is vegetarian, that the ape man of the first stages was partly vegetarian, and that the evolving animal did not become real man until he was completely independent of roots, berries, and sprouts—that the first complete man was the first who was completely a hunter.

This reasoning continues by stating that to man as we know him (since he became about as disassociated from the rest of the anthropoids as he is now) the hunter's life has been the normal life, and meat the normal food. It was not until very recently, after the development of agriculture some 30,000 or 40,000 years ago, that it became possible for man to be sedentary and to live on a mixed diet consisting in some cases largely of things from the vegetable kingdom. The time since then has been too short, the argument runs, for man to evolve into full biological adaptation to a mixed diet. Not being fully adapted to it he is not fully healthy on it—and maximum happiness goes only with maximum health.

Branching from hunter to pastoralist, the reasoning continues that man as a herdsman has lived in the main direct from the animals, by eating their tissues. So far as diet goes he might as well have been still the hunter. For only in a few regions has milk also been important; and in any case milk is an animal fluid, not a vegetable.

It has been my own experience, and that of all those of my associates who were of active habit and so able to take their place acceptably in the Eskimo way of life, that we have been happier than usual while so living. But I confess never having connected this up with the diet until I had the experience of living with one colleague in New York City for a whole year exclusively on meat and water. The committee of scientists, under whose scrutiny we were, noticed both from measured reactions and from their general impression that we seemed to be in somewhat better health, and to that extent in better spirits, during the year of exclusive meat than we had been through an observed three-week period on the ordinary New York mixed diet. Both my fellow of the experiment, Karsten Andersen, and I agreed with the observers. And we were in a position to add that we seemed to ourselves to be more optimistic and in better humor than average—we looked forward to the next day or the next job with more anticipation; we faced difficulties with somewhat more than common relish.

It is not, of course, thinkable that it would be possible for all mankind (with the population of the world what it is) to live on an exclusive or even a high meat diet. But it is not beyond the limits of possibility that, with careful study and adaptation, we may be able to find a wholesome diet with little or no meat in it—some diet which tends equally toward happiness in that it gives the same or similar degrees of health, including stimulation.

On the basis of my years with the people of the Age of Stone, I feel my vote will have to be that, while there may be some rightness about some of the other explanations, the chief factor in the happiness of the Stone Age Eskimos was that they were living according to the golden rule.

In the Stone Age community those who were selfish lost standing. Those who were altruistic rose in the public esteem. A man who got things to use them himself was not frowned on so long as everybody felt that what he was using was not beyond his needs; but whenever anyone began to keep for himself more than by the usual experience was necessary for his comfort, he lost some of the community's good opinion; if he gave the impression that his main purpose for getting things was that he wanted to keep them, then he fell in standing rapidly. However, that situation never went far, in my experience, for I never actually knew anybody who had the "moral" courage to persist in the acquisitive type of unsocial conduct.

It is easier to feel that you understand than to prove you understand why it is man gets more happiness out of living unselfishly under a system which rewards unselfishness than from living selfishly where selfishness is rewarded. Because we are writing less than a book we might perhaps rest with suggesting in answer that man is more fundamentally a co-operative animal than a competitive animal, that his survival as a species has perhaps been through mutual aid rather than through rugged individualism. And somehow it has been ground into us by the forces of evolution to be "instinctively" happiest over those things which in the long run yield the greatest good to the greatest number.

My hope for the good life of the future, as I have seen it mirrored from the past by the Stone Age of northern America, does not rest wholly on a belief in cycles of history. It rests in part on the thought that a few more decades or centuries of preaching the golden rule may result in its becoming fashionable, even for the civilized, to live by the golden rule. Perhaps we could live as happily in a metropolis as in a fishing village, if only we could substitute the ideals of co-operation for those of competition. For it does not seem to be inherent in "progress" that it shall be inimical to the good life.

# JOHN STRACHEY

*John Strachey has established himself in his books, articles, and lectures as one of the most vigorous of current critics of our society, taking a Socialist point of view, as this contribution indicates. He was born in 1901, son of John St. Loe Strachey and cousin of Lytton Strachey. Educated at Eton and Oxford, he quickly made his entry into English politics, serving as Labour M. P. from 1929 to 1931. In 1931 he resigned from the Parliamentary Labour Party.*

*His most influential books include: 'The Coming Struggle for Power' (1932); 'The Menace of Fascism' (1933); 'The Nature of Capitalist Crisis' (1935); 'The Theory and Practice of Socialism' (1936); 'What We Are to Do' (1938), and 'The Economics of Progress' (1939).*

# *John Strachey*

MY PHILOSOPHY of life is simple. I know what I want for myself. I want the opportunity to live a reasonably secure and full life; the opportunity to contribute from whatever capacities I have to the common store and to receive, in return, the benefits of the capacities of others. In a word, I want Life, Liberty, and the Pursuit of Happiness; I am not aware that the thing has been better put since the time of your founding fathers.

I presume that other people want this too. I presume this because I do not believe that in these fundamental respects human beings differ very significantly, and secondly because I observe that, however confusedly, men's efforts are directed toward this end. I also note that up till now in human history by far the greater part of mankind has never succeeded in getting anywhere near the attainment of this end. I do not, of course, know what the world would be like if mankind as a whole succeeded in obtaining secure and reasonable conditions of life. Maybe nothing much would come of it. Maybe, as the poet of the late nineteenth-century disillusionment has it:

> *The troubles of our proud and angry dust*
> *Are from eternity, and shall not fail.*

Nobody can prove the contrary; and nobody but an ass believes that the attainment of satisfactory conditions of life would do more than make it possible for men to approach the most intricate and interesting problems of living. But for that very reason it may be, and I for one believe that it would be, that the attainment of such conditions of life would open up a new epoch of human history which would make our present concerns seem very small beer indeed.

What, pray, is there to do with one's life in this twentieth century of ours except to take part in the struggle to build a world of security and peace? The only practical alternative, for men and women of any vigor, is to try to get money and power for themselves. There is, to be sure, this old ideal of personal advancement, not indeed, from log cabin to White House—that is old stuff—but from slum tenement to director's room. There was a time, no doubt, when a reasonable man could feel not dissatisfied with such a career, for his own personal success in the struggle was, up to say 1914, genuinely bound up, to some extent at any rate, with the development of the community. A man could hardly make a great fortune or build up a financial empire without, if only incidentally, building great railroads or public utilities, or what you will, for his country. But today, who can doubt that the road to great personal wealth and power lies, in the representative examples, not so much through building anything as through preventing things from being built; not so much through the provision of more and better supplies of food or clothing, or what you will, to the community as through the cornering or restricting of such supplies as there are; not through the development of the community but through a holdup of the community?

Once that has become apparent, it seems to me that there must be something a bit queer about a man who can feel satisfaction in devoting his life to the struggle for money and power. He must be either so frightened of poverty that he can think about little else, or he must have a slightly pathological love of accumulation. Or again he must be so frightened of being powerless that he cannot feel safe unless he feels omnipotent—or something of that sort. There are no doubt lots of people with one or other of these kinks;

present-day conditions of life tend to breed them. But for more normal people the old success-story ideal must surely be profoundly stale. And what else is there, I repeat? Do you wish to turn your back on the whole world in despair? It is two or three centuries too late for that. The command, "Get thee to a nunnery!" makes no real sense today.

The above paragraphs have been intentionally written upon the hypothesis that it is possible for us either to live our own personal lives or to participate in the struggle to better the world. Already, however, for the great majority of the population of the world this is a false hypothesis. The true alternative for the people of the world is not either to live personal, self-regarding lives against a background of more or less tolerable, or at least stable, social conditions, or to take part in the struggle for social improvement. The real alternative is one of successful struggle to change the world for the better, or of the rapid regression of the world to incomparably worse conditions than any we have yet experienced. You may not see it quite so clearly in America as we can in Europe. But over here it is becoming almost impossible to doubt that unless we somehow manage to get together in a conscious effort to make things much better than they have ever been before, things will get intolerably worse.

No doubt it will be upon the great masses of the human race—the 40,000,000 British wage earners and their dependents (out of 47,000,000 inhabitants of Britain), for example, or the worker and peasant masses of Continental Europe, or the wage earners and poorer farmers of America —that this choice will bear most obviously and inescapably. If they do not manage to put things right, it will be appallingly the worse for them. Far from being allowed to carry on with their own private, individual efforts to better themselves, which, however feeble and however frequently frustrated, did offer them an object in life, they will lose the very possibility of reasonable existence. They will lose their jobs in slump, their liberties in Fascism, and their lives in war. Hence, the struggle to make a decent world is, for this overwhelming majority of humanity, not something which they may or may not participate in; it is something which confronts them; it is a battle which they must fight, but which they may either win or lose.

Moreover, if this absence of choice in the matter is true for the working masses already, it is becoming true for members of those upper and middle classes of the community, to which most of the readers of these words will belong. We may have guarded ourselves against the consequences of slump pretty successfully (we of the British middle class have so far succeeded in this a good deal better than you have in America, I fancy). We may have thought that, after all, the loss of our liberty to write or say what we think under some kind of Fascist regime, would be, though unpleasant, not really so very important. But what does get us is being faced with the prospect of unending wars between the struggling empires. For if we are not killed in the next war, well then, we shall be killed in the next but one, or in the one after that.

The British upper and middle classes, in particular, are for the first time facing up to this situation as a reality, at the time that this article is being written (1939). As one of them said to me recently, "It cost us a million lives to defeat German imperialism last time—now, within twenty-five years, we have apparently got to do it again. Perhaps we *can* do it again; but what would another victory lead to? Another twenty years breathing space, and then a third world war, or what?"

He had suddenly seen that an unending series of world wars was the logical and inevitable outcome of running the world in the way in which it is run today. Or rather, he had seen an unending series of world wars as logical and inevitable in themselves, for he could not even conceive of organizing the world differently to the way in which it is organized today. And he did not like the prospect. It is, above all, this prospect of unending imperialist wars which is turning the minds of a quite significant number of the younger members of the upper and middle classes in this country toward the idea of devoting their lives to the reconstruction of society.

There arises in the minds of such members of the middle and upper classes, a very old problem; but it arises in a new form. When I was at the University, the problem used to be put in this way. Those young men who showed a tendency to be interested in "problems" of one kind or another, who showed a tendency toward devoting their lives to some more or less impersonal end, were called "idealists" and were appropriately admired and despised by those undergraduates who were not interested in "problems"—or, rather, were interested in the one great problem of how they were going to get on in the world. Of course, everyone instinctively realized (the realization was carried in the very tones in which the word "idealist" was said) that the self-regarding realists and all they stood for would, however regrettably, brush aside the idealists and all they stood for. As long as the issue poses itself that way; as long as it really is to the personal interests of the most vigorous types to take the condition of the world as given, and make the best of it for themselves, then no other result can be expected. Slowly but surely, however, the condition of the world becomes so intolerable that the first, the most pressing, the most severely practical, interest of everybody becomes to change it. Once that has happened, the world will certainly be changed; but it will only be changed for the better if the people who do the changing have learned to understand what is wrong, and consequently, how to put it right.

The fact is that once a man gets mixed up in the main

contemporary struggle to create a decent sort of world, his own personal interests and the interests of his cause become so interwoven, both in the sense that they can support each other, and in the sense that they can conflict with each other, that it is almost impossible to separate them. What, then, I am asserting is not the super-truism that men have individual personal aims for which they struggle, but the proposition, often denied both in words and deeds, that men entertain impersonal motives which are yet sufficiently strong to make them act.

The trouble is that the people who believe in the possibility of this often go to the other extreme and assert that these "idealistic" motives are entirely impersonal. They assert, for instance, that to wish the general betterment of human life is a wholly impersonal motive. They often term it a religious impulse. Now such an impulse has often been, in America and Britain, and in the last three hundred years especially, closely associated with deep religious conviction. But for my part I am old-fashioned enough to consider religion as indissolubly connected with a belief in the existence of a deity; to consider that religion is essentially theology, not philanthropy. And the impulse to participate in the struggle for human improvement is independent, as numberless instances indicate, of whether a man believes in the existence of a deity or not.

The simple truth is that the so-called idealistic impulses are by no means impersonal. On the contrary, they are merely an extension of the most personal, the most severely self-regarding, impulses. A man will fight for himself because if he does not he will go under. He will fight for his family, his group, his nation, his class, for the same reason, once he has become convinced, and insofar as he has become convinced, that his own interests have become involved with the self-preservation of his family, group, nation, or class. The gradations between the most crudely self-interested and the most apparently idealistic actions are infinite; the interconnections infinitely subtle.

But this undeniable fact ought not even to suggest to us that we have been wrong in placing immense importance upon the cultivation of what we have called the idealistic motive; in calling, as we have, men good or bad, largely according to whether they acted from narrowly personal, or relatively impersonal, motives. For the extension of a man's emotional involvement, by successive stages, from himself to his family, his clan, his nation, to humanity itself, is the story of progressive evolution itself.

It is because this development is so infinitely precious that by far the greatest, and by far the worst thing, that has happened in the world for the past two decades is the appearance of the armed and organized Nazi heresy. I call it heresy advisedly, for the innermost core of Nazi doctrine is, precisely, a denial that men can identify their interests with those of humanity as a whole. The core of Nazi doctrine is the denial of humanity. And whether we like it or not, it is a historical fact that the concept of humanity appeared in a religious form; it appeared, above all, in the specific form of the Christian doctrine of the infinite worth of every human soul.

Moreover, and this is very much to the point in connection with the Nazi heresy, the Christian doctrine of the infinite worth of every single human being was the disguised expression of man's revolt against slavery, the basic institution on which the whole ancient world was founded. This doctrine was the dissolving agent—"the un-saying word"—which undermined the institution of slavery, and undermined with it the whole gigantic structures of the empires of antiquity.

Now it is, whether they realize it or not, the object of the Nazi leaders to drive the mass of mankind back to a new form of slavery, as a condition necessary to the continuance of the private ownership of fields, factories, and mines. It is the declared object of Nazi economic policy—and this is the first act of any Fascist government—to withdraw from men their right to sell their power to labor, freely and as they will. The first and decisive step in this withdrawal is to make it a criminal offense for workers to strike. This is clearly the first step in the introduction of compulsory labor; in a word, it is a first and long step in the reintroduction of slavery. Is it not intensely interesting, significant, and ominous that the Nazi philosophers (and do not make any mistake about it—there *are* Nazi philosophers, and important and powerful ones) have found it necessary simultaneously to attack the Christian idea of humanity and the infinite worth of every individual human being? For this was the idea which dissolved the old slavery. This, therefore, is the idea which must be overthrown if the new slavery is to be established.

It will, I am convinced, in the end become clear to every sincere Christian that, in spite of their apparently greater regard, not indeed for religion itself, but for the churches as institutions with property rights, the specifically Nazi, and generally Fascist, view of life is incomparably farther from, and more irreconcilable with, the Christian view than is the Marxist or Communist view of life. For the Marxist does, explicitly, accept the ideal of a united humanity as the ultimate object with which the individual must identify himself. The Christian clothes this belief in language and concepts which are so different from those of the Marxist that he may, and indeed almost always does, fail to see that at the bottom they stand for the same thing. Above all, the Christian is shocked by what he has been told of the Marxist doctrine of the class war. Now it is perfectly true that Marxists believe that the 90 to 95 per cent of the population of any community which does the work of that community has to take power out of the hands of that 5 to 10 per cent which lives by virtue of its ownership of the fields, factories, and land of the community, before the ideal of a united humanity can be realized. It is perfectly true that the Marxist believes, as a result of experience, that this 90 to 95 per cent of the population will only be able to achieve power by political struggle.

Now this Marxist view may be right or wrong, good or bad; that is not the point. The point is that the whole object of the class struggle, as conceived by the Marxist, is to achieve a united humanity. It is precisely this ultimate ideal which the Nazis specifically reject. Every Nazi philosopher, like every Nazi politician or statesman, reiterates that there is no ideal beyond that of the nation or race. Their ultimate world view is one of endlessly warring races. It is precisely in order to make such a future possible that the Nazi philosophers, both by writing their own books and, more concretely, by burning the books of former philosophers, make war upon any idea which includes that of a united human race. It is thus gravely to underestimate the scope and sweep of the Nazi movement to suppose that it is directed simply against Communist, Marxist, or Socialist thought, or even that it limits itself to attacking humanitarianism and liberalism. On the contrary, it is indispensable for the Nazis to attempt to eradicate every idea, including above all that basic element in Christianity, which tends, in however mystical a manner, toward the ideal of a united humanity. For so long as such ideas can reach men's minds the world cannot be made safe for slavery at home and war abroad.

Well, my philosophy is that this movement must be fought. Every year of the twentieth century which passes makes it more clear that humanity must move down this incomparably dark path if it does not succeed in the struggle to create a new world. For that very reason we now see that the enormous impetus, the overmastering drive, needed to create that new world is coming, not primarily from amiable "idealistic" people who want to make things better (they could never be anything like strong enough to do the job by themselves), but from millions of men who, though they may not see very clearly what they are doing or whither they are going, are determined at any rate not to go down the dark path. We realize that it is fear of, and horror at, the regression of the world to slavery and war which drives men to achieve a far higher basis of freedom and peace than they have ever yet known. It is precisely out of, and by means of, the gigantic defensive struggle against Fascism and war, for which world-wide forces are today massing, that the struggle for a new world is being generated.

I am bound to say that the basic problem seems to me almost embarrassingly simple. The problem is so to arrange the life of society that its members can get their livings in peace and security. Until and unless they can do that, there is no chance of their living decent lives. Is that so hard to see? Does one need to subscribe to some special interpretation of history to agree with that conclusion? Is it, for example, so difficult to understand that the citizens of Germany cannot today live very decent lives when their community is so arranged that the final object of all their work is the piling up of instruments of slaughter; when they are told that war and its preparation are the be-all and end-all of human life; when everything—material prosperity, truth, reason, science, and religious belief—must be sacrificed to that end? Or again, is it so very difficult to see that that great part of the citizenry of the United States which now, every ten years or so, is suddenly deprived of the opportunity to work or earn, and passes into a period of months or years of semi-starvation without having the slightest possibility of controlling, much less of averting, the catastrophe by anything which they can do—is it very difficult to see that, no matter what moral virtues are preached, people in such a situation will not be able to be very reliant, satisfactory, or hopeful citizens?

Nor, for my part, do I believe that there is any mystery as to why the people of Germany, for instance, are being maddened into the belief that war is the only object of human endeavor, or as to why the people of the United States periodically lose their livelihoods. The reason is that the means of production—the fields, the factories, and the mines, the capital, of their respective countries— have passed out of the possession of the mass of the population and have become the exclusive possession of a small class or group. It is this extraordinary and unparalleled concentration of the ownership of the means of production in the hands of a small class of persons which is making it impossible for the American people, for example, to get their livings at all, and for the German people to get them at any other task than armament building.

This is, of course, no place to attempt to prove this statement (the larger part of my written work is devoted to no other purpose than this), but again, is it so difficult to see that this extreme concentration of property in the means of production at one end of the social scale will produce just those monstrous results which we see around us? I do not know of any exact figure on the concentration of capital ownership in the United States of America. But in Great Britain, according to the latest figure—that of Messrs. G. W. Daniels and H. Campion, in their standard work, *The Distribution of the National Capital*—80 per cent of the capital of Great Britain is now owned by 6 per cent of the population. The concentration would not, I think, be quite so extreme in the United States, for you still have a fairly large class of independent farmers owning their own land; but there is no doubt that the American situation is rapidly moving in that direction.

For example, the census of 1930 revealed that four out

of five actively employed Americans were wage or salary earners. In a word, four out of five Americans today get their living by working for that small group of Americans who own the capital of the country. (But perhaps these four out of five wage-earning Americans themselves own the capital of the country, through diffused shareholding, and thus employ themselves, as it were; but no, according to that authoritative work, *America's Capacity to Consume,* "with the masses of the population, the income derived from investments is negligible." Hence the masses of the American population certainly do not own the capital of the country, for if they did, they would draw incomes from it.)

Now the fact that the ownership of the capital of every one of the great capitalist communities has got into the hands of a small class of from 5 to 10 per cent of its inhabitants would not matter in itself. It only matters because the ownership of capital inevitably carries with it the receipt of all the really large incomes. The maldistribution of capital necessarily carries with it a maldistribution of income so extreme that the system simply will not work any longer. In the case of America we have figures to show just how far that maldistribution of income has gone. In 1929 (notice the year) the 36,000 richest American families each got an income of over $75,000 a year. These families, taken together, got ten billion dollars. But there were twelve million American families which had each an income of less than $1,500 a year. And these twelve million American families, taken together, also got almost exactly ten billion dollars a year. "Thus it appears," write the authors of *America's Capacity to Consume,* "that 0.1 per cent of the families (at the top of the American social scale) receive practically as much as the 42 per cent of families at the bottom of the scale."

That is the kind of inequality in the distribution of income which the private ownership of the capital of the coun-

John Strachey

try by a small group of persons inevitably produces. When once income has become as maldistributed as that, the economic system must inevitably begin to break down. For that horrible, familiar situation arises in which it is impossible to sell the final products of industry and so keep the masses of the population in employment. The rich, the 0.1 per cent of families at the top of the social tree, will not buy this final product since they are already gorged with luxuries, while the 42 per cent of families at the bottom of the social scale, who taken together get no more than the 0.1 per cent, have no money to buy the final products, however bitterly they need them. And so nobody buys them; they are not sold, and the men and women who made them fall out of work and become poorer still.

There are all sorts of palliatives, many of them very useful, by which this situation can be dealt with. You can take some of the money, by one means or another, which flows into the hands of the 0.1 per cent of families and distribute it, by one means or another, to the 42 per cent of families. That is, I understand, what your President, Mr. Roosevelt, is attempting to do at the moment; and it is well worth doing. But is it not clear that this can be no more than an attempt to deal with the consequences of a fundamentally unsound system? The only real cure is so to alter the system that the initial maldistribution of income does not occur. And you cannot do that so long as between 5 and 10 per cent of the population own the means of production, the capital of the country. The only way to produce a distribution of income sufficient even to make it possible for the population to buy the total product of industry and so keep themselves in employment is, in the long run, to redistribute the means of production themselves, which are the source of income, to the mass of the population. But you cannot distribute big, modern means of production such as railways and power stations by cutting them up and giving little bits of them to individuals. You have got to place them in the collective ownership of the whole population. It will not be until you have done that that you will have made it possible for people to live decent lives. But that is all you have got to do. And that is socialism.

# JAMES THURBER

*To the writer of these lines—and he will take on all comers—Mr. Thurber, whether he writes or draws, is a first-rate humorist, which means that he is an important writer and an important man, two propositions Mr. Thurber would doubtless violently deny.*

*At any rate it is impossible to deny that he was born in Columbus, Ohio, in 1894, and that he attended its public schools and Ohio State University. It is true, though improbable, that he was a code clerk in the American Embassy in Paris from November, 1918 to March, 1920. After serving as a newspaperman, a somewhat odd one, on the 'Columbus Dispatch,' the Paris Edition of 'The Chicago Tribune,' and the 'New York Evening Post,' he found his true home on 'The New Yorker' in 1927. He has served as an editor, is now a contributor, and spends much of his time planning books and plays and losing the notes he makes for them.*

*His publications include: 'Is Sex Necessary?,' with E. B. White (1929); 'The Owl in the Attic' (1931); 'The Seal in the Bedroom' (1932); 'My Life and Hard Times' (1933); 'The Middle-Aged Man on the Flying Trapeze' (1935); 'Let Your Mind Alone' (1937).*

# *James Thurber*

EVERY man is occasionally visited by the suspicion that the planet on which he is riding is not really going anywhere; that the Force which controls its measured eccentricities hasn't got anything special in mind. If he broods upon this somber theme long enough he gets the doleful idea that the laughing children on a merry-go-round or the thin, fine hands of a lady's watch are revolving more purposefully than he is. These black doubts creep up on a man just before thunderstorms, or at six in the morning when the steam begins to knock solemnly in the pipes, or during his confused wanderings in the forest beyond Euphoria after a long night of drinking.

"Where are we going, if anywhere, and why?" It will do no good to call up the *Times* or consult the Britannica. The Answer does not lie in the charts of astronomers or in the equations of mathematicians; it was not indicated by Galileo's swinging lamp or the voices of Joan of Arc; it evaded Socrates and Archimedes and the great men of the Renaissance and it has evaded everybody else from Francis Bacon to John Kieran. The fearful mystery that lies behind all this endless rotation has led Man into curious indulgences and singular practices, among them love, poetry, intoxicants, religion, and philosophy. Philosophy offers the rather cold consolation that perhaps we and our planet do not actually exist; religion presents the contradictory and scarcely more comforting thought that we exist but that we cannot hope to get anywhere until we cease to exist. Alcohol, in attempting to resolve the contradiction, produces vivid patterns of Truth which vanish like snow in the morning sun and cannot be recalled; the revelations of poetry are as wonderful as a comet in the skies, and as mysterious. Love, which was once believed to contain the Answer, we now know to be nothing more than an inherited behavior pattern.

Before we can pronounce any judgment on Man's destiny, we must have a peek at the dilemma into which he has gotten himself. We must examine his nature before we can measure his hope of Heaven. For some curious reason Man has always assumed that his is the highest form of life in the universe. There is, of course, nothing at all with which to sustain this view. Man is simply the highest form of life on his own planet. His superiority rests on a thin and chancy basis: he had the trick of articulate speech and out of this, slowly and laboriously, he developed the capacity of abstract reasoning. Abstract reasoning, in itself, has not benefited Man so much as instinct has benefited the lower animals. On the contrary, it has moved in the opposite direction. Instinct has been defined as "a tendency to actions which lead to the attainment of some goal natural to the species." In giving up instinct and going in for reasoning, Man has aspired higher than the attainment of natural goals; he has developed ideas and notions; he has monkeyed around with concepts. The life to which he was naturally adapted he has put behind him; in moving into the alien and complicated sphere of Thought and Imagination he has become the least well-adjusted of all the creatures of the earth, and hence the most bewildered. It may be that the finer mysteries of life and death can be comprehended only through pure instinct; the cat, for example, appears to Know (I don't say that he does, but he appears to). Man, on the other hand, is surely farther away from the Answer than any other animal this side of the ladybug. His mistaken selection of reasoning as an instrument of perception has put him into a fine quandary.

The survival of almost any species of social animal, no matter how low, has been shown to be dependent on Group Co-operation, which is itself a product of instinct. Man's co-operative processes are jumpy, incomplete, and temporary because they are the product of reasoning and are thus divorced from the sanity which informs all natural laws. The lower animals co-operate in the interest of the preservation of their species. Man no longer has the natural, earthy sense which would interest him in the preservation of his species. The co-operation of the lower social animals is constructive, that of man destructive. "Group struggles to the death between animals of the same species, such as occur in human warfare, can hardly be found among nonhuman animals," says W. C. Allee in his enormously interesting *The Social Life of Animals.*

The animals that depend upon instinct have an inherent knowledge of the laws of economics and of how to apply them; Man with his powers of reason has reduced economics to the level of a farce which is at once funnier and more tragic than *Tobacco Road.* One has but to observe a community of beavers at work in a stream to understand the loss in sagacity, balance, co-operation, competence, and purpose which Man has suffered since he rose up on his hind legs. His grip on the earth and its realities began to lessen in that hour; he could walk, but he had lost the opposability of his hallux, and his feet were no longer prehensile. Two of his parts increased enormously in size: his gluteus maximus and his cerebrum. He began to chatter and he developed Reason, Thought, and Imagination, qualities which would get the smartest group of rabbits or orioles in the world into inextricable trouble overnight. Man, the aloof animal, has deteriorated in everything except mentality and in that he has done no more than barely hold his own for the past two thousand years. He no longer understands the ways of the lower animals and they no longer understand the ways of Man. Here again it is Man that has suffered the loss.

Next to reasoning, the greatest handicap to the optimum development of Man lies in the fact that his planet is just barely habitable. Its minimum temperatures are too low and its maximum temperatures are too high. Its day is not long enough and its night is too long. The disposition of its water and its earth is distinctly unfortunate (the existence of the Mediterranean Sea in the place where we find it is perhaps the unhappiest accident in the whole firmament). These factors encourage depression, fear, war, and lack of vitality. They describe a planet which is by no means perfectly devised for the nurturing, or for the perpetuation, of a higher intelligence. The effect of all this on Man is everywhere apparent. On his misfit globe he has outlasted the mammoth and the pterodactyl, but he has never got the upper hand of bacteria and the insects. "This is not even the age of Man, however great his superiority in size and intelligence," writes Mr. Allee, "it is literally the age of insects." It is surely not going too far, in view of everything, to venture the opinion that Man is not so high as he thinks he is. It is surely permissible to hazard the guess that somewhere beyond Betelgeuse there may be a race of men whose intelligence makes ours seem like the works of an old-fashioned music box. The Earth, it seems to me, may well be the Siberia, or the Perth Amboy, of the inhabited planets of the Universe.

Now that we have got Man down on his back, so to speak, let us look at the tongue of his intellect and feel the pulse of his soul. There is a great deal to be said for his intellect, in spite of the fact that it is unquestionably coated. It has produced Genius and out of Genius has come Art, the one achievement of Man which has made the long trip up from all fours seem well-advised. Most of the faint intimations of immortality of which we are occasionally aware would

*Shelburne Studios, New York*

JAMES THURBER

seem to arise out of Art, or the materials of Art. This brings us to God and Heaven, the last stop which this exploration into the known and the unknown will make.

Everybody is supposed to have some opinion as to whether there is life after death. Intelligent persons are expected to formulate "an integrated and consistent attitude toward life or reality"; this is known as "a philosophy" (definition 2c in *Webster's New International Dictionary*). Unfortunately, I have never been able to maintain a consistent attitude toward life or reality, or toward anything else. This may be entirely due to nervousness. At any rate, my attitudes change with the years, sometimes with the hours. Just now I am going through one of those periods when I believe that the black panther and the cedar waxwing have a higher hope of Heaven than Man has. The Dignity of Man and the Divine Destiny of Man are two things which it is at the moment impossible for me to accept with wholehearted enthusiasm. Human Dignity has gleamed only now and then and here and there, in lonely splendor, throughout the ages, a hope of the better men, never an achievement of the majority. That which is only sporadically realized can scarcely be called characteristic. It is impossible to think of it as innate; it could never be defined as normal. Nothing is more depressing than the realization that nobility, courage, mercy, and almost all the other virtues which go to make up the ideal of Human Dignity, are, at their clearest and realest, the outgrowth of Man's inhumanity to Man, the fruit of his unending interspecific struggle. The pattern is easily traceable, from Christ to Cavell.

In spite of everything, it is perhaps too easy to figure Man as merely an animal of the earth whose cerebrum developed extraordinarily, like the peacock's tail or the giraffe's neck, and to let it go at that. There is always Browning's "plaguy hundredth chance" that the mysterious inner eye which seems to see God, actually does see God; and that God sees it, too. There is always Browning's "grand Perhaps." If it is hard to Believe, it is just as hard, as our poet's Bishop Blougram points out to the cynical Mr. Gigadibs, to "guard our unbelief." You remember: "Just when we are safest, there's a sunset-touch, a fancy from a flower-bell," and all that sort of thing—and we believe again. And then there's a man with a little mustache, and a man with an umbrella, and all *that* sort of thing, and we are safe once more in our conviction that there can be no God watching over this sorrowful and sinister scene, these menacing and meaningless animals.

We come back, in the end, to all that we can safely feel we know: a monkey man in the Eolithic times, wandering through the jungle, came upon a jewel and stuck it into his head. Since that day his descendants have given off light, sometimes a magic and blinding light. The question whether the jewel was carelessly flung off from a whirling star or carefully planned and placed by a supernatural hand has engaged the interest of mankind for a million years. The question will go on and on: is this light a proof of God or is it no more remarkable than the plumage of a bird of paradise?

"Come, come, it's best believing, if we can," says the jovial Sylvester Blougram, over his wine. "Why not," he asks, " 'the Way, the Truth, the Life'?" Why not, indeed? It is all right with me, I say over my own wine. But what is all this fear of, and opposition to, Oblivion? What is the matter with the soft Darkness, the Dreamless Sleep? "Well, folks," the cheery guard may say, as the train rushes silently into a warm, dark tunnel and stops, "Here we are at good old Oblivion! Everybody out!" Come, come, what is the matter with that? I ask—over my scotch and soda.

# HENDRIK WILLEM VAN LOON

*Hendrik Willem van Loon has distinguished himself in so many fields that it is not easy to summarize his achievements. One might perhaps say that he is carrying on for our time the great tradition of enlightenment called to mind by such names as Voltaire and Diderot. He unites, both in his writing and his social intercourse, enormous erudition, unfailing sturdy common sense, and refreshing humor.*

*Born in Rotterdam in 1882, he was educated at private schools in Holland, and at the age of twenty-one came to the United States. It has since been his country. He studied at Cornell, Harvard, and Munich; worked as a foreign correspondent both before and during the World War; taught history and art in various universities, particularly Cornell and Antioch College. The tremendous success of 'The Story of Mankind' determined his future career, which has been that of a writer, varied by work on the lecture platform and before the microphone. There are today ninety-six editions of his books in twenty-one foreign languages, probably some sort of record. The major ones include: 'The Fall of the Dutch Republic' (1913); 'The Rise of the Dutch Kingdom' (1915); 'Ancient Man' (1920); The Story of Mankind' (1921); 'The Story of the Bible' (1923); 'R.v.R.,' a magnificent biographical novel about Rembrandt (1930); 'Van Loon's Geography' (1932); 'The Arts' (1937). Mr. Van Loon, who started life as a musician, has recently returned to his earliest avocation and has illustrated a number of song books—the most ambitious of which: 'The Last of the Troubadours: The Life and Times and Music of Carl Michael Bellman,' the great Swedish troubadour, appears this summer.*

*He prefers to call the following essay 'The Laughing Philosophers' and adds that it is a chapter from his "unpublished autobiography."*

# *Hendrik Willem van Loon*

For a great many years (and by a great many people) I had been asked to give some sort of account of what were supposed to be "my religious beliefs," and whether I had any "religion" at all. And invariably I had most carefully evaded the issue. Not because I did not have any "religious convictions," but because I had very little "religion" (in the accepted sense of the word) and furthermore, an instinct, born out of the necessities of living for a great many years in a country filled with all sorts of uncompromising soul searchers, had taught me at a very early age, to beware of those citizens who went around with blueprints of The Truth in their pockets.

I am all for truth. But The Truth, in the Pauline sense of the word, is as little to my liking as cyanide of potassium. For not only is it apt to be equally fatal, but, unlike cyanide of potassium, there are no legal restrictions upon its sale and distribution. Indeed, it is given away for nothing at all to even the meekest of applicants. It may be true that the meek will find special favor in the eyes of Providence, as the Good Book tells us, but in that case, Providence and I happen to disagree, as we do in a good many other respects.

I have lived under almost every form of government, from the totalitarian states of Italy and Russia on the one side to the democracies of the West on the other. But the one thing I have come to fear most of all is the terrible tyranny of the meek! Compared to the Reign of Terror as not infrequently established by the humble folk, the absolutism of an Adolf Hitler or a Stalin becomes a pale form of enlightened despotism. Hence my reluctance to give myself away! The parties of the second part would never have understood a word of what I said. But they would at once have observed that a few commas in my arguments were missing and their mote-searching eyes would have detected all sorts of strange grammatical irregularities in my text. After that, I would have become anathema in the sight of the Truly Righteous and they would have set out to make my life as miserable as possible. I had not the slightest doubt about their ability to do so and to do so most successfully. One Socrates is enough for a good many thousand years. And therefore I followed the example of my fellow townsman, the learned, and worthy Dr. Desiderius Erasmus. I merely told the curious ones a few funny stories and kept them guessing.

In the end, there is always a road that leads through even the most difficult of territories. I have most carefully stuck to it until now at last I have reached that pleasant spot from which one has a delightful and most restful view of the cemetery. At fifty-seven, a great many things no longer seem to matter as much as they did at twenty-seven or thirty-seven, and so today there is no longer any need for secrecy. I therefore shall include a chapter I had never intended to write and I shall try to answer the question: "What do I think of the world around me as related to the problem of Eternity?" or words to that effect.

But there is another reason why I feel compelled to give some sort of account of my own beliefs and disbeliefs. This is the year of Disgrace, 1939. On all sides I am surrounded by people who are in utter despair. The events of the last twenty years have completely destroyed their faith in the ultimate victory of right over might. Whatever spiritual baggage they had carried with them when they left the parental home and struck out for themselves had either been lost or stolen or blown sky-high by an enemy bomb.

Even their iron rations upon which they depended in case of an emergency (and which consisted of some sort of belief in an Almighty God, who, in spite of everything, meant well by his children and who ultimately would come to their rescue), these too were found to have been spoiled by that poisonous gas of hate with which our poor planet has been so copiously drenched by the prophets of the new gospel of violence, and they had to be thrown away as completely useless. Love, the very foundation of the creed to which most of them had been exposed during the days of their earliest childhood, had become a byword of contempt, a product of that maudlin weakness for which there was no longer room in the bright lexicon of youth and which had been replaced by a more manly ideal of brute force and arrogant self-assertion.

These poor, forlorn pilgrims could of course have availed themselves of one of the many substitutes which were being offered for sale (and on very easy terms) by the quacksalvers, charlatans, and mountebanks who are always to be found in the wake of a great disaster. But somehow or other, a remaining sense of decency bade them keep away from these doubtful nostrums which, even in the labels on the packages, betrayed their highly spurious origin. What made these unhappy people suspect that I might have something to offer which they needed is more than I could tell you. But every one of my books and articles and radio speeches is invariably followed by a small avalanche of letters from complete strangers who write me: "Last night (or in your most recent book) you made us hope that now at last you were going to lift the curtain upon your own beliefs just high enough to let us see what you are trying to hide. For we know, all along, that you are hiding something. We suspect that you believe certain things which might be of tremendous benefit to all of us if only you would let us share them with you. So won't you please—please—play fair with your audience just for once and tell us what is really in your mind. It is not right to keep us in the dark! We are all of us so completely at sea! If you have any sort of compass that can in any way show us the road to safety, then, for heaven's sake, show it to us, share it with us, and don't keep it for yourself!"

Now I have long since given up any desire to pinch-hit for the great Jehovah. Neither do I feel that my little compass can ever be of very much use to anyone but myself. But if my unknown friends think that it may be of some benefit to them, very well—I will add this special chapter (which I had never expected to write) and I will give them a fairly accurate description of the compass and the charts by which I try to steer my own little craft. I warn them, however, that should they suffer shipwreck, it will be their own fault and not mine!

For all matters pertaining to spiritual navigation are of a highly tricky nature and everything depends, in the last analysis, upon the man on the bridge who has to handle these delicate instruments. Wherefore, if my own particular compass (which is completely satisfactory for all my own purposes) should cause someone else to suffer shipwreck and to see his ship dashed to pieces on the uncompromising rocks of despair, let him not blame me for his disaster, for I have told him to beware.

And now, without any further ado, here is that chapter for which so many people have asked.

Since all of us are the immediate and inevitable product of our earliest surroundings, I ought to repeat a few of the things which I have already told my readers in those previous chapters which dealt with my childhood days.

I was born in a country which, with all its manifold faults and shortcomings, had yet somehow managed to associate itself rather closely with the ideal of tolerance and religious liberty. I do not claim that the masses of my Dutch neigh-

*Von Behr*

HENDRIK WILLEM VAN LOON

bors were in any way superior in the breadth of their point of view to the rest of Europe. They were the direct descendants of that race of rock-ribbed Calvinists who, by sheer force of their convictions, had upset the mightiest totalitarian state of all times, the Church of Rome. And they still considered themselves soldiers of that army of the "elect" which under the banner of John Calvin had never known when it was defeated, because it had invariably preferred death to surrender—and dead soldiers are no longer conscious of anything, least of all of the way in which they met their end. Even today, when I have very little reason to love those stern-faced Ironsides, I feel compelled to admire their indomitable courage. Like all liberals, I feel a profound debt of gratitude towards those men and women who were hanged, burned, quartered, and tortured in every possible manner, but who never for a moment hesitated or recanted and who gloriously departed this life chanting their hymns of defiance until the smoke of their funeral pyres choked them into insensibility.

But alas! that which had been a living faith in the days when our country had resembled a mighty fortress in a constant state of siege—it had become a mere hollow shell of its former self, once the foe had been forced to retreat before the muddy waters of the North Sea. And that same garrison which three hundred years before had so bravely saved the lives of all the inhabitants had degenerated into a common nuisance, a small group of professional busybodies, everlastingly berating its less bigoted neighbors in a strange tongue which no longer made any sense (the language of the old Zion) and bitterly persecuting the most harmless of citizens if they happened to prefer the God of Love of the New Testament to the wrathful Jehovah revealed by that other Jewish chronicle, which for sheer savagery and ferocity stands unsurpassed in the annals of religious revelations as they are known to me—and I have made a pretty careful examination of that sort of literature.

Of course, as I have just said, the old, irrepressible energy was still there, but since it could find no normal outlets, it got dammed up like a river filled with ice. It had become a constant menace to the safety of the country. No one could foretell when or where it would break its bonds, though everyone was only too familiar with the damage it could do upon such occasions. As a result, we were never quite able to forget its presence, although we ourselves (that is to say, I and my own family) lived within the comparative safety of those towers of reason which had been originally built by the ancient Greeks and which more recently had been completely reconstructed according to the plans and specifications of the great French philosophers of the eighteenth century.

Such spiritual shelters were of course only to be found in the larger cities. Fortunately, I was born in Rotterdam and I did not come in actual contact with the religious Reign of Terror of our small towns until much later in life. And when that happened I had accumulated enough inner resistance not to let myself be worn down or exhausted by the everlasting bickering, wrangling, haranguing, disputing, quarreling, and fighting of those incredible and preposterous burghers who had been born three hundred years too late and who would have liked nothing quite as much as martyrdom at the hands of some contemporary Torquemada, "bearing witness to the Truth until the very end."

My childhood days (as I have explained in the previous chapters) had not been very happy but the misery of those years was at least not caused by any serious inner conflicts, for, as far as I can remember, there was not a single member of my entire family who had not completely and definitely broken with every form of established religion. We were a long-lived race and I knew all my grandparents and all my uncles and aunts. None of them ever went to church. None of them had been married in church. They dozed off peacefully into their last sleep without any benefit of clergy. I am under the impression (I think my sister told me so) that I was actually baptized by a Lutheran minister. But that was due to the personal friendship which existed between my parents and the leading Lutheran dominie of that day, who also happened to be a man of education and a great liberal. In asking him to baptize me, my father and mother wanted to be polite but had no thought of insuring me against the fires of hell. Indeed, it was not until after my eleventh birthday, when the uncertain temper of my father made it impossible for me to remain any longer at home and I was sent to a dreadful boarding school (my people did not know until years later how bad it had been), that I came into any direct contact with the Deity as he had been revealed unto my ancestors.

For statistical purposes, I may here add that in the course of many years I have been exposed to nearly every one of the more important forms of faith. The one exception is Confucianism, with which I have only a paper acquaintance, as I have never been in China. But for the rest, I know them all from personal contact.

For four years I lived in the home of a local Protestant minister. For three years I attended a school run on a rigid basis of orthodox Calvinism. At another school I learned to recite the correct answers according to the Heidelberg catechism. At still another school (we were forever moving) we attended the French Huguenot church and our religious instruction too was given in French. I lived for five years in Bavaria, which before the days of the Nazis was a center of a completely medieval form of Catholicism. I was a student at the University of Munich when several of its professors were deprived of their office on account of their "dangerous modernistic tendencies." I spent a whole year in the old Russia (of evil but magnificent memory) and, loving the music and the theatrical setting of the church services under the Romanovs, I learned a good deal about that interesting if preposterous survival of the days of the Middle Ages (Byzantine Middle Ages at that!).

Next I had a year in Poland, when the persecution of the Roman Catholics by the Greek Catholics had forced the Poles to take their own Catholicism with a seriousness I had never experienced elsewhere, not even in Bavaria. I am not entirely unfamiliar with the doctrines of the Moslems, having had an opportunity to study the teachings of Mohammed, both in theory and in practice, in a great many parts of the world. I have been fortunate (or unfortunate) enough to observe the Hindu in his native lair and to see with mine own eyes to what incredible degree of foul perversion man can descend while inspired by what is sometimes rather erroneously called his "religion."

On the other hand, it has been my privilege to wander through the pleasant lands where the gentle Buddha had left behind evidences of his actual or spiritual presence. And I have watched the out-and-out heathen, the worshipers of sticks and stones, while going about their strange business of placating the evil spirits and doing this in a way which reminded me rather painfully of some of my Christian neighbors. And, of couse, a thorough training in the classics has nicely familiarized me with the beliefs of the ancients, insofar as a person of one era can ever hope to live himself into the minds of a people who belonged to a different age.

That is a fairly formidable list, but I regret to say that the sum total of all these experiences was exactly nothing at all, as regards making me a convert. They merely produced a complete indifference and profound boredom. They made me wonder that people, supposedly created after God's image, could actually make their lives so hopelessly unhappy and so immensely complicated and often quite so repulsive in the name of something which was supposed to be their highest spiritual aspiration. Here and there (and very occasionally) I came across a man or woman who, in spite of being a convinced follower of some definite creed, had nevertheless managed to maintain a spirit of tolerance and good will toward his fellow men. Now and then I have also met a priest (most of these belonged to the Church of Rome) who was cheerful and kind and ready to make certain allowances for the weaknesses of his less fortunate neighbors, who perhaps did not share his own views. I also remember at least two missionaries who did not insult the Almighty by speaking in a contemptuous fashion of this utterly lovely planet which has so generously been bestowed upon us as our temporary place of abode and which is capable of so much beauty and joy that we could establish our paradise right here on this earth, if we only had the courage of our own convictions and seriously decided to do something about it.

That, I fear me, was rather a lengthy sentence but I hope that I have made myself entirely clear. I believe in a most complete form of liberty of thought for every man, woman, and child. Like my good master, Baruch de Spinoza, I have most conscientiously endeavored never to say or do anything that could deprive one of my fellow travelers along the path of life of the faith upon which he had based his own expectations of salvation. Indeed, to the best of my somewhat limited abilities within the realm of the spirit, I have given myself great trouble to strengthen these good people in those convictions which seemed best suited to their own spiritual needs. For I humbly confess that since it will never be given unto any of us mere mortals to attain more than a vague approximation of the ultimate Truth, I have no way of proving that the others are wrong and that I myself am right, or vice versa. But for myself I have long since come to the conclusion that none of the so-called revealed religions will ever give me the slightest satisfaction. I was therefore obliged to evolve some sort of workable creed out of my own inner consciousness. I am profoundly grateful to say that I have succeeded in doing this as far as my own needs are concerned. But I hasten to repeat (what I said earlier in this chapter) that I do not advise any other person to follow my example. For these things are so completely personal and they are so delicately balanced in the soul of every individual that others might perish miserably if they tried to live according to those same tenets which (until now—knock wood!) have enabled me to maintain a positive attitude toward all the problems of existence and which, after some pretty ghastly blows of fate (for I have had my share) still make it possible for me to keep on smiling and to say quite honestly, "In spite of everything, life is good."

Have I been able to do all this out and of and by myself? Of course not. I owe this blessing to a strangely assorted company of men who, in the truest sense of the word, have been my teachers and whose humble disciple I gratefully confess myself to be, now and evermore, amen. Do you want to know who they are? Very well, I will tell you. They are that small band of human benefactors whom I would like to group together as the Companionship of the Laughing Philosophers.

And now of course you would like to hear whom I count among that blessed fellowship of my private saints. That too I will gladly tell you, although you must be prepared for some quite unexpected visitors.

In order to qualify as a member in the great and glorious Companionship of the Laughing Philosophers, my candidates must come up to certain very definite standards of thought and behavior. First of all, they must be completely human in their attitude toward the human race. And they must not put the cart before the horse. They should not start out with a race of supermen endowed with all the virtues and perfections of angels and thereupon bewail the sad downfall of these erstwhile dwellers in paradise and hold them up to public scorn and contempt. On the contrary, they should wholeheartedly accept the unflattering truth about our very modest origin, when we were but little removed from the apes, and they should feel a profound admiration for a creature which, in spite of its lowly origin, its utter physical helplessness, and its many moral handicaps, has achieved as much as it has done in really a remarkably short space of time.

This latter attitude makes for a much greater degree of humility than the former and it is a constant incentive to do better and better and to feel that it is up to us ourselves to look after our own fate and not leave it conveniently to some outside force.

My Laughing Philosophers must also confess that before the Unsolvable Riddle of Existence, it behooves all of us to express our complete and everlasting ignorance. They must have the courage to say, "We do not know the final answer, but we are grateful for our ignorance. For if we had everything down, black on white, life would no longer be the glorious adventure it is today and we could no longer avail ourselves of the greatest gift the good Lord has bestowed upon us—our freedom of will."

They should, of course, be gentlemen in the true sense of the word and as such should be able without any reservation to subscribe to the oath of Hippocrates or to the solemn promise made by those young men who were about to be admitted to an early medieval order of knighthood.

I realize that there are a great many doctors who were never in the least affected by the admonitions of old Hippocrates, just as there were a great many knights who lived despicable lives and who broke every one of those commandments they had sworn to uphold and defend. That, however, does not in the least change the fact that those two documents (the oath of Hippocrates and the knightly vows of the thirteenth century) are in my estimation to be ranked much higher than the taboos and interdictions of the Old Testament, for the latter dealt with things no decent person would ever dream of doing anyway. Furthermore, I am firmly convinced that in each one of us there dwells that "still, small voice of conscience" upon which Socrates (one of the best beloved of my Laughing Philosophers) based his conceptions of the good life. And if from this the reader should draw the conclusion that I greatly prefer Socrates to Moses, he would have guessed right the first time. I have never been an admirer of either the tyrant or the dictator; and Moses in his personal aspirations and his public fulminations was much too much like Adolf Hitler or Benito Mussolini to be admitted to my private Pantheon of those who were true prophets.

This leads me to still another question which no man of this Western world has been able to escape these last two thousand years: "What think you of the Christ?"

Fortunately, I can give you a completely straightforward answer. I think everything of him. I unqualifiedly accept him as one of the greatest of my gay philosophers. But I have always experienced great difficulties in getting at him because his figure was completely obscured by the dark shadow of that Paul of Tarsus who in his Pharisaic self-righteousness and arrogance had undertaken to explain him to the rest of the world as he thought he ought to be explained. The simple, lovable carpenter of Nazareth, so beautifully and sublimely unconscious of the practical world around him, so bravely fighting his lonely battle against those forces of malice and evil and greed which turn our lovely planet into a perpetual vale of tears—yes, he is a teacher whom I would most happily follow unto the ends of the earth. But not if Paul the tentmaker has to be one of our companions. For that brash individual would forever be pushing his unwelcome self between us, and instead of letting me listen to the Master, he would volunteer to explain what the Master really intended to say (even before he had said it) until in despair I would either have pushed him aside (in which case he would have called me a dirty Nazi or something equally unpleasant) or I would have been obliged to bid these wanderers farewell and strike out for myself—as indeed, I have been obliged to do.

That (as I am seriously convinced) is exactly what Paul has done to millions of other people. Like myself they very likely would have become good Christians if only Paul had let them. Now I am obliged to meet Christ in a sort of clandestine and roundabout way. That, however, has in no way diminished the welcome I receive. I sometimes even fear that he regrets our separation as much as I. But what can he do? For his compassion is so great that he can even understand and forgive Paul. Has he ever really liked him? I don't know, but I doubt it. I doubt it very much.

Now if all that be true, why was I not contented? Why did I look for others and why wasn't I satisfied with Him alone? Because Jesus too was a very sociable person who liked the presence of his fellow men. And so, in that hidden recess of my soul, where I sometimes entertain my friends of the Laughing Brotherhood (those who say "yea" unto life), you may come across a strangely assorted collection of human beings. There are, I regret to say, no theologians present. They would, of course, be most welcome but they have always refused to cross my threshold. Perhaps that is just as well, for now the rest of us can have a much better time,

And Lord have mercy upon us! How the dominies can spoil a party!

And who are the others, who are this "rest"? Well, there are quite a number of philosophers present: Socrates (whom I have already mentioned) and Spinoza and the amiable Immanuel Kant. The still sprightly M. de Voltaire occasionally drops in, though warned that the moment he tries to show us how terribly clever he can be, he will be thrown out on his ear. And there are also several writers who may be counted among the steady guests: Montaigne, who will only come if we promise to provide him with a glass of his beloved Bordeaux, and Erasmus, who prefers the milder wines from the valley of the Moselle, and Thomas More (ale, if you please) and occasionally, when he is not too busy, old Dr. Rabelais will drop in, although we are apt to have a little trouble with him. He is still very much occupied with his beloved Abbey of Thélème. It is an interesting experiment but rather more suited to the tastes of his Gallic neighbors than to ours. My own Flemish antecedents safeguard me against ever being shocked (except by willful vulgarity), but some of our friends were brought up differently, and why make them uncomfortable if it is not absolutely necessary?

There are, of course, a great many musicians among the steady guests, for they preached the greatest gospel of gaiety of all times, the one that can be understood regardless of the printed or spoken word. Bach and Haydn and Mozart and most of their contemporaries are there. Beethoven occasionally drops in but we have to watch him rather closely, for his manners are apt to be a little—let us say—democratic. Once, however, he no longer feels the necessity of asserting himself or of proving that in spite of his drunken and disreputable father he is really as much of a man as any emperor, king, or mere plain archduke, he is really a very simple and very loyal friend.

Schumann and Schubert, too, will come quite often, and once in a while, at the special request of old Johannes Brahms, we invite the whole Strauss family, and those evenings are well worth remembering. Breughel once made a picture of such a gathering and it hangs in the place of honor, right over the mantelpiece. For those painters, too, who did not take themselves too seriously are always welcome. So indeed is everyone who will accept us for what we are and who shares our belief that life was meant to be gay, and that it is only our own ignorance, our own cowardice, and our unwillingness to make use of our God-given faculties which prevents it from being so.

I might add that we are often honored with a visit from some fiddler or other virtuoso. Indeed, every sort of artist has occasionally made his or her appearance. With one exception. We never had any opera singers. They are not deliberately kept out, but somehow they seem to fear that we might occasionally laugh at them and they would not like that at all.

And that, I think, concludes my little chapter on what I believe. It is really surprisingly simple, but why should it be complicated? I cannot for the life of me think of my presence on this earth as anything very important. At birth I was provided with a small quantity of that cosmic energy which is the substance out of which our universe is made. Some of those small quantities of energy were given the shape of plants while others were disguised as weeds. Some of them were used to give us the figure of a Thomas Jefferson or a Goethe or a Pasteur, while others but served as the physical containers for the destructive energies of a Napoleon or Genghis Khan or the contemptible foulness of a Goebbels. But since that is the way nature seems to have chosen to perform her miracles, it is not up to us to find fault with this arrangement but rather to see what we ourselves can make of that temporary loan from the vast reservoir of energy which is the beginning and end of all things, from Betelgeuse to the microbe who some day will destroy us.

Perhaps you will call this a philosophy of resignation closely bordering upon despair. But there I disagree, and most profoundly. I do not feel that I would get much further or be much happier if I tried to solve that which was apparently meant to be unsolvable for all time, and spent my days endeavoring to discover who or what started all this and who or what will again make an end to it. I know that it was started by some force outside of myself but, having humbly accepted that fact, I refuse to waste my energies on a futile quest (which will never lead me anywhere anyway). I prefer to concentrate my powers upon that which it is within my reach to do: to make this world with its tremendous, with its incredible potentialities for beauty and happiness—a place in which every man, woman, and child will be truly able to say, "We are grateful that we are alive, for life indeed is good!"

Today that sounds like mocking blasphemy. A hundred centuries hence, it will make sense. For by then man will have acquired the courage necessary to see himself as he really is—as a being equipped with a power of intellect which will eventually allow him to penetrate into every secret of nature until he will truly be the master of all he surveys, and endowed with such a complete freedom of will that he himself—and no one else—is the true master of his fate and therefore dependent for his ultimate happiness upon no one but

HIMSELF.

# REBECCA WEST

*The great respect in which Rebecca West, both as critic and novelist, is held is out of proportion to the number of her books and in direct proportion to their excellence. She is distinguished for her psychological insight, her constant play of wit, and the beautiful surfaces of her prose.*

*She was born on Christmas Day, 1892. Rebecca West is a pseudonym, her name having been originally Cicily Isabel Fairfield. Educated at George Watson's Ladies' College, Edinburgh, she joined the staff of the 'Freewoman' in 1911 and established her reputation at once as a witty and original critic. She has since contributed constantly to the leading English and American journals.*

*Her major publications: 'Henry James' (1916); 'The Return of the Soldier' (1918); 'The Judge' (1922); 'The Strange Necessity' (1928); 'Harriet Hume' (1929); 'St. Augustine' (1933); 'The Harsh Voice' (1935); 'The Thinking Reed' (1936).*

# *Rebecca West*

I HAVE no faith in the sense of comforting beliefs which persuade me that all my troubles are blessings in disguise. I do not believe that any facts exist, or, rather, are accessible to me, which give any assurance that my life has served an eternal purpose. I do not find this distressing. That is not because my life has been so happy that its superficial import strikes me as satisfactory. My childhood and my girlhood were overshadowed by the tragedies of my elders, and my twenties were a nightmare of overwork and harassment. Not till my marriage, and I married in my late thirties, did I have one human being close to me who ever thought of saving me fatigue or pain or responsibility. Now that I am at last able to take pleasure in both my family and my work, it happens that not only myself but all those whom I love may before long meet a violent death either in the course of an idiot war or at the hands of idiot Fascists. There have been many worse fates than mine, but I cannot think it ideal.

Nevertheless, I feel no overwhelming anxiety to find some creed to assure me that all has been for the best, which will tell me that I have only to follow a particular path to be consoled by eternal happiness. It may be that I should feel such anxiety if I were stricken by a painful and incurable disease, but as yet I have not felt it. I do not even find in myself any great curiosity as to whether my soul is immortal or not. If I received definite and convincing information either way I should certainly be very interested, though not, I think, either extremely depressed or elated; but I do not feel the lack of such information as a hardship.

The real interest of the universe seems to me not to lie in

these directions at all. The reason I feel no hunger for a creed that shall reveal to me the secret of the universe is that I do not see how the existence of such a creed is compatible with the condition of humanity. I cannot understand how our minds, which have been formed by response to the emergencies of a small corner of space and time, could possibly comprehend a revelation of the total universe even if it were granted to them. I can understand that we might be given a mystical intuition of the nature of the universe, and this would penetrate to the core of our being, which lies far beneath the level of our consciousness, and would determine our thoughts and actions—indeed, I believe that we must have received such an intuition, for otherwise we would not so often love life when by all logical criteria it is unlovable. But creeds claim to do much more than convey or support mystical intuitions. They pretend to explain the total universe in terms comprehensible to the human intellect, and that pretension seems to me bound to be invalid. I feel this as strongly about the non-Christian and anti-Christian creeds as about the Christian creeds, insofar as they make the statement, which seems to me the lie of lies, that seeks to cut down the growing tree of life before it has borne fruit, "All is now known."

I have, as I have said, no faith, in the sense of a store of comforting beliefs. But I have faith in a process, in a particular process that is part of the general process of life, though it is sometimes annulled by it. I find an ultimate value in the efforts of human beings to do more than merely exist, to choose and analyze their experiences and by the findings of that analysis help themselves to further experiences which are of a more pleasurable kind. I use the word pleasurable in its widest sense: to describe such experiences as come from good food and wine, exercise, the physical act of love-making, the practice of a beloved craft or art or science, a happy marriage, the care of children or the sick or

*Madame Yevonde, London*

REBECCA WEST

the old by those who enjoy it, the service of valid ideas or the administration of worthy institutions or the pursuit of agreeable sensations. *Trahit sua quemque voluptas.* By indulgence in these experiences life is made more pleasant from day to day. That is in itself of the first importance. That end would be worthwhile pursuing if no other benefit were obtained. But it also serves the purpose of furnishing each human soul with access to the avenue along which it can advance farthest toward the comprehension and mastery of life. Pleasure is not arbitrary; it is the sign by which the human organization shows that it is performing a function which it finds appropriate to its means and ends. I take it as a prime cause of the present confusion of society that it is too sickly and too doubtful frankly to use pleasure as a test of value.

There is, of course, the objection that man's tastes are so inherently vicious that if pleasure is taken as a standard he would exhaust his vital powers in drunkenness and sexual license. I do not believe this to be true of humanity as we know it in our civilization. It obviously is true in certain circumstances which prevent the development of alternative amusements. Convincing evidence of that is given in John Morris' anthropological study, *Living with Lepchas,* but the evidence speaks of a restriction of general appetite quite as remarkable as the indulgence of these particular appetites. I have observed human beings for a number of years in the United States and in all countries of Europe, except Russia, Poland, Rumania, and Turkey; and I do not find that dissipations of this sort are their special temptation. The mass of people who drink are found in the groups who, either by reason of extreme wealth or poverty, are cut off from the normal process of exploiting knowledge and capacities; and even of those groups they form an extremely small proportion. There is little evidence to show that sex is a greater danger than alcohol. It is doubtful whether Western men and women have any marked excess of sexual potency over and above what is required in a monogamous relationship. Certainly men and women require a certain amount of sexual intercourse, and in modern times they own to this need, and many insist on satisfying it in unsanctioned means if social and economic barriers stand between them and the sanctioned means; but there are few signs that either men or women want to indulge in sexual intercourse to an extent that is damaging either to themselves or society. Except where the peasantry are so poor that it has to count its daughters as livestock in order to survive, the number of women in any community who become prostitutes is small; and those that do rely for custom chiefly on travelers and men who are obliged to work far from home. There is about as much reason to suppose that mankind is likely to wreck itself by drunkenness and lechery as there is to suppose that it will extinguish itself by vegetarianism, teetotalism, and celibacy.

The fear that pleasure is an unreliable standard because the common man will identify pleasure with debauchery has two sources, neither of which is discreditable. First, there is the recollection of the difficulty found in more elementary stages of society to distract man from concentration on the simpler forms of animal gratification. This is strong in people who have been involved with a deprived proletariat, either as a despised member of that class or as one of the despising *bourgeoisie*. Secondly, there is the exaggerated consciousness of a real twofold difficulty in education. It is certainly not easy to convince young people that the simple and direct pleasures of "having a good time" will pale before the more complicated pleasures of adult life, which may even involve having quite a bad time. There is no way of giving a pinafored child a certain proof that ultimately it will like many kinds of food and drink far better than an ice-cream soda, or assuring a boy of sixteen that some day he may find working in a tropical hospital just as enjoyable as speeding in an automobile, or a girl of sixteen that some day she may find just as great happiness in looking after several children on small means as she does in dancing. It is also difficult to persuade young people to undergo the preliminary training necessary for them to enjoy adult pleasures, since this is often temporarily painful. The elementary stages of musical education are usually intensely boring, even to those who are best able to profit from it later. On both these sources of fear candor can shine with a helpful light. We need not be afraid that the drunkenness and promiscuity of the slums reveal the common trend of human life if we admit to ourselves that the greater decorum of the *bourgeoisie* is the result not of renunciation, which is indeed not a process we can count upon, but of command over more refined and satisfying means of self-indulgence. The educational difficulty is much graver. It can never be easily solved; if adults admitted to children that they lived for pleasure, of the value of which every child has an intuitive knowledge, instead of for some undefined value which is served by renunciation, children would put much more trust in the good faith of adults and accept their advice about the most useful preparation for life.

It is of paramount importance that these difficulties should be faced and that pleasure should be recognized as a reasonable standard, for certainly chaos establishes itself if we do not. The belief that all higher life is governed by the idea of renunciation poisons our moral life by engendering vanity and egotism. It is actually the case with most of us that we are creatures of limited potency, with hardly enough capacity to carry out the regular routine to fulfill the responsibilities to which we were born. Our problem is to increase our vigor and to respect and aid those among us who are in possession of exceptional vigor, but we are distracted from our attack on it by our pretense that we have already solved a problem of a much more spectacular kind. A man of mediocre gifts, whose task it is to keep stoked the furnace of a moderate-sized dwelling house, is not likely to do it better if he is under the delusion that he has just extinguished a colossal forest fire. It is also actually the case that if we take gratification as our ideal we thereby impose on ourselves a program of self-restraint; for if we claim that we are under the necessity of learning all that we can about reality, and that we learn most through pleasure, we must also admit that we are under the necessity of hearing what our fellow creatures learn about it and of working out a system by which we all curb our pleasures so that they do not interfere with those of others. If, however, we claim that it is by renunciation that we achieve wisdom, we have no logical reason for feeling any disapproval of conditions that thrust pain and deprivation on others. It is easy thereafter to fall into the depths of humbugging greed and dishonesty, especially in regard to the maintenance of inequitable economic situations. The premises of this philosophy make it possible to gratify all the baser impulses under a cloak of propriety by saying: "I am a rich man, but I have this and that individual sorrow which keeps me a saved and spiritual man. It is true that the source and extent of my wealth are such that others have to go poor in order that I should have it, but this is a good thing, as it provides them with the barrier between them and their desires which is necessary for salvation."

This attitude inevitably engenders hatred. Where the inequality of economic conditions is too marked, where a faulty system holds a number of workers on the subsistence line, it becomes necessary for the rich to pretend that the poor are a separate and wicked race, who would certainly be damned if they were not given this opportunity for purification through misery. This is a point of view which was openly expressed in all Western literature during the eighteenth and nineteenth centuries; and though that class at which it is now fashionable to sneer, the intellectuals, have jeered at this hypocrisy till it rarely dares show its face in print, it is repeatedly expressed in the conversation and oratory of the possessing classes.

But indeed we need no further argument in favor of taking pleasure as a standard when we consider the only alternative that faces us. If we do not live for pleasure we will soon find ourselves living for pain. If we do not regard as sacred our own joys and the joys of others, we open the door and let into life the ugliest attribute of the human race, which is cruelty. I believe this vice to be as much of a shame and a doom to humanity as the original sin of the theologians; and I believe it to be the root of all other vices. I do not believe people are cruel because they are greedy; I am sure they invent greed as a pretext for cruelty. I am as sure that the sexual caprice which makes people desert still loving mates or thrust their attentions on those who are offended by them has not its origin in the pure sexual instinct, but is a use made of it by cruelty, seeking an instrument. I take it that cruelty is an early error of the mind, which becomes a confirmed habit before reason can disperse it. Hatred necessarily precedes love in human experience. After the tideless peace of prenatal existence the child is born into a world of uncomfortable physical experiences and terrifying uncomprehended controls. It must feel that in order to preserve itself it must lay about it, it must beat with its hands, and plot evil against the aggressors. Thus a habit is initiated; thus a fantasy is engendered. It is imagined that it is right to inflict pain, which is given the most intricate and noxious ramifications by early experience. When one inflicts pain on the surrounding world one is punished, one is treated as guilty. This does not rob pain of its majesty; one suffers a greater pain than one inflicted, for punishment is pain, and punishment is acclaimed as good and holy. Is it not a way of salvation to be punished?

This last question the mind, being no fool, transforms quickly into another. If it did not do so, the human race would quickly become extinct, rushing forward to impale itself on expiatory tortures. Out of the instinct for self-preservation, and logically enough, it asks, "If it is a good and holy thing to be punished, must it not also be a good and holy thing to punish?" It answers that it is; and our earth becomes the hell it is. Thus we human beings plant in ourselves the perennial blossom of cruelty: the conviction that if we hurt other people we are doing good to ourselves and to life in general. It determines the course of all history, the forms of our institutions, the pattern of our lives; and the effect of it in all these spheres is death. It cannot have any other result, since pain is a warning that something is being done to the organism which is inimical to its well-being.

To destroy this cancer of our spirit is our real problem. Since its destruction means the correction of the whole structure of life down to the foundations that were laid when it first became self-conscious, it is a problem which is almost certainly beyond our power ever to solve completely. When we put our hands to this problem we must abandon all hope of success, certainly in our time, possibly in eternity. This is, however, of no importance. Any success achieved against cruelty is in itself absolute. I mean by this that it gives us and those from whom the cruel act has been averted an intense pleasure which could not be increased by a quantitative increase of the success. To pretend that those of us who hate cruelty are martyrs pledged to fighting a hopeless battle is humbug. We are liable to feel great anger and distress and to be put in prison and physically injured by cruel people. But actually we have a great deal more pleasure in our lives than those who pretend that the only problem before us is to curb an imaginary tendency toward intemperance and excessive copulation. Perhaps because they are perpetually confronted with evidence disproving their case, since the mass of human beings are sober and continent and nevertheless life is horrible, they are hagridden by irritability and intolerance.

I was made aware of the part cruelty plays in the world during my childhood, because I grew up in the shadow of the Dreyfus case. I am of pure Aryan descent. Though naturally I now feel a certain shame in confessing this, I must mention it here to make it quite clear that the Dreyfus case was discussed in my home circle with complete detachment. My father had been an army officer, and would have been a great criminal lawyer had he chosen another career, and he could judge both the military and legal aspects of the trial; and my mother was a woman of brilliant understanding and considerable experience of Continental life. They had talked over the case from the beginning, and later they had a special insight into it when the great journalist, G. W. Steevens, with whose family mine was very friendly, was sent to Rennes to report the trial. The earlier stages of the trial took place when I was too young to follow it; but I suppose I absorbed it through the pores, and I certainly remembered its later stages, culminating in the return from Rennes and the rehabilitation of Dreyfus. Therefore I learned early that a people, saddened by defeat and thirsting for a miraculous restorative draft, fancied that it could administer such to itself by the simple process of punishing a man for an offense of which they could not possibly believe him guilty: that is to say, the severest form of punishment conceivable, punishment on a pretext which the victim knows to be unjust.

I confirmed the existence of this human tendency in my youth when I examined certain laws laid down by society for the regulation of the position of the sexes. I realized that the subjection of women serves no purpose whatsoever except to gratify the desire for cruelty both in women and in men. This is obvious in connection with one common phenomenon springing from the sexual instinct. Exceptional circumstances make certain young women unable to find mates in the normal way among men of nearly their own age; they can fall in love only with older men. If these older men have enough vitality to attract these other women they are likely to have already formed matrimonial ties; so the obvious course is for an illicit relationship to follow. Such women are obviously far from fortunate. They cannot hope to have as easy or pleasant lives as ordinary women. But society, instead of letting them get on with their imperfect lives as they can, sets about visiting them with every petty annoyance that it can think of, as if they had found out some way of living that is enormously enjoyable and likely to be followed by all women if they are not discouraged by the spectacle of persecution; the reason for this odd behavior is plain when it is observed that an intoxication, a perversion of pleasure similar to that given by drugs or drink, fills and inflames all the people who take part in these attempts at annoyance. The majority has, in fact, found a minority which it is safe to hurt. Such women are bound to form only a small proportion of the population; the inducements to normal sexual behavior, the possession of a young husband and the first claim on his affections and economic resources, are likely to overcome all but the strongest compulsions. Therefore the majority of women who are not as these, and the entire male sex, have here a safe object for their aggressive instincts.

Much incidental suffering follows; but what is even more important is that the public mind has been sidetracked from working out a system of morality by which the genetic interests of the human races are subserved. If you say to a man and woman today, "You must exercise self-control for the sake of your children," they will instantly see a picture of themselves refraining from having sexual intercourse with some attractive members of the opposite sex, who would probably never look at them in any circumstances; and naturally you will find it hard to gain their sympathy or even their attention while you explain that what you mean is that the time has now come for adults to curb their appetites and make the provision of the goods necessary for the development of sound children a first charge on the economic resources of society, thus buying milk and peace before luxuries and adventure.

But it is important not to make the mistake of supposing that you can make people exchange a sexual morality that serves the interest of cruelty for one that serves the interest of love without imposing real and hideous suffering on them. I reiterate that cruelty is a part of our structure, that naturally we function by it. The proof lies in consideration of another aspect of the feminist movement. All over the world men put women to great inconvenience by pretending that women are as inferior to them in mind and character and social value as they are in muscular strength. I myself used to think this to be a caprice springing from vanity, which could be as easily corrected as a girl's belief that she is not only very beautiful but the most beautiful girl in the world, without any catastrophic results. I am now sure that I was quite wrong.

In the economic depression that befell Europe and America after 1929, many men fell into unemployment and were swept with their wives and families to the brink of starvation; but some men who lost their employment had wives who, by reason of some special talents or aptitude for industries unaffected by the depression, were able to earn wages and support themselves and their husband and children. In any sane world the men in the second group would have been happier than the men in the first. They would realize, sometimes very painfully, that society is wise in at least one of its conventions and that it saves a lot of trouble as a general rule if men go out to work and women stay at home; but they would be glad that a temporary suspension of the general rule had saved themselves and those whom they loved from hardship, and proud that their wives possessed the talent which made this possible. But in fact this was not so. The men of the first group, who had suffered and seen those whom they loved suffer, were damaged far less by their experiences than the men in the second. Many of them were spoiled by them, it would seem forever. Some fell into infantilism and wanted to remain in a permanent state of dependence; and others formed a deep feeling of resentment against their wives which was sometimes so intense that it led to divorce.

This seems to mean that a large number of men need to believe that the reason that wives do not go out to earn a living is that they cannot. Yet it cannot mean that. A man might sincerely believe that his wife or any woman cannot scale the heights of achievement which have been reached by man: he may doubt that a female Mozart or Shakespeare can exist. But he really cannot sincerely believe that women, who keep the race alive by their competent performance of the tricky jobs of tending babies and the sick, and who undertake a large part of its education, are incapable of reaching the comparatively low standard of capacity demanded by the capitalist system from the mass of its employees. What he needs is to pretend that they could not, and to pretend that even if there were certain women who could, the particular women in his family could not.

This allegation of inferiority, when it is unfounded, amounts to the same sort of cruelty as keeping an animal in a cage too small for it; and it is cruel to the same degree as anti-Semitism, since the victims know themselves undeserving of such pain. But, like anti-Semitism, it fortifies the soul of those who inflict it, so that a man who was deprived of this fortification just at the moment when the economic system had defeated him, really suffered a serious injury of the soul. The converse can be seen in a society where men have played as virile a part as anywhere in the world.

The Christian men in the East of Europe, who were conquered by the Turks and, largely by the connivance of the Western powers, left in their power for five hundred years, were during all that time starved and misgoverned and despised. They preserved their culture and their courage untainted so that they never let die the knowledge and the hope of freedom, and in the Balkan Wars took back their land and re-established their civilization as if there were no death, as if life was an indestructible condition which nothing could threaten. Living among them, one perceives they are sustained by a certain kind of primitive Christianity, by music, by the subjection of women. There is no reason why the Balkan man should be angry with the Balkan woman—there is no competition between the sexes; she is loving and thrifty, her embroideries put her among the world's great artists. Yet in theory she is regarded as if she were an idiot, unhelpful, a beast that has to be fought back lest it turn dangerous; and in practice she is often treated so. She suffers immensely, but it is plain the suffering has not been wasted. It is so much red blood in the veins of her menfolk.

It may be argued that if a need to inflict cruelty is so inherent in our nature, and its satisfaction such a stimulus to performance, there can be nothing more useless and dangerous than to interfere with it. That is exactly the issue, it seems to me, on which we have to part company with the obvious and convenient if we are to be morally respectable. It is not tolerable that humanity should continue to pay such a price for well-being. Nor is it a simple matter of continuance, for an appetite grows by what it feeds on, and there is no knowing to what hell our developed love of cruelty may lead us before the earth cools and we come to an end.

It is not a question of submitting to the subjection of women, and taking that as so much coin to be painfully put down. It might perfectly well happen that some scientific discovery and some change in the environment might put women into a position of power over men, and that women might find it immensely stimulating to develop a theory, and enforce it in practice, that men were happiest if they ran about on all fours with their posteriors painted like mandrils and were never allowed to learn to read. There is no end to the cantrips we may indulge in if we do not eradicate this cruelty from our nature, or to the deterioration of our history that may result; for if cruelty is a stimulus to action, it also determines the quality of our actions.

There are certain general ideas which seem to me to be imposed on us by the recognition of this cruelty. One is the necessity for freedom of speech and the arts. We have to scrutinize all the advances of society to judge whether they are cruel or frustrate cruelty, and for that purpose we must hear the evidence of all persons affected by their operation and of all persons qualified by experience or learning or speculative gifts to form an interesting opinion on what those operations might be. It is therefore necessary that all classes of men should be given the fullest opportunity to express themselves without constraint, not out of admiration for an abstraction, but as a practical measure toward human survival. It is also necessary that the artist, of whatsoever kind, should be free to anatomize the spirit, so that we can comprehend the battlefield that is this life, and which are the troops of light and which of darkness, and what light may be, and what darkness. For the essence of our human plight is confusion. Those who love cruelty dress themselves up as its enemies, and those who hate it appear to be, and sometimes are, its servants.

This deception is crystallized in its most pictorial, in its most horribly important form, by the history of Christianity.

The spectacle of the rise of Fascism, and some contact with the Eastern Church, which is many centuries nearer primitive Christianity than the Western Church, have made it clear to me that the life of Christ should have been an incomparable blessing to man and a revelation of the way he must follow if he is not to be a beast, and a failure at that. Christ was an incarnate denunciation of cruelty. He was sinless, he was full of love, he was ingenious in devising prescriptions of mercy; he was what the world needed, he could have taught us how to make life a perpetual pleasure. Society could find nothing better to do with him than kill him. Here was a man who could have saved his life if he had dissimulated his virtue. He unveiled it, knowing that he made himself a target for man's arrows. Just as a great artist finds the perfect myth to symbolize the truth he has discovered, that shall sum it up in a form that is acceptable by the human faculty of attention, so his crucifixion demonstrated exactly what the assault of cruelty on the innocent means; and the subsequent services devised by the early Church commemorated the beauty of the virtue that was slain and the beastliness shown by the slayer, and reiterated the warning that this was the kind of crime man was inherently likely to commit unless he watched himself. There could be no more proper medicine for the human disease.

But the Church has poured as much of the draft as possible down the drain by its attempts to develop a doctrine to account for the crucifixion of Christ as an atonement for the sins of man instead of a demonstration of them. These attempts were founded on the primitive idea of the magical value of sacrifice for propitiating the powers that be, and they were initiated by St. Paul, out of the legalistic quality of his mind. They were carried further by the Fathers of the Church, and given lasting authority by St. Augustine, the first theologian to be dominated by St. Paul. He was one of the greatest of geniuses and a most lovable character, but he was also a violent man, in love with violence and unrepelled by cruelty. He therefore found great pleasure in imagining a gross drama in which the devil held humanity in his power by reason of its sins and would have condemned it to death wholesale had he not killed Christ, after which he could not claim the blood of humanity since in the divine life of Christ he had been paid so much more than it owed him. Since God is omnipotent, He is of course responsible for this whole arrangement, and Augustine admits that He could have arranged for the redemption of man by other means, and that He chose this one only because it proved His love for humanity. In fact, a crime which should have shamed humanity into virtue is shown to be the contrivance of the highest good, and the criminals to have served the most mystical and exalted of ends. The doctrine involves so many absurdities that no church, not even the Roman Catholic Church, has ever formulated it even to its own satisfaction. But vaguely as it is held, it nevertheless has poisoned the Western mind with the suggestion implied in the word atonement. Cruelty has made the forces of its chief enemy work in its service.

It is the intellect which performs this perversion, though we are most familiar with its effects in the emotional sphere, with the disagreeable substitution of exaltation for the shame and pity we should feel at the sufferings of Christ on the cross which is indulged in by all the Western churches. But we see it also directly inscribed on life by conduct, notably in connection with sex and politics. The desire of men and women to be cruel to the people who commit themselves to their mercies in a sexual relationship is gratified by the existence of at least as many men and women who find it possible and indeed preferable to love those who treat them ill; and these last are as much responsible for the evil situations in which they are involved as those who initiate them. They complain of cruelty, the whole of literature echoes with their sighs; but they present themselves in such numbers and so stoutly endure the unendurable that the balance of sexual life, save where it is generously subsidized by nonsexual elements, is on the side of suffering.

The history of people shows a not less discreditable balance sheet. Again and again civilization cancels its own advance; so that it is more often than not a half-forgotten idea instead of a developing theme. This is the consequence of a pervasive weakness in the liberal forces that oppose cruel races or systems of government. Their policy is unworthy of their intellectual level, they envelop themselves in organizations which lead to dissension and betrayal, and above all they do not use the full energy that must be at the disposal of such a quantity of persons of such quality. The curious failure of European liberals to stiffen their opposition to militarist tyranny after the Great War of 1914, though that very soon, certainly by 1925, showed itself to have been an indecisive campaign, is typical of a score of passages in the Christian era; such as the frivolity with which the Christian European powers refused to unite against the invading Turks when they came out of Asia.

In the sexual and political spheres alike these defeats are due to the refusal to recognize pleasure as the supreme value in human life. This refusal leaves man to indulge in some of his characteristically false logic. His mind, which is quite inadequate for the purpose of mastering his environment and therefore always oversimplifies, sees the universe in antitheses, in dichotomies. He says, foolishly enough, for one cannot cut into clean halves two substances that pass into each other by insensible gradation, that there is light and darkness, life and death, pleasure and pain. He feels a need to identify these antitheses one with another, and since he is not allowed to make the obvious identification between pleasure and life and light, which would be rough indeed but sound enough save for the most crude and diseased character, he comes to the conclusion that the universe is a queerer place than he thought it, and he agrees with the cruel that life and light are pain. But there is that in all the more decent sorts of human beings which warns them that it is a filthy thing to inflict pain, and therefore all that are most likely to give themselves that warning and take it are likely to put themselves in the position of those on whom pain is inflicted; to be a beaten wife, a cheated husband, is better than being a bullying husband, an idle and spendthrift wife; to be put into a concentration camp is better than to put others into it. This must inevitably happen unless the emphasis is transferred to pleasure. Then only can a good man feel himself at ease in happiness with an unmalignant partner, and in victory over a bad man; then only will the human species have a chance to practice some other art than suicide, and creation oust nothingness.

To live by this philosophy is more difficult than following the old. Pain is always at hand in some form or other, but pleasure is harder to find; and these antitheses are protean and treacherous, always pretending to be one another. Birth control, for example, is a means of pleasure for women in certain circumstances: it enables them not to have more children than they can feed and clothe and adequately love. In other circumstances it can be the means of preventing them from knowing pleasure: it can enable a masculinist society to deny women the right to have any children at all, and keep them as starved and sterile producers and consumers of worthless goods in large towns, and in this second form it affects to make the same offer of freedom as the first, though in fact it enjoins slavery. But more dangerous than the protean nature of environment is the protean nature of our own souls, that constantly avails itself of these changes to pursue its own passion under cover.

It is because of the ineradicable persistence of cruelty in the human species, which may be incorrigible, that I should never be saddened to be warned of its passing. I can imagine no better news than to hear that there had emerged from the South American forest or the Australian desert specimens of a new species which would, by reason of some new organ or adaptation of an organ, be able to dominate man as man has dominated the other animals. They might, particularly if their reproductive systems were differently planned, be less morbid. Our lives would seem more tolerable and more honorable if we could know ourselves a transitional form, superseding what was worse and being superseded by what was better. Not that I feel our lives to be entirely intolerable and dishonorable. The living philosophy which really sustains us, which is our basic nourishment, more than any finding of the mind, is simply the sensation of life, exquisite when it is not painful.

# LIVING PHILOSOPHIES REVISED: BRIEF STATEMENTS BY THE CONTRIBUTORS TO THE ORIGINAL "LIVING PHILOSOPHIES," 1931.

# *James Truslow Adams*

When asked to say whether I had changed my opinions from those expressed in the volume of *Living Philosophies* in 1931, I naturally read over what I had then written, and which I had not looked at for seven years. I find that I then stressed what seemed to me to be the sheer necessity for our having some more or less generally accepted ethical code if human society was to function. We had, I said, to be able to count on all those with whom we came into business or social relations conforming more or less generally to a certain common ethical standard. I admitted that such codes and standards changed gradually over long periods of time to meet changed conditions, but that there was great danger, in periods of sudden alterations, of bringing about social breakdown if an ethical code were scrapped before another generally accepted one could be substituted in its place. A large element of tradition was essential in a code because individuals could not build up entirely *de novo* a new one to which they would instinctively react in all the problems of complex life; and that if each individual were to try to do so, and to replace the accepted "I ought" in a society by his wholly unpredictable "I want," we could have no confidence in each other or in society as a whole.

As I review the history of the past seven years since I made those statements, I am more than ever convinced that they are true. Today the world is gripped by fear, fear of war, of economic collapse. Greatest of all, underlying all other fears, is the fear that we can no longer trust individuals or nations to act according to the ethical code on which the whole of our civilization had been built. In the economic world we have seen such a complete undermining of contractual obligations that we have lost faith in contracts, and do not dare to make any long-time move in business or investment. In the political world we have seen that the most binding pledges given can no longer be relied upon. In the world of international relations the most solemn treaties drawn up by great nations, our own included, are not worth the paper they are written on when a nation decides to break them for convenience or profit.

We have had great economic depressions before but never in recent centuries such a complete abandonment of our traditional ethical code. It seems obvious to me that if we can no longer trust the plighted word or good faith of others, civilization must descend into anarchy. The armament race with the threat of world suicide in another war is simply the most striking forerunner of this impending anarchy, and is largely due to the fact that we can no longer believe the written promise of any nation. But the same breakdown is to be noted in all other fields. If a trade-union cannot believe in a corporation nor a corporation in a trade-union, the economic struggle descends into war. In business, if we cannot trust in contracts with individuals, corporations or governments, business simply will collapse with resultant social and political anarchy.

I said in my first article that it is impossible to carry on even social life with individuals whose conduct is utterly unpredictable from moment to moment, and who have no ethical code or standard of values which we may come to rely upon. What has happened is that the world has suddenly run into the danger which I predicted of throwing over an accepted code without having developed anything in its place which can be counted upon and form the basis of mutual confidence between individuals or nations. As I look over the present world condition it seems to me more essential than ever that we somehow re-establish our ethical code if we are to avoid complete chaos and collapse. In fact, the necessity for doing so is no longer a religious or ethical question, but one of the life or death of civilization. I have changed my opinion on many things in the past seven years, but in reading over what I wrote for *Living Philosophies*, as to my attitude toward ethics and life, I see no reason to change it at all. I would write it again today, except that the course of the world has provided me with many examples and allusions which I might include. Until we can—every one of us, whatever our position or job—do a little more thinking about our duties and less of our "rights," until we get in the way of saying more often again "I ought" instead of "I want," until we can restore some of the old-fashioned virtues like honesty and good faith—in a word, restore some of the discarded ethical code of the past—I see no chance for real happiness or satisfaction in life for anybody.

# *John Dewey*

My contribution to the first series of essays in *Living Philosophies* put forward the idea of faith in the possibilities of experience as the heart of my own philosophy. In the course of that contribution I said, "Individuals will always be the center and the consummation of experience, but what the individual actually *is* in his life experience depends upon the nature and movement of associated life." I have not changed my faith in experience nor my belief that individuality is its center and consummation. But there has been a change in emphasis. I should now wish to emphasize more than I formerly did that individuals are the finally decisive factors of the nature and movement of associated life.

The cause of this shift of emphasis is the events of the intervening years. The rise of dictatorships and totalitarian states and the decline of democracy have been accompanied with loud proclamation of the idea that only the state, the political organization of society, can give security to individuals. In return for the security thus obtained, it is asserted even more loudly (and with much greater practical effect) that individuals owe everything to the state.

This fundamental challenge compels all who believe in liberty and democracy to rethink the whole question of the relation of individual choice, belief, and action to institutions, to reflect on the kind of social changes that will make individuals in actuality the centers and the possessors of worth-while experience. In rethinking this issue in the light of the rise of totalitarian states, I am led to emphasize the idea that only the voluntary initiative and voluntary cooperation of individuals can produce social institutions that will protect the liberties necessary for achieving development of genuine individuality.

This change of emphasis does not in any way minimize the belief that the ability of individuals to develop genuine individuality is intimately connected with the social conditions under which they associate with one another. But it attaches fundamental importance to the activities of individuals in determining the social conditions under which they live. It has been shown in the last few years that democratic *institutions* are no guarantee for the existence of democratic individuals. The alternative is that individuals who prize their own liberties and who prize the liberties of other individuals, individuals who are democratic in thought and action, are the sole final warrant for the existence and endurance of democratic institutions.

The belief that the voluntary activities of individuals in voluntary association with one another is the only basis of democratic institutions does not mean a return to the older philosophy of individualism. That philosophy thought of the individual after the analogy of older physical science. He was taken to be a center without a field. His relations to other individuals were as mechanical and external as those of Newtonian atoms to one another. Liberty was supposed to be automatically acquired by abolition of restraints and constraints; all the individual needed was to be let alone.

The negative and empty character of this individualism had consequences which produced a reaction toward an equally arbitrary and one-sided collectivism. This reaction is identical with the rise of the new form of political despotism. The decline of democracy and the rise of authoritarian states which claim they can do for individuals what the latter cannot by any possibility do for themselves are the two sides of one and the same indivisible picture.

Political collectivism is now marked in all highly industrialized countries, even when it does not reach the extreme of the totalitarian state. It is the social consequence of the development of private capitalistic collectivism in industry and finance. For this reason those who look backward to restoration of the latter system are doomed to fight a losing battle. For the tendency toward state socialism and state capitalism is the product of the economic collectivism of concentrated capital and labor that was produced by mass production and mass distribution. The inherent identity of the two forms of collectivism is disguised by the present angry and clamorous controversy waged between representatives of private and public collectivism, both claiming to speak, moreover, in the interest of the individual, one for his initiative, the other for his security.

The strict reciprocity that exists between the two collectivisms is also covered from view because they are promoted in the respective interests of different social groups. Roughly speaking, the "haves" stand for private collectivism and the "have nots" for state collectivism. The bitter struggle waged between them in the political arena conceals from recognition the fact that both favor some sort of collectivism and represent complementary aspects of the same total picture.

Between the struggles of the two parties, both purporting to serve the cause of ultimate individual freedom, the individual has in fact little show and little opportunity. Bewildered and temporarily lost anyway, the din of the contending parties increases his bewilderment. Everything is so big that he wants to ally himself with bigness, and he is told that he must make his choice between big industry and finance and the big national political state. For a long time, what political agencies did and did not do in legislation and in the courts favored the growth of private capitalistic collectivism. By way of equalizing conditions, I do not doubt that for some time to come political activity will move in the direction of support of underprivileged groups who have been oppressed and made insecure by the growth of concentrated industry and finance. The imminent danger, as events of recent years demonstrate, is that political activity will attempt to retrieve the balance by moving in the direction of state socialism.

Indeed, many persons will ask how it is possible for political action to restore the balance except by direct control over and even ownership of big industrial and financial enterprises. The answer in general is that political activity can, first and foremost, engage in aggressive maintenance of the civil liberties of free speech, free publication and intercommunication, and free assemblage. In the second place, the government can do much to encourage and promote in a positive way the growth of a great variety of voluntary co-operative undertakings.

This promotion involves abolition or drastic modification of a good many institutions that now have political support, since they stand in the way of effective voluntary association for social ends. There are tariffs and other monopoly-furthering devices that keep back individual initiative and voluntary co-operation. There is our system of land tenure and taxation that puts a premium on the holding of land—including all natural resources—for the sake of private profit in a way that effectively prevents individuals from access to the instruments of individual freedom. There is the political protection given to return on long-term capital investments which are not now accompanied by any productive work, and which are, therefore, a direct tax levied on the productive work of others: an almost incalculable restriction, in its total effect, upon individual freedom.

The intrinsic likeness of political and private collectivism is shown in the fact that the government has had recourse to promotion of a regime of scarcity instead of increased productivity. It is evident on its face that enforced restriction of productivity, whether enforced in the name of private profit or of public relief, can have only a disastrous effect, directly and indirectly, upon individual freedom. But given existing conditions, it is the sole alternative to governmental activity that would abolish such limitations upon voluntary action as have been mentioned, a list that would easily be made more specific and more extensive.

Moreover, the principle of confining political action to policies that provide the conditions for promoting the voluntary association of free individuals does not limit governmental action to negative measures. There are, for example, such political activities as are now represented by provision of public highways, public schools, protection from fire, etc., etc., supported by taxation. This type of activity can doubtless be extended in a way which will release individual liberties instead of restricting them. The principle laid down does not deter political activity from engaging in constructive measures. But it does lay down a criterion by which every political proposal shall be judged: Does it tend definitely in the direction of increase of voluntary, free choice and activity on the part of individuals?

The danger at present, as I have already said, is that in order to get away from the evils of private economic collectivism we shall plunge into political economic collectivism. The danger is so great that the course that has been suggested will be regarded as an unrealistic voice crying in the wilderness. It would be unrealistic to make light of the present drive in the direction of state socialism. But it is even more unrealistic to overlook the dangers involved in taking the latter course. For the events of recent years have demonstrated that state capitalism leads toward the totalitarian state whether of the Russian or the Fascist variety.

We now have demonstrations of the consequences of two social movements. Earlier events proved that private economic collectivism produced social anarchy, mitigated by the control exercised by an oligarchic group. Recent events have shown that state socialism or public collectivism leads to suppression of everything that individuality stands for. It is not too late for us in this country to learn the lessons taught by these two great historic movements. The way is open for a movement which will provide the fullest opportunity for co-operative voluntary endeavor. In this movement political activity will have a part, but a subordinate one. It will be confined to providing the conditions, both negative and positive, that favor the voluntary activity of individuals.

There is, however, a socialism which is not state socialism. It may be called functional socialism. Its nature may be illustrated by the movement for socialization of medicine. I think this socialization is bound to come anyway. But it may come about in two very different ways. It may come into existence as a state measure, under political control; or it may come about as the result of the efforts of the medical profession made aware of its social function and its responsibilities. I cannot develop the significance of the illustration. But as an illustration, its significance applies to all occupational groups; that is, to all groups that are engaged in any form of socially useful, productive, activity.

The technocrats of recent memory had a glimpse of the potentialities inherent in self-directed activities of autonomous groups performing necessary social functions. But they ruined their vision when they fell into the pit dug by Wells and Shaw, that of rule from above by an elite of experts—although according to technocracy engineers were to be the samurai. The N.I.R.A. had a glimpse of self-governing industrial groups. But, quite apart from its conflict with the existing legal system, the plan loaded the dice in favor of the existing system of control of industry—with a few sops thrown in to "labor." At best it could not have worked out in the direction of freely functioning occupational groups. The Marxists professed the idea, but they held it as an ultimate goal to be realized through seizure of political power by a single class, the proletariat. The withering away of the state which was supposed to take place is not in evidence. On the contrary, seizure of political power as the means to the ultimate end of free individuals organized in functional occupational groups has led to the production of one more autocratic political state.

The dialectic that was supposed to work in solving the contradiction between increase of political power and its abolition is conspicuous by its absence—and inherently so. The Fascists also proclaim the idea of a corporate state. But again there is reliance upon uncontrolled and irresponsible political power. Instead of a corporate society of functional groups there is complete suppression of every formal voluntary association of individuals.

Before concluding that in America adoption of the method of voluntary effort in voluntary associations of individuals with one another is hopeless, one should observe the course of history. For if history teaches anything it is that judgments regarding the future have been predicated upon the basis of the tendencies that are most conspicuous at the time, while in fact the great social changes which have produced new social institutions have been the cumulative effect of flank movements that were not obvious at the time of their origin.

During the height of expanding competitive industrialism, for example, it was freely predicted that its effect would be a future society of free individuals and of free nations so interdependent that lasting peace would be achieved—*vide* Herbert Spencer. Now that the actual result has been the opposite, it is prophesied on the basis of the tendencies that are now most prominent that increased control of industrial activity by the state will usher in an era of abundance and security. Nevertheless those who can escape the hypnotic influence exercised by the immediate contemporary scene are aware that movements going on in the interstices of the existing order are those which will in fact shape the future. As a friend of mine puts it, the last thing the lord of the feudal castle would have imagined was that the future of society was with the forces that were represented by the humble trader who set up his post under the walls of his castle.

I am not optimistic enough to believe that voluntary associations of individuals, which are even now building up within the cracks of a crumbling social order, will speedily reverse the tendency toward political collectivism. But I am confident that the ultimate way out of the present social dead end lies with the movement these associations are initiating. Individuals who have not lost faith in themselves and in other individuals will increasingly ally themselves with these groups. Sooner or later they will construct the way out of present confusion and conflict. The sooner it is done the shorter will be the time of chaos and catastrophe.

# *Theodore Dreiser*

SUBSTANTIALLY, my feeling about life amounts to just what it did when I first tried to express it for this series. And so this essay will be more of the same, only, apropos of mechanism, I will try to meet some of the arguments which have been suggested to me.

It seems to me in the first place that although many find something intrinsically displeasing in the very idea of a mechanical universe, there is nothing unesthetic about it. The ugliness of a machine in a special sense is apparent only because of a limited idea of a machine. A man who is repelled by the concept of machinery is not considering universal machinery but something like a factory—with goods which are known going in one end and coming out the other, reformed. Yet it should be obvious that nothing like the end or the beginning or the whole utility of the universal machine is known. All we think we know is some process, however small, but definitely a mechanical process, and of this we are a part. There is nothing unesthetic to me in this idea, nothing degrading to man, nothing to besmirch or belittle the grandeur and mystery of life which is the direct evidence of sense.

Invert the analogy of the machine which comes from science and think of the special form as derived from the general form, and this cloak of pettiness falls off mechanism. In any case, the word "machine" implies a misunderstanding of it.

Thus a flower is as much a mechanism as a sewing machine; a rainbow as a dynamo; the mechanical processes in all are easily traced or diagrammed. Given elements and moisture, heat and light, and the chemisms that can function in this environment do function. Remove light, or heat—establish what we look on as cold or dark—and nothing that our limited senses can register appears; though that there are many things registering themselves *on one another* beyond our limited sensory reactions, we know.

But law! It governs everything from the speed of light and the spaces between island universes, to the floating of the minutest mote of dust in any space—the accurate physical and chemical laws accompanying these same being as mathematically deducible as those governing the floating of a battleship in water or an airplane in air (the limits of experimental science ever broadening). More, the chemical and physical accuracy and finish that go into the designing, coloring, and functioning of a beetle's wing, a fly's eye, a spider's web, a stalk of grass or a bird's feather, involve what we have come to look on as mind or science or knowledge as those are expressed in invention, designing, and constructing here. So that what one sees everywhere in nature or space suggests endlessly more of genius than man has ever achieved or is likely to.

And beauty! Involved in all things! Beauty of design, beauty of color, beauty of motion, beauty of sound, and beauty of finish, as recognized by the five senses—though how, in ourselves, we come by this sense of or reaction to "beauty" in ourselves, we cannot know, since we are plainly mechanisms designed to respond in the way that we do.

Which brings us back to the problem of mind or individuality, or individual thinking, since none of these things to which we respond are in use other than as processes, designs, compulsions, necessities, reactions, which cause in us the illusion of what we call mind, individuality, individual thinking. But plainly these are illusions only. All derive from various embodying or governing forces and conditions and materials, which, in their totality, we variously refer to as the Universe, God, or the Vital Force.

But, having said so much, where are we? Back to the Creator or God of the Bible? Or Brahma of the Hindus? Almost, if not quite, I should say. But with these exceptions. For into the speculations or reactions of humanity in regard to creation or God, has come science which has resolved the onetime "supernatural" so-called, into the natural, although not entirely. A vast body of data as to substances and forces has been assembled and is now known to many men, and by not a few of them used to advance their own functions and purposes. Science suggests that what we see or sense as the universe is not the instantaneous sum or result of a creative will, but an evolutionary process, which is none the less creative in a relative sense, in that it involves change. That it may or may not always have been as man senses it—even in its totality—is not necessarily to be apprehended ever—even by an evolving mechanism such as he is. He may retrograde and disappear. What has appeared through science is that, with man on this planet, plus all the protoplasmic chain of creatures, animal and vegetable, that have either preceded or now accompany him here, special environing conditions have been necessary, and that as these have changed so has he. Thus a little more heat or cold either develops or destroys at either end of the measure.

That man has improved and is even the epitome of the solar if not universal creation is the belief or reaction of some. That man is an evolved mechanism peculiar to this solar system and its environment and is likely to improve or decay with it, is the chemic reaction of others. That man is no more than a balanced equation between various forces, and that he cannot possibly exist save in a world which presents and must present endless and opposing contrasts or variations, is the profound conviction of others; i.e., that there is not and cannot be, if we are to have life *as we know it,* either absolute good, or absolute evil, but only relative good and relative evil—in other words, the now reigning description of relativity. So too with strength and weakness, as this applies to the various creatures that inhabit the earth, for an all-powerful creature could not possibly be opposed by another all-powerful creature. The result would be deadlock, stalemate, no suggestion of life whatsoever. So again with truth and error or falsehood, for in order to know truth there must be that by which it can be measured. For without the existence of relative error, or illusion, how could truth be known? What would there be to set opposite in order that its truthfulness should be plain? Hence for the possibility of life, here, *as we know it,* there must be relatively (not absolutely) good and evil, courage and fear, love and hate, joy and sorrow, beauty and ugliness—a balanced or fairly proportional quantity of each, even though it be true, as Christ said, "Woe to him by whom the evil cometh."

My personal reaction to all this, and to all science, as it relates to life on this planet, not elsewhere, is that this is true, and that from it there is no escape. What there is elsewhere, we, balanced mechanisms, so organized to respond, are in no position to say. For, in order to have wisdom we must have ignorance. For what or where would wisdom be without its contrary? The enlighteners of ignorance would do what? Whom would they enlighten? Where?

And just here a word as to progress. For "progress" or change there is of sorts—a relative progress or change merely as I see it, although others are sure that the "progress" that brought us into being, playing and enjoying or suffering at this interesting or miserable game as each sees it is far superior to the forces—their state or mentality—which brought us into being.

Yet how can that be?

Is the creator less than the created? Or merely different?

As a child I wondered at houses, tents, lampposts, wagons,

sidewalks, and the whole array of mechanically devised implements or utensils with which we have surrounded and aided ourselves (principally in numbers or masses) the better to pleasure ourselves. Later, because in connection with the coming of these and our use of them I heard of progress, I wondered why. Why progress? From what to what? One already carefully balanced condition to another. For before ever my day was, were endless others crowded with wonders, as stupendous as any I was witnessing. So where the progress? Was not Egypt as amazing as America, or China, or India? And before ever they were, the entire evolution of man, beast, fish, flower, bird, tree; compare our airplane to a bird—a gull or eagle. Our rate of speed to that of light, or the earth. We laugh at or commiserate the savage; but he neither laughs at nor commiserates himself. He is adjusted to his environment, just as we are to ours, just as the Egyptians were to theirs, just as every living or physical and mental (so-called) thing is adjusted to its. So to talk of progress instead of change would be to assume that so stupendous a process as Life, Nature, the Universal Creative Force, could or had to learn something, from something else! Us, for instance? Whereas it makes us.

The point of all this is that I have been awakened to and convinced of the unity of all processes, forms, variations, motions, and activities of matter, or matter energy, the staggering wisdom and care or fixed condition that evokes, directs, controls, and maintains their presence, harmony, beauty, order, or seeming disorder, as some rearrangements sometimes seem. Also, that both relativity and mechanism are but processes of this immense creative something which, if not compelled so to function, still does so. Also that for all this seeming cruelty and brutality of some of the creative processes, real enough to the subjects or victims of the same, there is still holding in this governing synthesis called Life, some balancing good; and this is a necessity by reason of which what we see here on earth—and all the sensations we experience—can be. Without this dualism, this mechanism, and this relativity of all things, this altogether dramatic and glorious force that, for any or no reason, involves and evolves, would not be what it is—the multiple and thrilling, or pleasing or painful, series of sensations called life.

To be sure, this poses the question as to what can be the value of our lives if all this should be so. How are we to evaluate anything, since everything seems to depend ultimately on some unknown, but inevitable, source? Do not the values of all things fall away? Civilization and the products of all thought and human effort? Nevertheless, at this point I wish to show that in spite of this devaluation, we are ourselves organisms, and we are as helpless to cease desiring or not desiring, as ever we were. Hence, we cannot be solely the *contemplators* of all this, as Schopenhauer would have us be, or ride roughshod over life, constantly aware of its valuelessness, as Nietzsche proposes, or even adhere to any standard of values set up arbitrarily by and through us, or our religionists, with knowledge that they cannot have any absolute meaning.

For law, the precepts of religion, and art, and creeds, and directions of all kinds, appear thus to have been set up in vain, and as we all know, quite all of them give way before one another. And so that which is outside of us, goading us to one action or another, comes to have no meaning in itself; that is, the individual items of the universe outside of us do not always have the same effect on us. In other words, possessions, people, travel, art, the vision of nature and knowledge, leave us with different feelings at different times. They are seen to be alternative to each other in producing what is, I must finally conclude, *our* only reality. And that is the succession of states of mind, of moods, of emotions, which all must undergo.

However, as you can see, it is this succession of contrasts in our own reactions which means *life* to us, joy and sadness, pleasure and pain, courage and fear, desire and indifference, etc. Life is what it *seems.* We inevitably *feel* these things. The equation of the universe—the fact of contrasts outside of us—corresponds to this interior cycle; but no individual item outside or inside of us can assure us of the perpetuity of any single reaction. It is for this reason, it seems to me, that if there is any practical value to philosophy at all, we might *feel* better, in the course of ages, perhaps might even come to a scale of values—no different in the absolute equation than what we have now—but which would relate solely to a consideration of *reactions* as such, without any relatively meaningless considerations of what may be done in the exterior world of causes and actions.

The larger my conception of it, if it can be called large, the more I am able to fit what might seem conflicting evidence into one whole pattern. All the contrasts of life—good and evil, beauty and ugliness, joy, sorrow, big and little, knowledge and ignorance—all these fall away as evidence of any inherent dualism or cross-purpose in nature, just as does the idea of the individual or the importance of the individual, or of life, or of any special aspect of the universe which men have from time to time singled out for their egotistical attention. It will be seen that we, men, or any one of us, cannot be regarded as ends in ourselves, or for that matter, there does not seem to be anything that can be singled out as a "purpose." It will be seen at the same time that the illusions of value which make up the cycle of our life must be necessary and evidently are functional to some other end, unknown to us. It will be seen that our wildest dreams such as perfectibility, free will, progress, love, justice, truth, goodness, God, the importance of man, of intelligence, are not created by us but are mere derivations suggested by partial evidence—I say partial because not one of the above but has its "enemy" so-called—its opposite in degree, at least—some other dream inconsistent with it. Even mechanism, which seems to me the fruit of as disinterested contemplation as I am capable of, depends entirely on the existence of illusions which oppose it, and but for which I would never have considered the proposition seriously!

# *Irwin Edman*

THE editor of this volume has invited me to say in a thousand words what changes, if any, I have to report in the philosophy I professed in three thousand words almost a decade ago in the first series of *Living Philosophies*. I have just reread what I wrote then, and I find that, on the whole, my opinions are the same, for though fashions and governments may change in a decade, the world and human nature are less variable than that. And it was my conclusions—or intuitions—about man and nature that I was then trying to state.

There is not much in discovery or thought or in the contemporary disheartening human spectacle to have caused me to change my opinions. I still feel a philosophy both honest and realistic must begin with a recognition of the mechanical order which, if not the ultimate reality, is the basis for human action and understanding. I still feel that we are nervous specks of stardust on a remote planet in an infinite solar system among infinite other systems. It still appears to me that our aspirations are rooted in our animal impulses, and that our animal impulses flower out into moral passions, poetry, and science. It appears to me as much as ever that life, though it has no single meaning, generates as many meanings as human wit and sensibility may devise and realize in action, art, and thought. No less than before I look to art, imagination, and companionship for my chief goods. I still feel death is the finis to mortal life but that mortal men may, while briefly living, experience immortal things. It seems to me, even now, that intelligence united to good will might render life reasonably content for most human beings, and that, though it lead to no far off divine event, life may be the transient vehicle of beauty, companionship, and wisdom.

All these things seem to me still true, and I cannot believe that the ugly terrors of a civilization possibly in its death throes make them less so. Civilizations have died before, but men continued to live, and there arose in turn other civilizations. The world does not come to an end each time an individual dies, nor does it end each time a form of civilization decays. It is a tragic moment to be alive, but nature has outlived tragedies before our own. What I have said above as to my general beliefs was said in essence by Democritus in Greece before Christ, Lucretius in Rome not long after the birth of Christianity, by Spinoza in Holland in the turmoil of the seventeenth century. Nature continues to breathe evenly while men and nations suffocate and pass away. The truth does not vary because men forget or ignore or traduce it.

But ambitious as a man may be to take the perspective of eternity, he realizes that he is rooted in a given time in a given age, in a given juncture of circumstance. I presume an editor of a book such as this one wishes to have one state the "philosophy" by which one lives as well as that by which one merely speaks. Unless one is content to treat philosophy as pure spectacle, and thinking as "pure" contemplation, one must draw certain consequences from a general conception of the world, and define one's feelings with respect not simply to the universe but also to the society in which one actually lives.

I should, therefore, revise a little the accent, the emphasis, the hopes, and fears I expressed eight years ago. For eight years, while a short time geologically, are a long time humanly, especially now, with the tragic acceleration of political events. I am more conscious than I used to be of the social and economic matrix of even (or especially) the freest art and contemplation. The life of the spirit, of joy, insight, and contemplation are, I know, dependent on a commonwealth that nurtures or kills these things. Spinoza was not primarily interested in politics, but he insisted with great force on civil liberty as a condition of spiritual freedom. And civil liberty, we know now, is only insured by economic equality and freedom. Even a philosopher must take his stand somewhere or philosophy itself will be, as in present-day Germany and Italy and Japan, impossible. In metaphysics I am content to be above the battle; in morals and politics, since there is a battle, I must be on the left, meaning by the left those who wish to participate in the adventure of a co-operative life for mankind. Discouraging as are the portents, I cannot give up the hope that men of good will, aided by intelligence, may still convert the shambles of the contemporary world into a garden and a society of friends. That faith seems fantastic, I know, right now, but right now is not forever, and the good experiment has not yet been tried.

With reference to one other, perhaps an ultimate, matter. Intelligence—or scientific method—seems to me still the only technique, but I sense more vividly now the deep, unplumbed sources of vitality and energy from which what we call a system of nature is merely an abstraction. I look, therefore, to the scientists for *method*, but more than ever to the poets and the prophets for insight. The latter speak with the tongues of men and angels, and while in no orthodox sense do I believe in any gods, for moral wisdom I still turn to the oracles, the poets, and prophets of divine things.

# *Albert Einstein*

READING once again the lines I contributed almost ten years ago to the volume *Living Philosophies,* I receive two strangely contrasting impressions. What I wrote then still seems essentially as true as ever; yet, it all seems curiously remote and strange. How can that be? Has the world changed so profoundly in ten years, or is it merely that I have grown ten years older, and my eyes see everything in a changed, dimmer light? What are ten years in the history of humanity? Must not all those forces that determine the life of man be regarded as constant compared with such a trifling interval? Is my critical reason so susceptible that the physiological change in my body during those ten years has been able to influence my concept of life so deeply? It seems clear to me that such considerations cannot throw light upon a change in the emotional approach to the general problems of life. Nor may the reasons for this curious change be sought in my own external circumstances; for I know that these have always played a subordinate part in my thoughts and emotions.

No, something quite different is involved. In these ten years confidence in the stability, yes, even the very basis for existence, of human society has largely vanished. One senses not only a threat to man's cultural heritage, but also that a lower value is placed upon all that one would like to see defended at all costs.

Conscious man, to be sure, has at all times been keenly aware that life is an adventure, that life must, forever, be wrested from death. In part the dangers were external: one might fall downstairs and break one's neck, lose one's livelihood without fault, be condemned though innocent, or ruined by calumny. Life in human society meant dangers of all sorts; but these dangers were chaotic in nature, subject to chance. Human society, as a whole, seemed stable. Measured by the ideals of taste and morals it was decidedly imperfect. But, all in all, one felt at home with it and, apart from the many kinds of accidents, comparatively safe in it. One accepted its intrinsic qualities as a matter of course, as the air one breathed. Even standards of virtue, aspiration, and practical truth were taken for granted as an inviolable heritage, common to all civilized humanity.

To be sure, the World War had already shaken this feeling of security. The sanctity of life vanished and the individual was no longer able to do as he pleased and to go where he liked. The lie was raised to the dignity of a political instrument. The War was, however, widely regarded as an external event, hardly or not at all as the result of man's conscious, planful action. It was thought of as an interruption of man's normal life from the outside, universally considered unfortunate and evil. The feeling of security in regard to human aims and values remained, for the main part, unshaken.

The subsequent development is sharply marked by political events that are not as far-reaching as the less easily grasped socio-psychological background. First a brief, promising step forward characterized by the creation of the League of Nations through the grandiose initiative of Wilson, and the establishment of a system of collective security among the nations. Then the formation of Fascist states, attended by a series of broken pacts and undisguised acts of violence against humanity and against weaker nations. The system of collective security collapsed like a house of cards—a collapse the consequences of which cannot be measured even today. It was a manifestation of weakness of character and lack of responsibility on the part of the leaders in the affected countries, and of shortsighted selfishness in the democracies—those that still remain outwardly intact—which prevented any vigorous counterattack.

Things grew even worse than a pessimist of the deepest dye would have dared prophesy. In Europe to the east of the Rhine free exercise of the intellect exists no longer, the population is terrorized by gangsters who have seized power, and youth is poisoned by systematic lies. The pseudo-success of political adventurers has dazzled the rest of the world; it becomes apparent everywhere that this generation lacks the strength and force which enabled previous generations to win, in painful struggle and at great sacrifice, the political and individual freedom of man.

Awareness of this state of affairs overshadows every hour of my present existence, while ten years ago it did not yet occupy my thoughts. It is this that I feel so strongly in rereading the words written in the past.

And yet I know that, all in all, man changes but little, even though prevailing notions make him appear in a very different light at different times, and even though current trends like the present bring him unimaginable sorrow. Nothing of all that will remain but a few pitiful pages in the history books, briefly picturing to the youth of future generations the follies of its ancestors.

# *J. B. S. Haldane*

MY PHILOSOPHY is the philosophy of Marx and Engels, of Lenin and Stalin. It is a living philosophy all right. Millions of men and women live for it and, when the need arises, die for it. And on the intellectual level, too, it is alive and growing. Although it includes theory, it puts practice first; and one can only learn Marxism at all fully by acting as a Marxist, though conversely one cannot act as a Marxist without some knowledge of the theory.

Marxism is concerned with change. So an account of how I changed over to it is not out of place here. As a scientist I was concerned with matter. I even experimented on myself, and treated myself as a material system obeying physical and chemical laws. If these laws had not held for me as they do for chemicals in a bottle I should probably have killed myself. In fact, I was betting my life that materialism was true.

But I could not believe in materialism, because every account of that doctrine which I had read reduced me to a machine, or to something that merely behaved. Now I knew that I did more than behave. I felt and knew, I willed and planned. Then I read Engels' books, *Feuerbach* and *Anti-Dühring*, and found that there was a kind of materialism which bridged the gap between matter and mind, without denying the reality of either.

So far so good. But I found that when this dialectical materialism is applied to society it predicts that our existing economic system will cease to work; and that so far from the necessity for a thorough change being recognized by the ruling class, such a change can only come about through a revolutionary struggle by the workers. I didn't like this theory. As a professor I was in a securer position than most people. I hoped that if necessary there could be a gradual change to socialism by the successive nationalization of railways, mines, land, banks, and so on. I wanted to get on with my job as a scientist, and to keep out of politics except for voting and occasionally speaking. I looked on at politics with interest and a mild contempt, as many professors still do.

And then Donald Duck stepped off the screen and hit me on the jaw. Hitler started dismissing my German colleagues because they happened to be Jews, Catholics, Protestants, Socialists, liberals, or merely honest men. I had to find jobs for some of them. And the moment I started making anti-Hitler propaganda I found myself associated with all sorts of Reds, of whom the Marxists seemed to have the best grip of the situation.

I still said, "It can't happen here." But I noticed the amazingly rapid growth of corruption in England, which began to impede my scientific work. I also noticed that the British government was systematically breaking treaties and other pledges such as the League Covenant in such a way as to help Hitler and Mussolini.

In December 1936 I went to Spain to give technical advice to the Loyalists. I found that as a result of British policy the British volunteers, armed with Canadian rifles dating from the nineteenth century, were facing up-to-date German tanks, that the rebel Spanish ports were becoming German naval bases, and that everything for which I had fought from 1914 to 1918, including the rights of small nations and the safety of the world for democracy, was being handed back to the German militarists. It didn't make sense.

But from the Marxist angle it does make sense. So I had to take the political and economic side of Marxism seriously, including the theory that the state is at the bottom a product of the class struggle, serving to keep one particular class on top. This explains why the British Empire will commit suicide, as it is now doing, rather than risk a change in its class structure. And in Spain and elsewhere I found that although men and women of many different political views were fighting for democracy, there was a hard core of Marxists, many of them communists, who were an example to the rest of us both in their understanding of the situation and in their capacity for self-sacrifice. So I became a Marxist both in theory and in practice. In the next few years millions of others will follow a similar path.

Here is the philosophy in tabloid. Reality is something that happens. Nothing just exists in its own right. There is nothing behind nature, though there is infinitely more in nature than we know at present. There is no supernatural, and nothing metaphysical. Our minds are real, but there was matter before there was mind. The sensations and thoughts in our minds mirror reality, though imperfectly. We are always getting nearer to absolute truth, but never get all the way.

Reality is full of contradictions. When we say the earth is at rest and that it is in motion, both statements are true in their different ways, and correspond to realities. Pitch is both a solid and a liquid. Man is both good and bad.

Change may be continuous or abrupt. When anything increases to a certain point there is sudden change. Water boils at 212° F. The last straw breaks the camel's back. Atoms only give out energy in quanta. Creative change always arises from struggle. Men don't become good by being kept in cotton wool, but by fighting difficulties and temptations. The most important conflicts and contradictions are internal, and the most important changes come from inside.

The most fundamental thing about a society is its method of production. Capitalism did not arise because capitalists stole the land or the workmen's tools, but because it was more efficient than feudalism. It will perish because it is not merely less efficient than socialism, but actually self-destructive. It is shaking itself to pieces at the present moment in a series of economic crises like the oscillations of a shaft that is whirling too fast.

Each economic system develops its own system of thought, law, ethics, and politics. We can't think like medieval men today, even though we try to. Nevertheless, man is not the slave of economic or any other sort of fate. Freedom is the recognition of necessity. This is a paradox, but a truth. The man who realizes that there is bound to be an earthquake because his home town is on a fault clears out or gets himself a quakeproof home. The man who trusts to luck gets caught when the quake comes.

If enough people see that capitalism is cracking up, study the philosophy that predicted its doom, and act together, we can make the transition without too much trouble. If we think it is none of our business, and wait for the crash, we shall have to face one of two alternatives. The first is Fascism, leading to a series of international wars and a lowering of cultural and economic standards, ending, as I believe, in a final disaster. The other is a prolonged and bloody civil war, as in Russia. I am an optimist. I believe that there are peoples which will take the third path, the difficult path of reason. Such peoples will be able to carry what is best in their old culture into a new economic system. But they will only do so by clear thinking and brave action. And they will have to decide quickly.

# *Hu Shih*

WHAT do I now think of my own philosophy of life of almost ten years ago? Have I grown dissatisfied with it? Or has it grown more real to me as a result of maturer experience?

Needless to say, these last ten years have been soul-stirring and heartrending years in the annals of man and in particular of my own people. I lived through the Japanese aggressions of 1931, 1932, 1933, and 1935. In November and December of 1935, the Japanese military attaché at Peiping repeatedly served demands on the mayor of Peiping that I be "deported" from North China, together with the chancellor of my university because we were opposing and exposing Japanese intrigues to sever the Northern provinces from the rest of China. In 1936, when I passed through Japan on my way back from America, the Japanese press greeted me as "the most powerful leader of anti-Japanism in China." Yet, in all those years, I was frequently criticized and attacked in my own country for being too moderate and too pacifistic, and for advocating too great concessions to Japan. In 1937, both before and after the outbreak of the undeclared war, I worked hard for an eleventh-hour effort to settle the outstanding issues between China and Japan by peaceful methods. During the first months of the war, I witnessed the first thirty-one air raids on Nanking, and on two occasions I was within short distances from where huge bombs exploded. When it became apparent that the conflagration was beyond control, I gave up my futile efforts of peace and openly supported China's war of resistance to Japanese aggression. I have temporarily forsaken my work in historical research and taken up war service, first as an unofficial observer abroad, and now as Ambassador to the United States.

In short, during these years, I have had to think and write seriously about the problems of national policy and international relations—problems of war and peace. Both as a citizen and publicist, and as a personal friend and critic to leaders in the government, I had to think and advise on issues which concerned the national welfare and even the national existence of China.

This experience has given me many occasions to test out one of the chief tenets of my own credo. Under the influence of Huxley and Dewey, I had worked out what I termed the concept of intellectual responsibility—the idea of holding one's self morally responsible for what one thinks and says. I had said: "To think sluggishly, to think without strict regard to the antecedents and consequences of thought, to accept ready-made and unanalyzed concepts as premises of thinking, to allow personal factors unconsciously to influence one's thinking, or to fail to test one's ideas by working out their results is to be intellectually irresponsible." "The discovery of a microscopic bacillus may benefit millions of people, but a wrong theory of political or social reconstruction may cause centuries of bloodshed." Huxley expressed it even more emphatically: "The most sacred act of a man's life is to say and feel, 'I believe such and such to be true.' All the greatest rewards and all the heaviest penalties of existence cling upon this act."

When in the last ten years I was compelled to think and write about national and international problems, I was fully aware of the *tremendous responsibility of all social and political thinking*, which to me means thinking and planning for a whole society, for a whole population of hundreds of millions, and in some cases for the whole world. All social and political theorizing deals with situations wherein a careless and dogmatic theory, if taken seriously—as many a careless and dogmatic theory has been taken seriously—may bring about an incalculable amount of confusion, retrogression, and misery. These situations and problems always remind me of the prince who asked Confucius if it were really possible that one saying could build up a state and another might ruin a country. We who live twenty-four centuries after Confucius can cite numerous examples of writings which at one time or another have made or unmade states and empires.

In a sense, philosophers *are* kings. Kings reign only a short time, but philosophers sometimes may rule the mind and the destiny of mankind for ages. And all who now write or talk on social and political subjects and who advise the public on national or international polity are taking the place of ancient philosophers who had no voice in the affairs of the day but who thought and wrote only for a distant posterity. We who have a much better chance than the ancients to be listened to by the public, by the legislators, and by the governments, therefore, should be all the more imbued with a sense of moral responsibility for what we think and broadcast.

Very often I have tried to remind myself and my friends that we who pose to think and plan for the nation, should discipline ourselves in what may be called "responsible thinking." Responsible thinking implies at least, first, the duty to verify our facts and check our evidences; second, the humility to admit the possibility of error of our judgment and to guard against bias and dogmatism; and, thirdly, a willingness to work out as thoroughly as we can all the possible consequences that may follow the acceptance of our theory or policy, and to hold ourselves morally responsible for those consequences.

Some such discipline seems particularly imperative when one thinks and advises a nation on matters as grave as war and peace. More often than not, pacifists are just as irresponsible in their thinking as the warmongers. And very often it is not wars but the bad peace resulting therefrom that have caused more lasting resentment and hatred and sown the seeds for future wars. Those statesmen, for example, who made the Peace of Versailles, and those American pacifists and isolationists who defeated Woodrow Wilson, discredited Wilsonism, and weakened the new world order that had cost eight and a half million human lives to bring forth, have probably just as much to answer for the sorry state of the world today as the men who now dictate the policies of the aggressor nations.

I do not say that such an attitude of intellectual responsibility will free us from error or fallacy in social and political thinking. Nor do I imagine that I myself was able always to practice such a discipline with success. I merely wish to state my own conviction born of almost ten years of painful observation and experience, that we who think for the public should have the sense of public duty to cultivate as far as possible such an attitude of responsible thinking.

After all, this attitude is not new. Confucius said long ago: "Do your work reverently." And elsewhere he illustrated this attitude of reverence in these words: "When you go out of doors, act as if you were receiving a most honored guest. When you employ the people, act as if you were officiating at a great sacrificial ceremony." When we are called upon to speculate and plan in matters that involve the life and welfare of millions and generations, how dare we think irreverently?

# *Sir Arthur Keith*

"SUCH a creed as mine must grow and change as knowledge grows and changes." With this sentence I concluded my contribution to *Living Philosophies*—written almost ten years ago, when I was in my sixty-fourth year. And now I am in my seventy-third year. What has happened to my creed in the interval? Knowledge has certainly grown apace, but something else has also grown: the intervening years have brought experience—bodily suffering and death to my most loved. In the shaping of our inner beliefs what we are made to suffer and to endure counts more than all we may glean in the realms of science.

When I wrote last I was still in the full tide of my life's work, helping in every way open to me, both by encouraging the young and by personal endeavors to further our knowledge of the human body, particularly that kind of knowledge which paves the way for the advance of surgery. I was then living in London—a city which gives to the individual thinker a greater measure of freedom than any other in all the world. For it is only in great cities we can be intellectually and socially free; in lesser and more compact communities we are fettered by local opinion. So intently are neighboring eyes focused on us that only the stout and resolute dare think aloud. And I, as already confessed, am one of the herd; I am never really at peace with myself unless I am in agreement with those around me.

And now I am—and have been these past five years—a member of a village community in the green and wooded chalk uplands of the County of Kent, England, situated under the shadow of London. Here has been a separate, self-contained community these thousand years past, but now the tentacles of suburban London threaten us. Ours is a famous village, the village of Downe, the home of Darwin. Indeed I have but to rise from my chair and look from my study window and there just before me, half hid by its screen of trees, is Darwin's house. Thanks to my good friend Sir Buckston Browne, it is open to all who may care to visit it. Just beyond the orchard which surrounds me lives a company of young surgeons engaged on research. I have a laboratory still at my disposal. My young friend Mr. Theodore D. McCown of the University of California and I have just brought to an end a long research on fossil human bones. They were dug out of the caves of Mount Carmel, Palestine, and reveal a people who lived there at least one hundred thousand years before the time of Elijah. They were very different from any people now alive on the earth. My readers will thus realize that although I am now "retired" and a member of a village community, I am still in touch with the outer world.

How has my creed fitted into its new surroundings? Quite comfortably, so far as I am concerned. Allowances are made for me. The vicar of the parish, a man of my own age, is my nearest neighbor. We are on good terms, notwithstanding his persistent assertion that all I have thought and written concerning the evolution of man is "pure supposition." I like our village church with its squat square tower built from flints, dug from the chalk. I should miss the peal of its bells and so I subscribe to the fund that keeps them ringing as well as to that which keeps the parson preaching. Church and chapel decorate our village. Life to be enjoyed has to be decorated. Bare subsistence is not enough. You may call me pagan, agnostic, atheist, or what you will, but I should be distressed to think that, were I to return a thousand years hence, I should find churches and churchmen had been swept from the face of Kent.

This attitude of mine toward the church and to all organized forms of religion is a bone of contention between me and many of my fellow rationalists of England. Many of them are militant. "Is it not the duty of everyone," they demand, "to fight for the truth and to destroy error—in season and out of season?" On such occasions I am pacifist. I hold that truth has to make its way in its own right without browbeating. A forced truth, like a forced peace, has no enduring value.

Another bone of contention with my fellow rationalists has been an unhappy phrase which crept into my creed as I stated it about a decade ago. "Whether we are laymen or scientists," I wrote, "we must postulate a *Lord of the Universe*—give him what shape we will." I felt then, as I do now, that "Lord" is a dangerous word—too apt to assume a human shape, and this shape it did assume in the minds of my critics. My fellow contributors are happier in their choice; they speak of "an immortal essence," "a pervading spiritual force," "a principal of guiding good," "a Great First Cause."

My difficulty is that which the late Lord Russell had to face when he sought to teach his younger brother Bertrand the elements of Euclid. Lord Russell maintained that his pupil had to accept certain axioms before they could begin their study. Bertrand refused; so no beginning could be made. We who seek to explain the evolution of the universe and all that is therein, living and dead, must postulate certain conditions as axiomatic. We must postulate a universe already in existence—permeated and controlled by certain qualities and forces which were capable of evolving and changing until the universe assumed the state and form in which we now find it. How and why the universe came into existence is beyond our present reach. It is childish to say it is the work of a potter who stood outside his clay. We have to postulate a "Lord" that is inside the clay—just as life is an inherent quality of living matter. The poet may be justified in speaking of the universe as God's visible garment, but such a God or Creator is one to which science applies an altogether different nomenclature. Nevertheless my choice of the word "Lord" was an unhappy one.

Of the twenty-two men and women who contributed originally to these pages, only two regard the Creator—God, the One, omnipotent and personal—as having the form and properties set forth in the book of Genesis. These were Mr. Hilaire Belloc and Dean Inge; perhaps I err in bracketing Dean Inge with Mr. Belloc. All the others, if they postulate a God at all, give Him the pervading, inherent universal nature I have indicated above. Yet I am far from claiming that the anthropomorphic God is dead; the most we can say is that he is dying. We humans are weak-kneed beings. Most of us still demand a God, cast in our own mold—one who can give succor when approached in prayer. An emotional need has called Him into being.

Since I wrote almost ten years ago I have been in trouble with fellow rationalists over another matter. In the exuberance of youth I believed that reason, and reason alone, should determine our beliefs and our conduct. Some forty years ago I began to investigate the conditions and forces which had raised man to his unique position. I was then driven to the conclusion that among the chief determining factors of his rise were his inborn instincts and predispositions, particularly that which has come to be known as the "herd instinct." Closely allied to that instinct are the feelings which lead us to love our own land and our own people. I do not see, as the world now is, how man can throw away these crutches; without them he would have been still in the jungle. Hence I pleaded that a prejudice—such as patriotism—should be given a recognized place in modern civilization. But I never said—nor thought—that prejudice should dominate reason. Our instincts, our feelings, our passions, and prejudices should serve us but not master us.

A majority of the contributors to this work are—or claim to be—determinists. If by determinism is meant that we have no power to do this rather than that—that man has no power to choose—then I am not a determinist. For every day—almost every hour—alternative modes of action arise; after due consideration, I take the one way rather than the other. The choice is often ethical in its nature—as to whether I should satisfy self or sacrifice self. It is sophistry to say my choice was already determined. Determinism is a criminal doctrine.

One point more and I have finished. Among those who have contributed to these pages, as among mankind in general, some are militant and impatient, eager to impose their beliefs on all; others are calm, patient, and gentle, willing to let what they regard as truth make its way into men's minds by virtue of its own merit. I hope to be given a place in the tolerant group.

# *Joseph Wood Krutch*

A GLANCE at the first series of *Living Philosophies* serves to remind me that my contribution was a rather glum (and rather elementary) statement of some of the premises of a skeptical naturalist. I do not see how even the terrifying course of events during the ten years just past can have made that statement either more or less adequate as a description of the most fundamental aspect of the human predicament, but if I were to rewrite it today the implied estimate which emerges of the worth of human life at the moment of writing would bear a decidedly different emphasis.

In 1929 one took for granted, and therefore failed properly to value, certain opportunities and privileges which are extraordinarily rare, precious, and precarious. Among them are of course the material comfort and apparent security which the most fortunate among us still seem to enjoy. Among them are also the right to express one's own thoughts and, within limits which we now realize to be remarkably wide, to lead one's own life. Both the latter rights no longer seem things to be taken as a matter of course but privileges which the next generation may possibly find almost inconceivable. To be alive in a world where, even as a member of an admittedly limited class, one may work in peace, think in freedom, and play with a light heart is to have been born more extraordinarily fortunate than any of us was likely to realize in 1929. What we assumed as minimal conditions of a tolerable existence now appear as blessings for which one ought to be perpetually and wonderingly thankful.

The very fact that about ten years ago I could lay the major emphasis upon the existence of certain conflicts between what I believed to be the deepest desires of man and the cold universe of nature in which he finds himself is an indication of the extent to which I took it for granted that these deepest desires would continue to be recognized as at least theoretically legitimate in any civilization I was ever likely to know anything about. But tolerance, detachment, sympathetic understanding, and the pursuit of truth for its own sake have already ceased to be counted officially as virtuous throughout the major part of what was then regarded as the civilized world; and it is at least quite possible that what I somewhat naïvely assumed to be human traits stable enough to establish a contrast between the human being and the nonhuman universe will soon cease to be anywhere openly recognized as modes of feeling or judgment which ought to be cultivated.

To recognize this fact ought logically, perhaps, to lead to a lower estimate of the value of human existence and a gloomier attitude toward the worth of one's own individual experiences in living. Psychologically, however, the effect is quite different. The privilege of living in a world where there is still a considerable company of one's fellows united in valuing certain precarious things seems far more precious than it did when one failed to realize that the privilege was one which might soon entirely cease to exist. The fact that what we think of as humane living and humane thinking exist at all now seems more important than the fact that they are based upon standards of value which correspond to nothing demonstrable in the universe outside of man.

Had the question then been raised I should probably have said, even ten years ago, that the human animal could be regarded as a success only if we considered its artistic and intellectual achievements apart from that ghastly record of crimes and failures which constitutes the largest part of what is commonly recounted in history; that of the records man has left behind him, only his record as thinker and as artist could possibly be regarded with anything except horror. But today the contrast between man's success as poet and philosopher and his all but utter failure as manager of his own material world forces itself upon the consciousness as, within my lifetime at least, it never had before, and makes it seem less likely than it did ten years ago that those activities which do him honor can continue to be carried on at all in a world mismanaged as badly as that of the immediate future seems in danger of being.

I was always called an individualist even in the days when the designation was not necessarily vituperative. I am still as much of an individualist as I ever was and that is merely to the extent of still believing that really conspicuous virtue or achievement must always be exceptional, unpredictable, and not to be planned for. But I am aware, more acutely than I was aware before, that though no social or economic conditions can assure the birth or development of the finest kind of human being there are, on the other hand, social and economic conditions which can come very near to making impossible the existence of any such human beings. I can, in other words, imagine no society in which virtue and happiness would not still be difficult to achieve, but I can imagine societies in which any virtue I would accept as such and any happiness I could be able to understand would be nearly impossible. "There was never yet philosopher could bear the toothache patiently." Men must be saved one by one but they can be damned wholesale.

The American writer whom I admire more than any other once allowed himself to be so carried away by his contempt for superfluities as to proclaim this astounding generality: "Money is not required to buy one necessary of the soul." But Thoreau was wrong. There is at least one "necessary" of the soul which only money or its equivalent can secure, one material *sine qua non* for the soul's existence. That necessary is, of course, a body.

# *H. L. Mencken*

MY CONTRIBUTION to the first edition of *Living Philosophies*, written in 1930, was in substance no more than a summary of what I had been writing since 1905. Rereading it today, I see no reason for altering a single item of it. If I were formulating it again, I'd formulate it in almost precisely the same terms. The cases cited would be later and different ones, but the doctrine preached would be unchanged.

The great infirmity of mankind, it seems to me now as then, is its colossal capacity for believing the palpably not true. So far as I am aware, no other race of mammals shows anything of the sort. The lowly mouse (*Mus musculus*) appears to view its earthly environment with a highly realistic and, on the whole, accurate eye. There is no evidence that any faction of mice maintains as an article of faith that cats are really benign creatures, or argues that so maintaining is a virtue. Mice, to be sure, are sometimes trapped, but never, it appears, willingly, never with hallucinations of glory: they always try to escape, and most of them probably do. If they fight one another it is honestly and rationally, for immediate gain, and not as martyrs to manic ideologies.

So with all God's other creatures, save only man. Man, in the main, takes another course. It is his peculiar boast and grandeur that he can imagine worlds better than the one he lives in; it is his peculiar disease that he has only a small talent for distinguishing between his imaginings and reality. Thus his history is a history of constant and costly blunders. He is forever mistaking (to borrow from the argot of divinity) the species for the substance, or vice versa. The process, of course, is not without its valuable by-products. Out of the whirlwind of illusion a steady drizzle of new facts rains down. These new facts, seized upon by a minority of abnormal (and, by the general standard, wicked) men, supply the raw material for what is called human progress—a strange and beautiful phenomenon, unmatched in the animal kingdom and perhaps in the universe. But the overwhelming majority of men have no hand in it, and do not relish it. They are dragged along unwillingly, and on occasion they resist with great pertinacity.

At the moment the preponderance of resistance is exerted against (*a*) a fact first noted, I gather, in the eighteenth century, and (*b*) an idea based upon it. The fact is that government, in its essence and invariably, is inimical to all competent and well-disposed men, and the idea is that the only way to make it endurable to such men is to limit its powers. That idea is all that is sound in modern democracy: the rest is only illusion. It is not a fact that all men are created equal, it is not a fact that they are able to choose their rulers wisely, and it is not a fact that their judgments on public matters, taking them in the mass, are prudent and valid, or even worth hearing. But it *is* a fact that they are better off, the stupid along with the intelligent, when the scope of government is rigidly limited, and its agents have no prerogative outside narrow and clearly marked bounds. This is the fact that is now under attack everywhere in the Western world. It is rejected as false and abominable in all the principal nations, not only by the common run of men but also by groups pretending to be informed and even wise. It remains sound none the less.

The effects of the attack begin to be visible. What is false in the democratic theory devours the one thing that is true, and there ensues the threat of chaos. The accumulated wealth of great peoples is wasted upon enterprises so preposterous that it is difficult to describe them in rational terms. The highest places in presumably civilized nations are resigned to obscene demagogues, each hawking his brummagem Utopia and reaching out for more and more power. No decent value in all the scale of human values is safe, and neither is any decent man. The human race, once more and surely not for the last time, is engaged in an heroic effort to give the authority of gospel to the palpably not true.

Will it succeed? I am optimist enough to think not. The damage that is done by such upsurgings of imbecility sometimes lasts a long while, but so far it has always been remedied soon or late. Intelligence is at work all the while, though from time to time it has to go underground. Let us hope that it will emerge once more anon, and pull the reluctant race along another peg.

# *Robert A. Millikan*

A *correct* philosophy is like the law of gravitation in that it withstands all the assaults of time, but it is also like that law in that new and more refined observations and more minute and painstaking analysis may be expected to bring refinements and extension, rather than replacement. In contributing my bit to *Living Philosophies* some years ago, I saw the three great discoveries which have underlain the progress of mankind as: (1) the discovery of the golden rule, or, more broadly, of the altruistic ideal; (2) the discovery of the idea of natural law, or of the scientific method of approach to knowledge; (3) the discovery of the idea of continuous, age-long growth, or evolution.

Let me amplify and refine and extend somewhat these ideas as they apply to the present year. The discovery of the golden rule finds its beginnings in "the dawn of conscience," i.e., in the development of a sense of duty or responsibility to something more significant, more fundamental, more enduring than oneself—the devotion to which justifies unselfishness. Where and how this altruistic idea developed, we can only conjecture. Perhaps it is an outgrowth of mother love found in all mammals and birds but apparently not in fishes, for beneath the surface of the sea there seems to be no heart, no pity. This altruistic ideal that underlies the word "ought" is the common element in all religions. It springs from the feeling or the conviction that there is something more important even than the life of the individual, something that justifies his devotion and his self-sacrifice. This attitude is at the base of all *personal* morality—the willingness to listen with Socrates to "the inner voice." It is clearly a matter primarily of the emotions and the will.

This *attitude or feeling of good will* is clearly absolutely essential to human progress, but *it is not sufficient.* Head, as well as heart, is necessary for *social* well-being. Indeed, the sincere and devoted fanatic has often been a terrible world scourge. Social morality has nothing to do with individual morality. It is *social results* alone that we are here concerned with, not *attitudes.* And it was here that the second discovery—that of the scientific method—made its stupendous contribution to human progress. Though adumbrated in Greek times, it essentially came into being about 300 years ago. It starts with two fundamental assumptions: (1) that nature acts consistently, not capriciously, as all the preceding animistic philosophies, ancient and medieval, had assumed; and (2) that man by sufficiently intensive study is capable of understanding to some extent, at least, her processes and turning them to his own social needs. We have now had 300 years of testing of these assumptions first and most elaborately in the fields of physics and astronomy, then in chemistry, in engineering, in geology, in biology, and, much more recently and less completely, in economics and the social sciences, with results so uniformly consistent as to justify the assertion that the scientific method, with its uniform technique of hypothesis, careful analysis, prediction and experimental test, and verification, is the only method by which definite, dependable, practical knowledge has been obtained; that in all the fields in which it has been applied there already exists a core of well-established, noncontroversial fact and law; and that human progress must henceforth be made, primarily if not exclusively, by standing on this core of the already known, and slowly gathering into this core in all fields, by the continuous use of the scientific method, more and more from the surrounding zones of the controversial and the unknown. The procedures and the attitudes are essentially the same in the social as in the natural sciences, but the techniques are different. In the former we are able in our laboratories to separate and isolate the various factors and obtain controlled conditions. In economics and the social sciences long and elaborate statistical studies must be made in order to eliminate the disturbing factors and thus obtain the controlled conditions. We are just beginning to have available through the National Bureau of Economic Research and other similar agencies, a large amount of such definite, dependable, statistical knowledge in economics.

While the first of my three elements in human progress, unselfishness, stems from the emotions and the will, the second is the child of man's intellect alone. The first leads him to *do* right *as he sees it,* the second gives him knowledge of what *is* socially right—a purely scientific problem on which he is slowly making progress, although, alas, the definite knowledge of which he is already in possession is vastly greater than what he has thus far been willing to use, since we see him every day, under the lure of the demagogue and the sincere but ignorant rabble rouser, advocating and voting for the use of both physical and economic perpetual-motion machines and the like.

My third great element in human progress involves both the intellect and the emotions. The facts of evolution have been demonstrated intellectually, but nothing stirs the soul of man to wonder and to reverence more than the contemplation of the extraordinary orderliness and unity of nature more and more clearly revealed as man's studies go deeper and deeper, and above all the inescapable evidence that he finds, not of random and unprogressive change, but of definitely directed movement toward the age-long development of higher and higher forms culminating in man himself. Most scientists, I think, will join with Einstein in his combination of emotion and intellect when he says, "Enough for me to contemplate the mystery of conscious life perpetuating itself through all eternity, to reflect upon the marvelous structure of the universe which we can dimly perceive, and to strive humbly to understand even an infinitesimal part of the *intelligence* manifested in nature."

May I now add one new political element to my social philosophy which is inspired by recent world's events and is essentially a corollary to the second of the foregoing elements?

The most important social question that faces the civilized world today is, "Can free representative government survive anywhere in the face of the reactionary influences that are now pushing the whole world back toward the despotisms from which it began to free itself 300 years ago, when the method of modern science first began to let in the light, to free the spirit of man, and to destroy the authoritarianism of both church and state which had kept mankind in ignorance and bondage throughout most of recorded history?" These reactionary forces mask under the names of Communism, National Socialism, liberalism, even democracy; but while the hands are Esau's, the voice is Jacob's. The suppression of the freedom of the individual to speak, to write, even to think, reveals in every case the deception. This alone tells the story of whether a given country has actually turned the clock of progress back 300 years or not. No other criterion is needed.

By this test we in this country are still free, but the reactionary influences are rolling in in waves from Russia, from Germany, from Italy, from Japan. Will they engulf us? New moves toward socialisms and collectivisms—these are only the vanguard of despotism as one can see by observing what the countries that profess them have become—are reported in the papers every day. If Longfellow were alive today he would write more anxiously than he did seventy-five years ago:

*Humanity with all its fears,*
*With all its hopes of future years,*
*Is hanging breathless on thy fate.*

For Communism, Fascism, Nazism, totalitarianism in all its forms, mean simply "despotism," and *despotism means eternal war.* That is where we are headed, unless through the public school, which in this country now reaches practically the whole of the oncoming generation, and through the press, which now reaches a large part of the present population, and through all other available agencies, we can so educate the people of the United States while it still has the ballot, to use that ballot to *preserve* our American liberties. It all comes back to you and me—the voters. If we have rotten government it is because we, by our ballots, put corrupt men into control. If we have an insidious and disgraceful patronage system which corrupts the public and private morals of the nation and renders us callous even to the wholesale use of public funds for political purposes it is because we, the voters, tolerate it. If we have stupid, incompetent, untrained, unscientific, ununderstanding men in office, it is because our ballots put them there.

The only possible hope for the preservation of our American liberty obviously lies in the development of an educated, an intelligent, a scientifically minded, an objective electorate. That is what, in the last analysis, our schools and colleges primarily exist for, and the most direct and effective approach to the problem of rational, objective, intelligent living is through the spread throughout our whole population of an increased familiarity with the way in which modern science has developed, for it is here that the problem of obtaining real, dependable, workable knowledge as a guide to conduct, in place of hunch, superstition, prejudice, and emotion, has come most near to a solution. If our educational institutions of all types can rise to their responsibilities and do their jobs rightly our America can be saved. If they cannot do it we are doomed.

# *Lewis Mumford*

ALMOST a decade has passed since I first set down the outlines of what I believe. Meanwhile, death has crept nearer, and every living philosophy must reckon with the fact and the meaning of death.

For death as a natural event in the development of the individual, which he shares with all other living things, there is only one appropriate mood: that of smiling resignation. The secret of this smile—if I can pass on a secret that needs constant relearning—is to live from day to day so that any moment might, without a bitter sense of frustration, make an appropriate end. Browning's Grammarian wished to postpone living till he had mastered the intricacies of Greek grammar and "settled *hoti*'s business." Such postponement, such sacrifice, tends to be a mark of all specialized competence: carried to the extreme, it becomes a kind of voluntary death that robs the organism of its just satisfactions, and ultimately disables the very proficiency it seeks to further. My philosophy, by its emphasis on life's many-sidedness and its effort to achieve balance, is the opposite of the specialist's; and whereas the Grammarian left now to dogs and apes, because "man has forever," I hold that "now" is a fair sample of eternity. It is those who have chosen death as their mode of life who have reason to shrink most from the final encounter.

The increasing nearness of personal death, then, makes no new demands upon my philosophy. But meanwhile something quite different has been spreading through the world: the *will* to die, the will to die and to inflict death upon others: an attempt to salvage life's defeats and frustrations by a collective glorification of war, slaughter, savagery, and irrational sacrifice. This cult has existed sporadically in many forms; but the most sinister challenge today comes from Fascism. In 1930 the threat of barbarism was still only a latent one. Gradually men were modifying the injustices embodied in the peace treaties and removing the atavisms that had been spread through the world by the first World War. Spengler had indeed freely predicted the rise of brutal military dictatorships; but despite the frog-puddle boasts of Mussolini, Spengler's prophecy seemed mere reactionary wishfulness. Today his forecasts have been justified on two counts: not merely have the Nazis trampled with sadistic boots upon millions of decent men and women, but the nerveless absence of resistance upon the part of the cowed, bewildered democratic groups has given to barbarism a victory it probably had not the strength to earn.

Now, my own philosophy is based on the domestic, one might almost say the parental virtues: its deepest postulate is the sacredness of life. It calls for love and democratic co-operation and emotional balance and rational understanding; while it recognizes conflict and struggle as a salutary condition of growth, it seeks to transfer struggle from the sordid plane of brute force to that of "mental war," to use Blake's phrase, in which both sides profit, no matter which way the battle turns. What has such a philosophy to say to the Fascist's cult of death with its paranoid delusions, its cold violence, its systematic savagery, its co-ordinated barbarism? Shall one let one's rational hatred of warfare keep one from answering Fascism with the only argument its demented creed respects—namely, superior force? Shall one fold one's hands, and prepare for the universal concentration camp as the Christian martyrs once prepared for the torture of the arena?

No: one has a duty to life which transcends one's immediate distaste for adopting, even in self-protection, the barbarous methods by which alone Fascism prevails; one has a duty to protect life against those who are inimical to all its humane and cultivated forms. There is something worse than the temporary barbarism of war: that is the all-devouring and compulsive and enduring barbarism of the Fascist state. Totalitarian systems of government, by reason of their systematic suppression of minorities and their complete censorship of expression and their viselike hold over the action of individuals and groups, wall themselves up against the common forces of civilization. Fascism thus fortifies itself not merely against the challenge of humane ideas, but against the residual humanity of its own subjects. There is no means of co-operating with this systematic barbarism, except by co-operating with our own suicide. On the contrary we must resist it; resist it with a soldierlike firmness. If, facing that resistance, the Fascists force war upon us, it is better to accept the challenge than to submit to the ultimate degradation and humiliation of a Fascist "peace."

So there comes into my philosophy of life a hard note of necessity: the grim willingness to meet with decisive force the Fascist "heroes" who have marched from victory to victory over the weak, the defenseless, the divided, and who exult publicly in the destruction they inflict, from safely heroic distances, in their one-sided fighting. We who do not believe in physical force must be ready to fight in order that those who do believe in it shall not rule the world. In this tragic issue, we accept battle reluctantly, remembering A.E.'s aphorism, that a man becomes the image of the thing he hates; but it is the nature of tragic issues that they leave no easier alternative. Only by this firm readiness to face danger can the values and goods of a truly human life be secured against the cancerous spread of Fascist barbarism. Once the danger is confronted boldly by men of good will, who represent the majority of mankind, it is already, even without the necessity of striking a single blow, more than half conquered.

# *George Jean Nathan*

ALTHOUGH, with the passing of the years and the changing of the world we live in, certain convictions which I entertained in other and younger days have undergone some alteration, I find that the body and essence of my beliefs remain, for good or ill, very much what they were. There are some things which I no longer believe, but they are of relatively lesser importance in the general fabric, and it may even happen that as time again passes and as the world again changes I may revert to my earlier hold with them. So the qualifications and amendments may be accepted as being possibly temporary.

No man can live through the upset and agony of our time and remain insensible to it. The sounds of barbaric cannon, the cries of starving and helpless masses of men, the tears and curses of humanity reach to even the remotest ivory tower. And the human mind, however independent and self-frontiered, must find its aloof contemplations invaded and shattered by them, as the pounding G minor chords and roaring drum invade and shatter the air-drawn mood of the Requiem. It is thus that philosophy is emotionalized out of some of its steel; it is thus that that eternally greatest enemy of cold, hard meditation, the heart, beats its sympathetic tune into the toughest and most gasconading brain.

Once—and still to a considerable extent—content to let the rest of the world manage its own concerns and to devote myself humbly to an attempt to manage my own, I accordingly find myself touched by the whirlpool that touches us all. In the midst of death, we are in life; and the mortal wounds of civilization fleck us with their blood. Ivory towers show red stains.

Although conceivably not all, as the indignant sentimentalists proclaim, in Fascism is bad, I am against Fascism in any of its phases, whether good or bad. Although not all in Communism, as the rashly arbitrary contend, is conceivably bad, I am equally against Communism, whether good or bad. Believing more fully than ever in individualism and autonomy, I compromise with my philosophy to the degree of persuading myself that, of all present forms of government, what goes roughly by the name of democracy is the least discommodious and the most satisfactory. There may be a better form in one's philosophical imagination, but this is a pragmatic age and we are not privileged to dwell in a land of our philosophical imagination. Its flag is too brilliantly hued for these harsh, drab days. It isn't that we must take the world as we find it. That we must never do. It is rather that we must try, vainly or successfully, to devote our efforts to make the world one day take us as we find ourselves. A lovely job, that!

With honor and decency to so appalling an extent forgotten and contemptuously dismissed on every hand, with so many of the nations of the world breaking their faith, their promise, and their word to one another, and with men in high office and position the world over turning traitor, welcher, thief, and poltroon, anyone who holds with honor and decency is likely to be looked upon today as either something of an eccentric or something of a dubious poseur. For there are fashions, paradoxically enough, in honor and decency, and they change with the changing times like fashions in clothes, dances, the lighter therapeutics, and anatomical morality. Yet I cannot believe in a world that does not accept and adhere to the old, unchanging concepts of honor and decency, and have only an acute disrelish for one that seeks apologetically to live by paraphrases.

I am no pacifist; far from it. To be a pacifist in today's world is akin to looking under the bed at night for Bérylune. This is an age of swords and guns, whether we like it or not, and swords and guns are not to be too happily met with sentimentalized logic and prayers. A cannon a day keeps the undertaker away. Let us be prepared to the teeth and when the time comes, as it is sure to come, let us make further certain that our teeth are in good, sharp, biting condition. Diplomacy is simply procrastination. History, despite Henry Ford and H. G. Wells, is not a liar.

But under and beyond all such matters, it remains my conviction that in one's own work, whatever it may be, lie one's only salvation, one's only true purpose on earth, and one's only measure of self-justification and happiness. That there is in such a conviction a deplorable selfishness and an even more deplorable taint of vanity I duly appreciate, but I believe it still today as I believed it yesterday. There may come irresistible and necessary interruptions; there may be times when extrinsic phenomena for the moment cast doubt upon the integrity of one's conviction; but as God created man in His own image so man in turn creates his work in his own image—and that is the least reciprocity that he may humbly vouchsafe to his Maker.

Nor, as I have suggested, have the majority of my other earlier credences and conclusions altered. Some of my opinions on minor matters have experienced minor changes, obviously enough in view of internal changes in those matters themselves. But by and large I am what I have been and shall doubtless continue to be. For I persist in believing that men do not, basically, much change. Suddenly and for a spell they may now and again veer from the straight line of their imposed or self-imposed destiny, but soon thereafter you will generally discover them once again following their ingrained, traditional and established paths, whether mental, emotional, physical, or spiritual—or all four together.

# *Julia Peterkin*

THE last decade has changed none of my beliefs but has deepened some of my convictions. For example, I think that the chemistry of a human being's body determines in large measure his traits of character, that his ductless glands or malnutrition or infection may be responsible for his good or evil traits.

I believe that an excellent person invariably demands more of himself than of anyone else, that an inferior person demands more of others than of himself, but I doubt that an inferior person is so from choice nor do I think that he can change himself into a superior one simply by choosing to change.

I doubt that mechanical inventions have increased human happiness. For example, while means of communication have multiplied enormously, safeguards against misinformation have not multiplied proportionately. I realize as I write this, that what now seems to me to be true may not be true at all. However, I believe that the man who told us to "Know the truth" gave us good advice, and that peace of mind depends upon discovering as much of truth as is possible even though what we discover fails to be reassuring.

# *Bertrand Russell*

Nothing that has happened in the world since the first appearance of *Living Philosophies* has caused me to alter any of my beliefs, but some events have led to a change of emphasis. In ordinary life we do not have to proclaim vigorously that two and two are four, because we do not find it questioned; but if important governments put people to death for asserting it, we might have to devote time to the multiplication table which otherwise might be better employed. So it is at the present time. It had seemed, to my generation, that certain principles were definitely accepted in politics, e.g., that Jews and Christians should have the same social and political rights; that a man should not be deprived of life or liberty except by due process of law; and that there should be freedom of opinion except in so far as some interference might be necessary in time of actual war.

These principles, in whole or part, are now rejected by the governments of Germany, Italy, Russia, India, and Japan, not to mention many smaller countries. Those who disapprove of their rejection in one case very often approve of it in another. Communists are shocked by the tyranny in Fascist countries, but think it quite right that Stalin should be able to execute his colleagues whenever the humor seizes him. Fascists are horrified by the sufferings of Russian kulaks, but think that Jews deserve no mercy. The world grows more and more fierce, and fewer and fewer people object to atrocities committed by their own party.

In these circumstances, those of us who still believe in tolerance and democracy are told that we are condemning ourselves to futility, since victory must go either to the

Fascists or to the Communists. I think this point of view quite unhistorical, but in any case I could not accept it.

To begin with the historical argument. For a time, the Western world was divided between the followers of Luther and the followers of Loyola; all governments were on one side or the other, fierce wars were fought, and the few who, like Erasmus, remained neutral might have been thought negligible. But after about a hundred years of slaughter without victory to either side, people got tired of the whole business and just stopped. To us, in retrospect, there seems very little to choose between persecuting Protestants and persecuting Catholics: we should divide the world of the seventeenth century into fanatics and sensible people, putting the opposing fanaticisms together as analogous follies. So, in retrospect, will Communism and Fascism appear. The ultimate victory is never to the fanatic, because he tries to keep men's emotions in a state of tension which the great majority, in the long run, find unbearable. The eighteenth century—the age of reason—was a period of relaxation after the excitements of the wars of religion. So, I doubt not, the modern wars of ideologies will be succeeded by another age of reason, in which, once more, people will not be willing to persecute in the name of beliefs for which there is no evidence.

Fascism and Communism, when analyzed psychologically, are seen to be extraordinarily similar. They are both creeds by which ambitious politicians seek to concentrate in their own persons the power that has hitherto been divided between politicians and capitalists. Of course they have their differing ideologies. But an ideology is merely the politician's weapon; it is to him what the rifle is to the soldier. This is still true, psychologically, even if the politician is taken in by his own eloquence. The technique of both parties is the same: first, to persuade a minority by an ideology which appeals to hate; then, by some trick, to confine military power to this minority; and finally, to establish a tyranny. The method, so far as the modern world is concerned, was invented by Cromwell.

The defects of the method are obvious. Since it appeals to hate, it involves, internally, cruelty and suppression of every kind of freedom, and externally, a vehement reaction of fear and preparation for war. Owing to its revivalist's technique, its success, like that of analogous religious movements in the past, cannot be more than temporary; before long, enthusiasm gives place to corruption, and zeal degenerates into the activities of spies and informers. The ruler, terrified of assassination and palace revolutions, is the prisoner of his own secret service; everyone else comes to know that the road to success is to denounce relations and friends for imaginary conspiracies. There is nothing new about all this; it may be studied in the pages of Tacitus as well as in recent accounts of Russia.

It is a great misfortune that so many radicals should have persuaded themselves that the millennium is to be reached along such a road, and should have closed their eyes to the similarity of different brands of totalitarian states. The mentality produced by the Great War has encouraged an excessive belief in what can be achieved by violence, without the concurrence of the populations concerned; and at the same time impoverishment has stimulated the desire to find an enemy to whom misfortunes may be attributed. The cure for the crisis due to the Great War is thought to be a still greater war; all the disillusionments of idealists at Versailles and after are forgotten. In this there is no wisdom. It is not by violence and cruelty and despotism that the happiness of mankind is to be secured. In 1914 the world started along a wrong road, which it is still traversing, faster and faster the longer the end of the journey remains out of sight. Perhaps the blind alley will have to be followed to the very end, as in the wars of religion, before men discover that it leads nowhere. But in the meantime those who retain the use of reason should not encourage the frantic stampede toward disaster.

# *Beatrice Webb*

In 1930 I was honored by an invitation to contribute to a series of essays—essays assumed to express the contributor's philosophy of life, whether from the standpoint of man's relation to man, or man's relation to the universe. So far as man's relation to the universe was concerned, I had no creed by which I lived: I was an agnostic; I simply did not know. But I confessed to an instinctive and unreasoning faith in a force that makes for righteousness at work in the world. In all that relates to the mortal life of man on this earth, including his relation to other men, I believed in science as the salvation of mankind; my own specialism being the analysis and description of social institutions past and present. But science reveals the processes by which things happen: it cannot tell you what you wish to happen, or, as some would say, what ought to happen. Hence, if the science of society is to be applied so as to maintain or change the existing social order or create a new social order, it has to be supplemented by a scale of values of what constitutes the good life, alike for the individual and for the community. The ideal that inspired my day-to-day work was the maximization of the health, happiness, artistic culture, intellectual adventure, and loving-kindness of every member of the human species, irrespective of color or race. I was in fact a humanist.

Now it so happens that since the publication of *Living Philosophies* my husband and I have spent our energies in studying the political, economic, and cultural organization of the U.S.S.R.; our conclusions being embodied in 1400 pages of somewhat unreadable detail.[1] In this postscript I shall not attempt to summarize these conclusions, unfavorable or favorable; I shall limit myself to what seems to us a vital discovery in social science made and in process of being applied by the Soviet government, throughout their vast territory with its 170 million inhabitants. If it be desired to maximize the production of services and commodities and to distribute them in a way that will bring about a healthy, happy, and cultured life, for all the inhabitants, irrespective of race or occupation, the exploitation of man by man, whether by landlord, capitalist employer, trader, or financier, must be made a penal offense, to be prevented, prohibited, and if persisted in, punished, exactly as theft and fraud are dealt with in capitalist states.

Why must profitmaking be made a crime? Because the Bolsheviks believe that the profitmaking motive leads inevitably and universally to a corruption and perversion of the economic system; that it divides the community into two nations, the rich and the poor; that it concentrates power in the hands of the wealthy, and keeps the wage earners and the peasants in a state of poverty and dependence; that it produces a disastrous alternation of booms and slumps, with a permanent army of unemployed persons, tragically deteriorating in health and happiness, skill and character. This profitmaking motive even leads to the destruction of natural resources, and turns forests and fertile plains into sand-swept deserts.

What is the substitute for the profitmaking motive? The alternative has been discovered in planned production for community consumption. This does not mean the abolition of private property, or having all things in common. On the contrary, there has been and still is a steadily increasing amount of private property in the U.S.S.R. But it is distrib-

[1] *Soviet Communism: A New Civilization,* 2nd Edition, 1938, by Sidney and Beatrice Webb: Scribner's, New York.

uted among the whole population, it is not heaped upon a class of rich persons. It does not mean the universal engagement at wages, by the state, or the consumers'-co-operative movement. More than half of all the families of the U.S.S.R. are not working for wages at all, but are working with their own instruments of production, either individually or co-operatively, living in their own houses and sharing among themselves their own products—for instance, in the quarter of a million collective farms. But they must not hire labor, or engage in trading or speculation, or let their property to rent-paying tenants.

The scant space of a postscript does not permit an explanation of the constitution and working of the central planning department (Gosplan) at Moscow, with its elaborate statistical and audit departments, and its subsidiary regional, industrial, agricultural, and cultural departments, scattered over the huge territory of the U.S.S.R. The purpose of Gosplan is to combine the maximum of production with the minimum of expenditure in the shortest possible time. Hence it develops its own type of efficiency movement, and its own brand of rationalization. Judged by the amount produced, whether in capital or consumers goods, in railways or canals, in hospitals or universities, in scientific research or holiday resorts, this planned production for community consumption has been brilliantly successful. Remember that the Soviet government started with an immense territory, inhabited by 160 millions; the vast majority being poverty-stricken, illiterate, and deplorably superstitious. For the first two or three years it was confronted, not only by civil war, but by invading armies, the Germans, then the British, American, French, and lastly the Japanese. In the ensuing fifteen years the Soviet government has built up a great manufacturing industry, today in aggregate output second only to that of the United States; they have mechanized their agriculture, thereby not only securing the nation's food supply, but also greatly increasing their harvests of flax and hemp, cotton and tea. Incidentally they have abolished mass unemployment. And now I come to the greatest achievement. From the Arctic Ocean to the Black Sea, from the Baltic to the Pacific, they have created a gigantic health and educational system, a universal network of crèches and schools, colleges and universities, clinics and hospitals, research institutes and sanatoria, always increasing in number and variety, and accessible to the whole of the population without class or racial discrimination.

This success is due to there being no enemy party. The General Council of Trade-Unions who take an active part in state planning, and are the supreme authority for settling wage rates, know that the amount available each year for wages and salaries will be estimated according to the past productivity of the workers by hand and by brain. Hence the trade-unions have started what is called "socialist competition"; each individual in each plant competes with other individuals and other plants, in seeking to produce more commodities for the wages received. They are all equally anxious to use any method of remuneration, or to introduce any machinery, lessening effort and increasing productivity. What is even more surprising is the device of "patronage." If one factory has beaten another factory in the race for increased production, it is in honor bound to send its best men, and even provide machines, to bring the other factory up to the level of production. This sounds romantic. But as the amount to be distributed depends *on the total production during the past year of all the workers in all the plants,* it is in the interests of each plant to increase the productivity of every other plant. That is obvious. And here we touch on the scale of values, the code of conduct, which inspires the planned production for community consumption. The dominant motive in everyone's life ought to be, not the pecuniary self-interest of each individual, but the wealth and consequent well-being of all the people, all the time. For it is clear that every man starts adult life in debt to the community in which he has been born and bred, cared for, fed and clothed, educated and entertained. Anyone who, to the extent of his ability, does less than his share of work, and takes a full share of the wealth produced in the community, is considered a thief and is treated as such. On the other hand, those who do more than their share of the work that is useful to the community, who invent or explore, who excel in the arts and crafts, who are able and devoted leaders in production or administration, are not only provided with every pecuniary or other facility for pursuing their chosen careers, but are also honored as heroes and publicly proclaimed as patterns of behavior.

Thus, in planned production for community consumption, the secular and the religious are one. The good life at which the citizen aims is the life that is beneficial to all his fellow men, irrespective of age or sex, religion or race.

# *H. G. Wells*

ALMOST a decade ago I contributed to a book entitled *Living Philosophies* my conception of what life is to me and why I live. That book is now to have a supplement and I am asked if there is anything I would like to alter or add to that statement I made. I have read it over and I find little to alter. But it was written originally to be read in a certain limited time, it had to be concentrated and a little superficial, and this question gives me an opportunity of adding to it a certain expansion of my political philosophy and certain recent and acuter developments of my social ideas. They are developments in response to recent events. The world has plainly become much darker and more dangerous in the intervening years. Open free speech has ceased over vast areas. There has been much almost promiscuous killing, much waste of natural resources and much economic disorganization. Violence has made headway against the world's peace and the level of civilized life is visibly sinking. The element of hope for a new way of living in Soviet Russia has dwindled. The call for positive activities to arrest this world-wide dissolution is much more urgent than it was. A decade ago one could write, "I am opposed to nationalism and war" and "I exalt science" and leave it at that. Now that does not satisfy. How long shall I be free to maintain these excellent attitudes if I do not exert myself to defend them? The political end of one's philosophy now has to be of a more practical quality. The question, What are you going to do about it? is more urgent.

In the fact of that urgency it no longer suffices merely to

disapprove of war and of the freedom of egotistical recklessness in the private exploitation of natural resources. The call to action requires a plan of action and a plan of action requires a diagnosis of the disorders we have to face. In that earlier statement I simply condemned war and nationalism, linking them together; now a much more precise consideration of their causes and particularly of their vast and steadily growing malignity is necessary. All war is not nationalist; abolish nationalist sovereignty and there would still be a social war on hand. Moreover, war changes its physical conditions and material effects monstrously, and so it follows that a philosophy intended to determine action must inquire what it is that has so greatly exacerbated the war danger at the present time. I find the answer to that inquiry, in a great release of human energy and a rapid dissolution of social classes, through the ever-increasing efficiency of economic organization and the utilization of mechanical power. As machinery and the material organization of life has improved social order has become deliquescent.

Let me state this idea as plainly as possible. Throughout the ages the processes of social life have been carried on by long-established and well-defined classes, professions, and types of functionary, priest, soldier, lawyer, artisan, merchant, peasant. They all had, in effect, time-sanctioned codes of behavior, codes that were almost universally understood and respected. A sort of rough social balance among these elements had stood the tests of several thousand years. There was balance during that period even in the structure and method of armies and the conduct of war, with cavalry, infantry, and an accessory artillery. Life adapted itself gradually to such gradual changes as were in progress. Gunpowder, for instance, was a small slow innovation compared with the airplane and the tank. Then suddenly came the onset of power machinery and a new scale of human operations. New wholesale mechanical methods, transport of commodities, gas, explosives, and so forth, have not only made war an entirely different and more catastrophic thing but—what is not so universally recognized—they have twisted the old functional classifications of mankind in peace or war almost out of recognition. We did not realize that was happening until quite recently, and we are still trying to run a new and imperfectly understood machinery of living, with the traditions, feelings, sentiments, morality, culture, of the time-honored old order. These traditions, almost all of them over-implemented now and many of them now plainly mischievous or reduced to utter futility, tangle us into the most alarming and sanguinary strains and stresses. Old classes change or vanish; new ones appear. The old-fashioned farmer who satisfied most of his needs by his own products has vanished over great parts of the world and we call the new cropgrower by his name and judge him by bucolic precedents. Really he has been as much industrialized as any factory hand. And everywhere there appears a new hitherto unheard-of stratum of able-bodied, unemployed, untrained, and aimless young men. We get them in great multitudes everywhere and our methods of distributing the products of industry neither employ nor satisfy nor dispose of them. What are we to do with them?

All the civilized communities suffer from a sort of cancer of irrelevant, useless, energetic young people. Their lack of function is a purely disintegrating force. We seem to have no better employment for them than to turn them over to war preparation, which must lead at last to their consumption in war. Human life has stalled; its organization is clogged with a growing surplus of human beings it can neither interest nor use. And it seems incapable of adapting its organization to the new demand upon it. The surplus energy produces violence and incoherent instinctive revolutionary movements of increasing gravity.

This condition of things was unanticipated. In three or

four decades it has rushed upon us and become the major problem that faces mankind. To my mind it seems plain that this problem of the reclassification of society and the reorientation of humanity to a new, vaster, richer, and more satisfying set of objectives, has to be tackled strenuously and immediately. I am amazed and distressed at the complete failure of social research, of education, and of statesmanship, even to recognize that this problem exists—much less to realize its priority. It towers over my mind, a stupendous menace. I realize it will not wait. Only an enormous intellectual effort throughout the whole world can now arrest the headlong deliquescence of human society that is now in progress. I clamor, and I clamor with an increasing shrillness for a gigantic effort to pull together the mind of the race before it is altogether too late. "Adapt," I say, "adapt yourselves to these greater demands or perish."

I find myself almost alone with my outcries. People about me drift, with a quiet and rather amused complacency, toward disaster. "Why worry?" they say. "Nobody knows exactly what has to be done. So what can we do? One man tells us this and another that." To which the only possible retort is: "Why not think for yourselves? Why not come into the thinking and planning before it is too late?"

But that is a hard saying for the common man. Yet it is precisely because we do not know, because of our lack of exactitude and co-ordination, that this passionate necessity to inquire, to think hard, to accumulate the definite will for a new order, arises. Study, clarify, educate, without haste indeed but without a moment's delay, interchange, and speak plainly; that now must surely be the primary rule of life for every rational man and woman, and whatever detracts from that must be evil. The hour is late, but still amidst the deepening shadows we may yet be in time. Build up an acceptable vision of a new world, make, not a flimsy gesture of good intentions, but set to work, to work hard, to produce a reasoned and tried and tested common plan that will hold human minds together in a new order in the world. The effort may seem well-nigh hopeless in the face of contemporary fatalism, but it is the only thing to do. That is why I say and repeat, first in this form and then in that, that an educational revolution, a new Encyclopedism, must be the basis of any better human life, and that failing that, we shall, as humanity, perish. At present all our efforts to produce a new human society are insufficiently implemented with knowledge. More science is needed, more interchange, and more mental synthesis. That is my philosophy of action; that is the general philosophy I stated in my previous paper, brought now to a cutting edge.

# BIOGRAPHICAL NOTES ON THE CONTRIBUTORS TO "LIVING PHILOSOPHIES" (1931)

*Biographical Notes on the Contributors to "Living Philosophies" (1931).*

*James Truslow Adams (1878– ), after a successful business career, became a widely known historian. Among his best known books are 'The Founding of New England,' 'The Epic of America,' and 'Our Business Civilization.'*

*John Dewey (1859– ), Professor of Philosophy in Columbia University, is accounted one of the greatest living figures in philosophy. His pragmatic viewpoint has influenced American and European thought greatly, particularly in the field of education.*

*Theodore Dreiser (1871– ) is the author of more than a score of books whose total impact has been of incalculable effect on modern American literature. Among his finest novels are 'An American Tragedy,' 'Sister Carrie,' 'Jennie Gerhardt,' 'The Titan,' and 'The Financier.'*

*Irwin Edman (1896– ) is Professor of Philosophy at Columbia University. He has established his reputation as teacher and essayist and has written many books of philosophical criticism and discussion. His most popular work is also his most recent one—the gentle and humane 'A Philosopher's Holiday.'*

*Albert Einstein (1885– ), generally ranked as among the greatest of scientists, living or dead, now makes his home permanently in this country.*

*J. B. S. Haldane (1892– ) since 1933 has been Professor of Genetics at University College, University of London. He ranks among England's greatest living scientists and popularizers of science.*

*Hu Shih (1891– ) is known as the 'Father of the Chinese Renaissance' and is largely responsible for the new sense of cultural responsibility alive in China today. His most monumental work is a 'History of Chinese Philosophy.'*

*Sir Arthur Keith (1866– ), famous for his researches in the antiquity of man, was in 1927 President of the British Association for the Advancement of Science.*

*Joseph Wood Krutch (1893– ) is the Dramatic Editor of the New York* Nation *and Professor of English at Columbia University. Perhaps his most influential book is 'The Modern Temper.' He has written widely on many phases of literature.*

*H. L. Mencken (1880– ) has influenced a whole generation of young Americans. The list of his works is long and varied, but it is possible he may be best remembered in years to come for his monumental 'The American Language,' which manages to be at once a work of wit and of scholarship.*

*Robert A. Millikan (1868– ) was in 1923 awarded the Nobel Prize for isolating and measuring the electron.*

*Lewis Mumford (1895– ) is one of our keenest art critics, social historians, and architectural authorities. Among his books are 'Sticks and Stones,' 'The Golden Day,' 'Herman Melville,' 'Technics and Civilization,' and 'The Culture of Cities.'*

*George Jean Nathan (1882–  ) is known on two continents as one of America's most learned as well as most scathing dramatic critics.*

*Julia Peterkin (1880–  ) has written out of her intimate and sympathetic knowledge some of America's finest tales of Southern plantation life. In 1929 her novel 'Scarlet Sister Mary' won the Pulitzer Prize.*

*Bertrand Russell (1872–  ) secured his early reputation through his work as mathematician and symbolic logician. He has developed it as educator, philosopher, and writer of many popular works on science and related subjects.*

*Beatrice Webb (1858–  ), in conjunction with her husband, Sidney Webb, is the author of many standard works on social problems, the most monumental of which is 'Soviet Communism—A New Civilization?'.*

*H. G. Wells (1866–  ) has achieved equal eminence as novelist, historian, social philosopher, and scientific popularizer. His tremendous output has not lessened, one of his finest books being his autobiography, published only a few years ago.*